An Introduction to
Computer
Simulation
Methods
Applications to Physical Systems
PART 1

HARVEY GOULD
Department of Physics, Clark University

JAN TOBOCHNIK
Department of Physics, Kalamazoo College

An Introduction to
Computer
Simulation
Methods
Applications to Physical Systems
PART 1

Addison-Wesley Publishing Company

Reading, Massachusetts•Menlo Park, California•New York
Don Mills, Ontario•Wokingham, England•Amsterdam•Bonn•Sydney
Singapore•Tokyo•Madrid•San Juan

This book is in the Addison-Wesley Series in Physics

Library of Congress Cataloging-in-Publication Data

Gould, Harvey, 1938-
　　An introduction to computer simulation methods.

　　Includes bibliographies and indexes.
　　1. Physics—Mathematical models. 2. Physics—Data
processing. 3. Stochastic processes—Mathematical
models. 4. Stochastic processes—Data processing.
5. BASIC (Computer program language) I. Tobochnik,
Jan, 1953–　. II. Title.
QC21.2.G67　　1987　　530′.072′4　　86–28825
ISBN 1-201-16503-1 (v. 1)
ISBN 1-201-16504-X (v. 2)

Reprinted with corrections, March 1988.

BCDEFGHIJ-AL-898

To the memory of
Sheng-keng Ma

ACKNOWLEDGMENTS

Many colleagues and students have generously commented on preliminary drafts of chapters of the manuscript and have given general encouragement and advice. We particularly wish to thank Harold Abelson, Daniel Ben-Avraham, John Davies, Hugh DeWitt, Lisa Dundon, Fereydoon Family, Jim Given, Jim Gunton, Marilyn Jimenez, Gabor Kalman, Tom Keyes, Robert Kilmoyer, Bill Klein, Peter Kleban, Roger Kohin, Christopher Landee, François Leyvraz, Jon Machta, Gene Mazenko, Bill Michalson, Robert Pelcovits, Joseph Priest, Stan Rajnak, Sidney Redner, Peter Reynolds, Qun Ru, David Stork, Oriol Valls, Gerard Vichniac, George Weiss, Pieter Visscher, and Ju-xing Yang. Needless to say, all errors, omissions and unclear passages are our responsibility.

The course on which this book is based could not have been developed without an initial donation of personal computers from IBM to Clark University and a small grant for course development from the National Science Foundation. One of us also wishes to thank the Mellon Committee of Clark University for support of curriculum development and the Digital Equipment Corporation for support of a related project involving the incorporation of computers into the undergraduate curriculum. We would also like to acknowledge the hospitality of the Department of Physics at Boston University where parts of the book were written.

Special thanks go to Stacey Bressler, Sherry Howlett, and Greg Smedsrud of the Apple Computer Corporation for their interest in our project. It would be difficult to imagine writing this book without the use of a Macintosh computer and an Apple LaserWriter, both donated to us by the Apple Computer Corporation. Many thanks are due to Bruce Spatz, former science editor at Addison-Wesley, for his support, interest, and patience, Sharon Van Gundy for finding some of our grammatical errors and to Mona Zeftel for producing the manuscript in camera-ready form. The text was produced using TEXtures and MacWrite; the figures were drawn by the authors using MacPaint, MacDraw, and Cricket Graph.

We are grateful to our wives, Patti Gould and Andrea Moll Tobochnik, and to the Gould children, Joshua, Emily and Evan, for their encouragement and understanding during the course of this work.

CONTENTS

PREFACE

Computer simulation is now an integral part of contemporary basic and applied science and is approaching a role equal in importance to the traditional experimental and theoretical approaches. Hence, the ability "to compute" is part of the essential repertoire of research scientists and educators.

The philosophy of this book is expressed well by the Chinese proverb (source unknown to us):

"I hear and I forget. I see and I remember. I do and I understand."

We ask not how can the computer be used to teach physics, but how can students be trained to teach the computer. Our primary goal is to create an environment in which the reader teaches the computer to simulate physical systems. Our experience is that an active involvement with computer simulations leads to a greater intuitive understanding of physical concepts. Other goals of the book are to introduce molecular dynamics and Monte Carlo methods, to integrate simple but realistic research-type problems into the undergraduate curriculum, and to teach by example structured programming techniques.

Much of the material in this text has been used in a one semester course entitled "Computer Simulation Laboratory" offered at Clark University. Prerequisites for the course are one semester each of physics and calculus. A background in computer programming is not necessary. The interests of the undergraduate and graduate students in the course have included physics, chemistry, biology, mathematics, computer science, geography and electrical engineering. The physics and programming background of these students has ranged from minimal to extensive. We have found that many computer simulations are accessible to those with a limited background in physics and that students with a stronger background can gain additional insight into material that they have already studied. The course is organized in the same way as other laboratory courses at Clark with two weekly lectures in which the subject matter is presented and student progress is reviewed. Programming methods are introduced in the context of a regularly scheduled laboratory. The course is project oriented and allows students the freedom to work at their own pace and to pursue problems consistent with their own interests and backgrounds.

We believe that computer simulation has become sufficiently important for courses of this kind to be taught at other institutions. However, other uses of this book might work equally well. For example, this book could be used as a supplement to an introductory physics course for honors students and in intermediate level courses on classical mechanics, waves, electricity and magnetism, statistical and thermal physics, quantum mechanics, and physical chemistry. The text can also form the basis of a numerical methods course. Although the book begins with basic concepts in physics and calculus, we believe that in general the most successful use of the book will be at the intermediate level.

The programming language used in the body of the text is True BASIC. Translations of several of the programs into Pascal and FORTRAN 77 are listed in the appendices to each part of the book. True BASIC is our language of choice because it is easy to learn and use, has "true" subroutines, excellent graphics capabilities, and is identical on the IBM PC and compatible computers and the Apple Macintosh computer. Readers familiar with "street" BASIC should have few problems adapting the programs in the text as long as they clearly distinguish local and global variables. In our view, the similarities of BASIC, FORTRAN and Pascal are much greater than their differences.

We believe you can learn programming the same way we did—in the context of a discipline. Although the book is as independent as possible of any particular brand of computer, we strongly recommend that readers with little programming experience should write their programs on a personal computer. Personal computers are easier to use than mainframe computers and also offer readily available graphics capabilities. The problems in the text should be done with a programming manual and a physics text as handy references.

Each chapter contains a brief discussion of the important physical concepts, followed by program listings, problems, and relevant questions. The discussion, programs and problems are interrelated and the discussions will be more readily understood after the problems are completed. We regard the program listings as text for the reader rather than source code for the computer. Our programs are designed to be simple and easy to read, rather than elegant or efficient. To do most of the problems, the reader must understand the logic of the programs and hence the logic of the underlying physical system. Most of the problems require at least some modification of the programs. We believe that typing in the programs line-by-line will help you learn programming more easily. Most of the programs are short and you are encouraged to change the programs. The problems are organized so that the earlier ones in a chapter provide the basis for the later problems in the same chapter and in following chapters. Problems denoted by an asterisk are either more advanced or require significantly more time than the average problem and are not a prerequisite for work in succeeding chapters. The recommended readings at the end of each chapter have been selected for their pedagogical value rather than for completeness or for historical accuracy. We apologize to our colleagues whose work has been inadvertently omitted and we would appreciate suggestions for new and additional references.

We emphasize classical physics in Part I and statistical physics in Part II. These areas reflect our own research interests but also are areas in which the methods of computer simulation can be introduced most easily. We also discuss waves, optical phenomena, electricity and magnetism, and quantum mechanics. Each part of the book contains enough material for a semester course on computer simulation. Part I of the text emphasizes the simulation of deterministic systems. Chapter 1 discusses the uses of the computer in physics and the nature of several popular computer languages. Chapter 2 introduces the Euler method for the numerical integration of first order differential equations. Since many readers are familiar with the Euler method, the main purpose of the chapter is to introduce the core syntax of True BASIC. Although this introduction might cover too much material for those without programming experience, remarkably little additional syntax is used in the remainder of the text. Chapters 3–5 use a modified form of the Euler method to simulate falling objects, planetary motion, and oscillatory motion. Chapter 5 also includes a section on electrical circuits and an appendix on other numerical methods for the solution of Newton's equation of motion. Chapter 6 introduces the method of molecular dynamics. Unless the reader has access to large scale computing (or the next generation of microcomputers), only a qualitative picture of thermal phenomena can be obtained from the simulations. However this method is important in physics and chemical physics and the ideas underlying it are straightforward extensions of the previous chapters. Chapter 7 introduces non-linear dynamical systems and the use of the computer to "discover" new knowledge. Chapters 8 and 9 mainly contain traditional material on oscillations and waves, and electrostatics and magnetostatics. Much of the material in these two chapters is oriented toward visual demonstrations.

Each chapter in Part II of the text applies a random sampling technique, known generally as "Monte Carlo" methods, to problems in statistical physics and quantum mechanics. Chapter 10 introduces Monte Carlo methods in the context of numerical integration. Although this chapter does not directly discuss physical phenomena, it allows us to survey the various methods in a well known context. Chapter 11 is devoted to random walks and their application to physical phenomena. Chapters 12 and 13 treat current research areas which are becoming important in many fields of science. In these chapters we discuss percolation, simple ideas of phase transitions and the renormalization group, fractals, local growth laws, and cellular automata. Many of the applications are not difficult to formulate but yield complex behavior which is visually interesting. Chapter 14 discusses an example of the approach to equilibrium and methods for computing the entropy. Chapter 15 uses a relatively new method to simulate the microcanonical ensemble and to "discover" the canonical Boltzmann distribution. Chapter 16 introduces Monte Carlo methods for simulating thermal systems. In Chapter 17 we discuss Monte Carlo and more traditional numerical methods for treating quantum systems. Chapter 18 briefly discusses how the same methods can solve many apparently unrelated problems.

The availability of personal computers and the demands from industry for meaningful computer literacy is putting pressure on all disciplines to incorporate computer related material into the basic curriculum. Thus far, most physics departments have used computers as a tool for data analysis and for demonstrations. Some physics departments now offer courses in computational physics and in measurement and control processes. However, the impact on the curriculum as measured by greater student understanding, increased numbers of physics students, or changes in textual material has been negligible. We realize that the nontrivial use of computers in physics education will take many years to accomplish. We hope that this book makes a contribution to that end, and we welcome your comments, suggestions and encouragement.

We have taken care to check our programs for errors and typos. It is our experience however that few programs remain error free forever, and we make no guarantee that the programs in this text are totally free of error. Instructors who adopt this book for a course may request a program disk (IBM PC or Macintosh format) at no charge from Addison-Wesley.

INTRODUCTION

1

The importance of computers in physics and the nature of computer simulation is discussed.

1.1 IMPORTANCE OF COMPUTERS IN PHYSICS

It is only necessary to read the research literature casually or to walk through a physics laboratory to see computers everywhere. For purposes of discussion, we can divide the use of computers in physics into four categories:

1. numerical analysis
2. symbolic manipulation
3. simulation
4. real-time control

In the numerical analysis mode, the simplifying physical principles are discovered prior to the computation. For example, we know that the solution of many problems in physics can be reduced to the solution of a set of simultaneous linear equations. Consider the equations

$$2x + 3y = 18$$
$$x - y = 4 \quad .$$

It is easy to find the *analytical* solution $x = 6$, $y = 2$ using the method of substitution and pencil and paper. Suppose we have to solve a set of four simultaneous equations. We can again find an analytical solution, perhaps using a more sophisticated method. If the number of variables becomes much larger, we have to use numerical methods and a computer to find a numerical solution. In this mode, the computer is a tool of *numerical analysis*, and the essential physical principles, e.g. the reduction of the problem to the inversion of a matrix, are included in the computer program. Since it is often necessary to compute a multi-dimensional integral, manipulate large matrices, or solve a complex differential equation, we see that this use of the computer is important in physics.

A less common but increasingly important use of the computer in theoretical physics is *symbolic manipulation*. As an example, suppose we want to know the solution to the quadratic equation $ax^2 + bx + c = 0$. A symbolic manipulation program can give us the solution in symbolic form $x = [-b \pm \sqrt{b^2 - 4ac}]/2a$. In addition such a program can give us the usual numerical solutions for specific values of a, b and c. Mathematical operations such as differentiation, integration, equation solution and power series expansion can be performed using a typical symbolic manipulation program. What will happen to education when such programs become readily available on personal computers? Will tables of integrals become as obsolete as slide rules?

In the *simulation* mode, the basic laws of the model are included in the program with a minimum of analysis. As an example suppose we give $10 to each student in a class of 100. The teacher, who also begins with $10 in her pocket, chooses a student at random and flips a coin. If the coin is "tails," the teacher gives $0.50 to the student; otherwise the student gives $0.50 to the teacher. Neither the teacher nor the student is allowed to go into debt. After many exchanges, we ask "What is the probability that a student has n dollars?" and "What is the probability that the teacher has m dollars?" Are these two probabilities the same? One way to find the answers to these questions is to do the experiment. However such an experiment would be difficult to arrange and tedious to perform. Although this particular problem can be solved exactly by analytical methods, not all problems of can be solved in this way. Another way to proceed is to incorporate the rules of the game into a computer program, simulate many exchanges, and compute the probabilities. After we obtain the computed probabilities, we might gain new insight into their nature and their relation to the exchanges of money. We can also use the computer to ask "What if?" questions. For example, how would the probabilities change if the exchanges were $1.00 rather than $0.50?

If we change the names of the players (e.g. money is energy) and change the rules of the game slightly, this type of simulation would be applicable to problems in magnetism and particle physics (see Chapter 15). During the past twenty-five years, the use of the computer in the simulation mode has helped us discover new simplifying physical principles.

In all these approaches, the main goal of the computation is generally insight rather than numbers. Computation has had a profound effect on the way we do physics, on the nature of the important questions in physics, and on the physical systems we choose to study. All three approaches require the use of at least some simplifying approximations to make the problem computationally feasible. However, since the simulation mode requires a minimum of analysis and emphasizes an exploratory mode of learning, we stress this approach in this text.

Computers are also important tools in experimental physics. Computers are often involved in all phases of a laboratory experiment, from the design of the apparatus, control of the apparatus during experimental runs, and the collection and analysis of data. This involvement of the computer has not only allowed experimentalists to sleep better at night, but has made possible experiments which would otherwise be impossible. Some of these tasks such as the design of an apparatus or the analysis of data are similar to those encountered in theoretical computation. However, the tasks involved in control and interactive data analysis are qualitatively different and involve real-time programming and the interfacing of computer hardware to various types of instrumentation. Consequently, a discussion of the use of computers in real-time control must be found in other texts.

1.2 THE NATURE OF COMPUTER SIMULATION

Why is computer simulation becoming important in physics? One reason is that most of our analytical tools such as differential calculus are best suited to the analysis of *linear* problems. For example, you have probably learned to analyze the motion of a particle attached to a spring by assuming a linear restoring force and solving Newton's second law of motion. However, many natural phenomena are *non-linear*, and small changes in a variable can produce large rather than small changes in another variable. Since non-linear problems can be solved by analytical methods only in special cases, the computer gives us a new tool to explore non-linear phenomena. Another reason for the importance of computer simulation is our interest in systems with many degrees of freedom or with many variables. The money exchange example described in Sec. 1.1 is an example of such a problem.

Developments in computer technology are leading to new ways of thinking about physical systems. Asking the question, "How can I formulate the problem on a computer?" has led to new formulations of physical laws and to the realization that it is both practical and natural to express scientific laws as rules for a computer rather than in terms of differential equations. Presently this new way of thinking about physical processes is leading some physicists to consider the computer as a physical system and to develop novel computer architectures which can more efficiently model physical systems in nature.

Computer simulations are sometimes referred to as *computer experiments* since they share much in common with laboratory experiments. Some of the analogies are shown in Table 1.1. The starting point of a computer simulation is the development of an idealized model of a physical system of interest. We then need to specify a procedure or *algorithm* for implementing the model on a computer. The computer program simulates the physical system and defines the computer experiment. Such a computer experiment serves as a bridge between laboratory experiments and theoretical calculations. For example, we can obtain essentially exact results by simulating an idealized model which has no laboratory counterpart. The comparison of the simulation results with an approximate theoretical calculation serves as a stimulus to the development of methods of calculation. On the other hand, a simulation can be done on a realistic model in order to make a more direct comparison with laboratory experiments.

Computer simulations, like laboratory experiments, are not substitutes for thinking but are tools which we can use to understand complex phenomena. But the goal of all our investigations of fundamental phenomena is to seek explanations of physical phenomena which fit on the back of an envelope or that can be made by the wave of a hand!

TABLE 1.1 Analogies between a computer simulation and a laboratory experiment.

Laboratory experiment	Computer simulation
sample	model
physical apparatus	computer program
calibration	testing of program
measurement	computation
data analysis	data analysis

1.3 IMPORTANCE OF GRAPHICS

Since computers are changing the way we do physics, they will also change the way we learn physics. For example, as the computer plays an increasing role in our understanding of physical phenomena, the visual representation of complex numerical results will become even more important. The human eye in conjunction with the visual processing capacity of the brain is a very sophisticated device for analyzing visual information. Most of us can draw the best straight line through a sequence of data points very quickly. And such a straight line is more meaningful to us than a "best fit" line drawn by a statistical package which we do not understand. Our eye can determine patterns and trends which might not be evident from tables of data and can observe changes with time which can lead to insight into the important mechanisms underlying a system's behavior.

At the same time, the use of graphics will increase our understanding of the nature of analytical solutions. For example, what does a sine function mean to you? We suspect that your answer is not the series, $sin\,x = x - x^3/3! + x^5/5! + \ldots$, but rather a periodic, constant amplitude graph (see Fig. 1.1). What is important is the visualization of the form of the function.

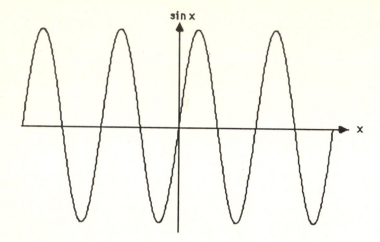

Fig. 1.1 Plot of the sine function.

1.4 PROGRAMMING LANGUAGES

We will use three programming languages in the text: BASIC, FORTRAN and Pascal. The BASIC programming language was developed in 1965 by John G. Kemeny and Thomas E. Kurtz of Dartmouth College as a language for introductory courses in computer science. Pascal was designed in 1970 by Niklaus Wirth of the Swiss Federal Institute of Technology and was also intended for teaching purposes. Both languages have since been adapted to many other purposes. FORTRAN was developed by John Backus and his colleagues at IBM between 1954 and 1957 and is the most common language used in scientific applications. The most recent version is known as FORTRAN 77. Many other programming languages, e.g. APL, C, LISP, Modula-2, PL/1, are also in use.

There is no single best programming language any more than there is a best natural language. Programming languages are not static, but continue to change with developments in hardware and theories of computation. As with any language, a working knowledge of one makes it easier to learn another. BASIC has the advantage of being easy to learn. The disadvantages of BASIC include its hardware dependence and more importantly its lack of modular programming features. Pascal is well structured and provides the ability to define a rich set of data structures. Pascal also imposes requirements which make it difficult to avoid writing modular programs. A disadvantage of Pascal is that these requirements make it more difficult to develop simple programs quickly. FORTRAN allows structured programming (we consider only FORTRAN 77), and much of its syntax is simpler than Pascal. The major disadvantages of FORTRAN are that it presently does not allow recursive subroutines, and data types are more limited than Pascal. Also, control structures such as DO WHILE or DO UNTIL are not standard in FORTRAN.

A new version of BASIC called True BASIC has recently been developed by Kemeny and Kurtz. True BASIC has subroutines similar to FORTRAN and has excellent graphics capabilities which are hardware independent. The identical True BASIC program can run on microcomputers as different as the IBM PC and the Apple Macintosh. Because of the introductory nature of much of this text and the importance of graphics, we assume that most readers will develop their programs on a microcomputer. For these reasons we have adopted True BASIC as the programming language in the body of the text. FORTRAN and Pascal versions of most of the programs are given at the end of each part of the text. Readers who already know a programming language will find the True BASIC program listings like "pseudocode" which can be easily translated into a language of their choice. Readers learning a programming language for the first time should compare the listings and attempt to acquire a passive understanding of FORTRAN and Pascal. A comparison of the core syntax of Microsoft BASIC, True BASIC, FORTRAN 77 and Pascal is given in Appendix A at the end of Part I. Short program examples are given in Appendix B.

1.5 LEARNING TO PROGRAM

If you already know how to program, try reading a program that you wrote several years (or even several weeks) ago. Many scientists would not be able to follow the logic of their program and consequently would have to rewrite their program. If you are learning programming for the first time, it is important to learn good programming habits and to avoid this problem. The programs in this text employ *structured* programming techniques such as the IF-THEN-ELSE constructs and avoid the use of GOTO statements. The programs are also written in *modules,* which are subprograms that perform specific tasks.

Because of their background, students of science have special advantages in learning how to program. The many cables and other hardware aspects of computers are already familiar to most of us and we know that our mistakes cannot harm the computer. More importantly, we have an already existing context in which to learn programming. The past several decades of doing physics research with computers has given us numerous examples which we can use to learn physics, programming, and data analysis. Thus we encourage you to learn programming in the context of the examples in each chapter.

Our experience is that the single most important criterion of program quality is readibility. If a program is easy to read and follow, it is probably a good program. The analogies between a good program and a well written paper are strong. Few programs come out perfect on their first draft, regardless of the techniques and rules we use to write it. Rewriting will always be an important part of programming.

1.6 HOW TO USE THIS BOOK

In general, each chapter begins with a short background summary of the nature of the system and the important general questions. We then introduce the computer algorithms, True BASIC syntax if necessary, and discuss a sample program. The programs are meant to be read as text on an equal basis with the discussions and the problems which are interspersed throughout the text. It is strongly recommended that all the problems be read, since many concepts are introduced after the simulation of a physical process.

It is a good idea to maintain a laboratory notebook to record your programs, results, graphical output, and your analysis of the data. This practice will help you develop good habits for future research projects, prevent duplication, help you organize your thoughts, and save you time. Ideally you will use your notebook to write a laboratory report or mini-research paper on your programs, results, data analysis and interpretation.

REFERENCES AND SUGGESTIONS FOR ADDITIONAL READING

Programming Manuals

We recommend that you learn programming the same way you learned English—by practice and with a little help from your friends and manuals. We list some of our favorite programming manuals here, but the list is by no means complete. Many of the manuals which are supplied with the programming language are also excellent.

Richard E. Crandall, *Pascal Applications for the Sciences, A Self-Teaching Guide,* Wiley Press (1984). This book is not a programming manual, but contains many examples of Pascal programs and a discussion of the nature of Pascal. Of particular interest are the discussions of three-dimensional graphics routines and Fast Fourier Transforms, topics not treated in our text.

Susan Finger and Ellen Finger, *Advanced Applications for Introduction to Pascal with Applications in Science and Engineering*, D. C. Heath (1986).

John G. Kemeny and Thomas E. Kurtz, *True BASIC*, Addison-Wesley (1985). The True BASIC reference manual is well written and essential. Other useful books on True BASIC include William S. Davis, *True BASIC Primer*, Addison-Wesley (1986), and Larry Joel Goldstein, C. Edward Moore and Peter J. Welcher, *Structured Programming with True BASIC*, Prentice-Hall (1986).

Vardell Lines, *Pascal as a Second Language*, Prentice-Hall (1984). Once you know structured programming, you can learn another language easily.

Michael Metcalf, *Effective FORTRAN 77*, Clarendon Press (1985). An excellent but advanced text. The author has had extensive experience in large-scale data processing in high-energy physics.

Robert Moll and Rachael Folsom, *Macintosh Pascal*, Houghton Mifflin (1985). One of many softcover books on Pascal.

Russ Walters, *The Secret Guide to Computers*, 12th ed. (1986). A three volume collection by one of the most original writers in the computer industry. You have never read a programming manual like this one before. May you enjoy computers and programming as much as Walters. Vol. 3 which discusses FORTRAN and Pascal is the most relevant. The books can be purchased by mail by writing to Walters at 22 Ashland St., Somerville, MA 02144.

Robert Weiss and Charles Seiter, *Pascal for FORTRAN Programmers*, Addison-Wesley (1984).

General References on Physics and Computers

Per Bak, "Doing physics with microcomputers," *Physics Today* **36**, No. 12, pp. 25-29 (December, 1983).

Alfred Bork, *Learning with Computers*, Digital Press (1981). Various strategies for using computers in education are discussed.

Robert Ehrlich, *Physics and Computers*, Houghton Mifflin (1973). This book and the one by Grossberg are excellent examples of pioneering texts which integrate computer applications into the undergraduate physics curriculum.

Robert G. Fuller, "Resource letter CPE-1: Computers in physics education," Am. J. Phys. **54**, 782 (1986). The author hopes that it is possible that the computer can bring more fun into the study of physics.

Alan B. Grossberg, *Fortran for Engineering Physics*, McGraw-Hill (1971). This laboratory manual treats mechanical and thermal systems.

Dieter W. Heermann, *Computer Simulation Methods in Theoretical Physics*, Springer-Verlag (1986). A discussion of molecular dynamics and Monte Carlo methods directed toward advanced undergraduate and beginning graduate students.

Steven E. Koonin, *Computational Physics,* Benjamin/Cummings (1986). The emphasis of this book is on applications of numerical methods. Many nontrival problems are given.

John R. Merrill, *Using Computers in Physics*, University of Press of America (1980). Areas discussed by Merrill and not covered in our text include applications to relativity, nuclear decay, snd solid state physics.

Herbert D. Peckham, *Computers, BASIC, and Physics*, Addison-Wesley (1971). Why did the pioneeering texts of the early 1970's not make a greater impact? Will the widespread availability of microcomputers make a difference?

Commun. ACM **28**, No. 4, pp. 352-394 (April, 1985). Special Section on Computing in Theoretical Physics.

Physics Today **36**, No. 5, pp. 24-62 (May, 1983). Special Issue: "Doing Physics with Computers". Articles by Donald R. Hamann, "Computers in physics: an overview"; Michael Creutz, "High-energy physics"; Jorge E. Hirsch and Douglas J. Scalapino, "Condensed-matter physics"; and Bruce I. Cohen and John Killeen, "Computations in plasma physics."

THE COFFEE COOLING PROBLEM

2

We discuss a simple numerical method for the solution of first-order differential equations and introduce several simple programming and graphical techniques.

2.1 BACKGROUND

In order to initiate ourselves into computer simulation methods, it is a good idea
first to sit down at a comfortable distance from a computer and enjoy a cup of
hot coffee (or tea). However, usually when we take our first sip, we find that
the coffee is too hot. If we are in a hurry, we can add milk. But if the coffee is
still too hot, we must wait for it to cool. If we want the coffee to cool as soon
as possible, is it better to add the milk immediately after the coffee is made, or
should we wait for a while before we add the milk?

The nature of the heat flow from the coffee to the surrounding air is complicated and in general involves the mechanisms of convection, radiation, evapora-
tion, and conduction. However, if the temperature difference between an object
and its surroundings is not too large, the rate of change of the temperature of
the object is proportional to this temperature difference. We can formulate this
statement more precisely in terms of a differential equation:

$$\frac{dT}{dt} = -r(T - T_s) \tag{2.1}$$

where T is the temperature of the body, T_s is the temperature of the surroundings
and r is the "cooling constant." The "cooling constant" depends on the heat
transfer mechanism, the contact area with the surroundings, and the thermal
properties of the body. The minus sign appears in (2.1) because if $T > T_s$, the
temperature of the body will decrease with time. The relation (2.1) is known
as *Newton's law of cooling.* Try integrating (2.1) to obtain a solution for the
temperature as a function of the time.

Equation (2.1) is an example of a *first-order* differential equation since only
the first derivative of the unknown function $T(t)$ appears. It is important to
know how to solve such equations, since many types of systems can be modelled
by differential equations. Let us consider a first-order equation of the form

$$\frac{dy}{dx} = g(x) \quad . \tag{2.2}$$

In general, an *analytical* solution of (2.2) in terms of well-known functions does
not exist. Moreover, even when analytical solutions do exist, our interpretation
of their nature will be aided by a visual display of the solution. For these reasons, we are motivated to seek approximate, but accurate, numerical solutions
of differential equations and to learn simple ways of visually representing the
solutions.

2.2 THE EULER ALGORITHM

The standard technique for the numerical solution of differential equations involves the conversion of a differential equation to a *finite difference* equation. Let us analyze the meaning of (2.2). Suppose that at $x = x_0$, y has the value y_0. Since (2.2) tells us how y changes at x_0, we can find the *approximate* value of y at the neighboring point $x_1 = x_0 + \Delta x$ if Δx is small. The simplest approximation is to assume that $g(x)$, the rate of change of y, is constant over the interval x_0 to x_1. Then the approximate value of y at $x_1 = x_0 + \Delta x$ is given by

$$y_1 = y(x_0) + \Delta y \approx y(x_0) + g(x_0)\Delta x \quad . \tag{2.3}$$

We can repeat this procedure again to find the value of y at the point $x_2 = x_1 + \Delta x$:

$$y_2 = y(x_1 + \Delta x) \approx y(x_1) + g(x_1)\Delta x \quad . \tag{2.4}$$

Clearly we can generalize this procedure to calculate the approximate value of y at any point $x_n = x_0 + n\Delta x$ by the iterative formula

$$y_n = y_{n-1} + g(x_{n-1})\Delta x \qquad (n = 0, 1, 2, \ldots) \quad . \tag{2.5}$$

This procedure is called the constant slope or *Euler* method. We expect the method will yield a good approximation to the "true" value of y only if Δx is sufficiently small; the degree of "smallness" of Δx depends on our requirements and must be left vague until we consider specific applications.

The Euler method assumes that the rate of change of y is constant over the interval x_{n-1} to x_n, and that the rate of change can be evaluated at the *beginning* of the interval. The graphical interpretation of (2.5) is shown in Fig. 2.1. We see that if the slope changes during an interval, a discrepancy occurs between the numerical solution and the true solution. Nonetheless the discrepancy can be made smaller if we choose a smaller value of Δx.

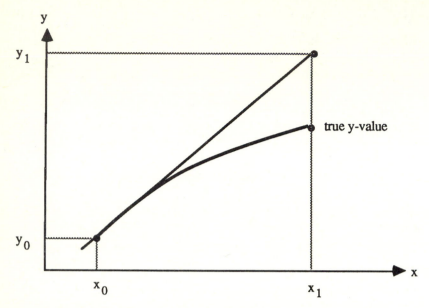

Fig. 2.1 Graphical illustration of the Euler method. The slope is evaluated at the beginning of the interval. The Euler approximation and
the true function are represented by a straight line and a curve respectively.

2.3 A SIMPLE EXAMPLE

To prepare ourselves for the coffee cooling problem in Sec. 2.5, let us use the
Euler method to compute the numerical solution of the differential equation
$dy/dx = 2x$ with the initial condition $y = 1$ at $x = 1$. We wish to find the
approximate value of y at $x = 2$. We choose $\Delta x = 0.1$ so that the number of
steps is $n = (2-1)/\Delta x = 10$. After we finish the calculation, we might find that
this value of Δx is too large and that we have to repeat the calculation with a
smaller value of Δx.

The calculation can be arranged as in Table 2.1. The condition $x = 1$ determines the initial slope $g(x) = 2x = 2$. The value of y at the end of the interval,
y_1, is obtained from y_0, the value of y at the beginning of the interval, by the
relation

$$y_1 = y_0 + \Delta x(slope) = 1 + 0.1(2) = 1.2 \quad . \tag{2.6}$$

This value of y is then transferred to the second line of Table 2.1 and the process is repeated. In this way we find that $y = 3.90$ at $x = 2$. In comparison, the true solution is $y = x^2 = 4$; the error is 2.5%. Convince yourself that a smaller value of Δx improves the accuracy of the solution by redoing Table 2.1 using $\Delta x = 0.05$.

TABLE 2.1 Iterated solution of the differential equation $dy/dx = 2x$ with $y = 1$ at $x = 1$. The step size is $\Delta x = 0.1$. Three significant figures are shown.

x	y	$g(x) = 2x$	$y_{n-1} + 0.1(\text{slope})$
1.00	1.00	2.00	$1.00 + 0.10(2.00) = 1.20$
1.10	1.20	2.20	$1.20 + 0.10(2.20) = 1.42$
1.20	1.42	2.40	$1.42 + 0.10(2.40) = 1.66$
1.30	1.66	2.60	$1.66 + 0.10(2.60) = 1.92$
1.40	1.92	2.80	$1.92 + 0.10(2.80) = 2.20$
1.50	2.20	3.00	$2.20 + 0.10(3.00) = 2.50$
1.60	2.50	3.20	$2.50 + 0.10(3.20) = 2.82$
1.70	2.82	3.40	$2.82 + 0.10(3.40) = 3.16$
1.80	3.16	3.60	$3.16 + 0.10(3.60) = 3.52$
1.90	3.52	3.80	$3.52 + 0.10(3.80) = 3.90$
2.00	3.90		

2.4 A COMPUTER PROGRAM

Now that we have obtained a numerical solution of a differential equation using the Euler method, we are ready to restate the method as a computer *algorithm*, i.e. as a finite sequence of precise steps or rules which solve a problem. We will then develop a computer program to implement the algorithm. The Euler method is specified by the following algorithm:

1. Choose the initial conditions, step size, and number of iterations;
2. Determine y and the slope at the beginning of the interval;
3. Calculate y at the end of the interval and print the result;
4. Repeat steps 2 and 3 the desired number of times.

Our first step is to write the program as a series of separate tasks which correspond to the above steps. For example we can write the main program in terms of two tasks:

```
CALL initial
CALL Euler
```

In True BASIC and FORTRAN these tasks are written as a series of *calls* to *subroutines*; in Pascal these tasks are denoted as *procedures*.

We next use True BASIC to implement each task. For simplicity we will consider the solution of the same differential equation, $dy/dx = 2x$, as discussed in Sec. 2.3. The initial conditions and the numerical parameters are specified in **SUB initial**.

```
SUB initial(y,x,dx,n)
    LET x = 1                 ! initial value of x
    LET xmax = 2              ! maximum value of x
    LET y = 1                 ! initial value of y
    LET dx = 0.1             ! magnitude of step size
    LET n = (xmax - x)/dx
END SUB
```

The following characteristics of True BASIC have been used:

1. A subroutine is defined by a **SUB** statement.
2. Assignments of variables are made with the **LET** statement.
3. Comment statements begin with **!** and can be included anywhere in a program. Use them freely to make your programs readable. They are ignored by the computer.
4. The end of a subroutine is denoted by the **END SUB** statement.

Our next task implements the Euler method and prints the result of each iteration:

```
SUB Euler(y,x,dx,n)
    FOR i = 1 to n                  ! iterate n times
        LET slope = 2*x             ! slope at beginning of interval
        LET change = slope*dx       ! estimate of total change during interval
        LET y = y + change          ! new value of y
        LET x = x + dx              ! increment value of x
        PRINT x,y
    NEXT i
END SUB
```

We used two additional statements in **SUB Euler**:

1. The **FOR** ... **NEXT** loop. The control variable in the loop is the integer i. Its initial value is set equal to 1. Each time the loop is repeated, i is increased by 1. The loop continues as long as i is less than or equal to n.
2. The **PRINT** statement displays the values of the selected variables on the screen.

The complete program is listed in the following:

```
PROGRAM example          ! beginning of main program
CALL initial(y,x,dx,n)
CALL Euler(y,x,dx,n)
END                      ! end of main program

SUB initial(y,x,dx,n)
   LET x = 1             ! initial value of x
   LET xmax = 2          ! maximum value of x
   LET y = 1             ! initial value of y
   LET dx = 0.1          ! magnitude of step size
   LET n = (xmax - x)/dx
END SUB

SUB Euler(y,x,dx,n)
   FOR i = 1 to n               ! iterate n times
      LET slope = 2*x           ! slope at beginning of interval
      LET change = slope*dx     ! estimate of total change during interval
      LET y = y + change        ! new value of y
      LET x = x + dx            ! increment value of x
      PRINT x,y
   NEXT i
END SUB
```

If you are not familiar with a programming language, run the program and see how it works. Note the following characteristics of True BASIC which have been used in **Program example**:

1. The first line of the main program has an optional heading.
2. The last line of the main program must contain an **END** statement.
3. *External* subroutines such as **SUB initial** and **SUB Euler** are listed after the **END** statement of the main program. They are separate program units and do not share variables with the main program unless the variables are passed to and from the main program. In both subroutines the variables y,

x, dx, n are passed. More examples of the use of external subroutines are given in the following.

4. The structure of the program has been emphasized by listing keywords in upper case and indenting the contents of subroutines and loops. True BASIC is not case sensitive and ignores extra spaces.

Program example is an example of a *modular* program, a program divided into separate tasks each of which can be written and tested separately. A complete program includes at a minimum a *main* program, containing executable statements. Usually the main program consists of a series of invocations or *calls* to subprograms. These subprograms are of two types, *subroutines* and *functions*. An example of the latter will be given in Sec. 2.7.

Whenever possible, we will use the features of True BASIC, FORTRAN and Pascal which emphasize the similarities of the three languages. Hence in True BASIC we will use only *external* subroutines and functions. External program units are defined in any order *after* the **END** statement of the main program. In order to understand the nature of external subroutines, we need to distinguish between *local* and *global* variables. A variable name represents a memory location in the computer. An external subroutine is a separate program unit and has its own *local* variables. If the same variable name is used in two program units, the name represents two different memory locations. As an example, **Program local** uses the variable names x and y in the main program and in **SUB add**.

```
PROGRAM local
LET x = 1
LET y = 1
CALL add
PRINT x,y
END

SUB add
  LET x = x + 1
  LET y = y + 2
END SUB
```

Since the variable name x is a *local* variable, the result printed for x in the main program is 1. The same result holds for y.

We also need to define *global* variables, variables that are known to two or more program units. In True BASIC, subroutines pass information to the main program and to other subroutines via arguments in the subroutine calls. The passing of information goes both ways. Thus, if a variable is passed from the main program to a subroutine and then changed by the subroutine, it is passed back to the main program with its new value. **Program global1** illustrates the passing of the variable names x and y.

```
PROGRAM global1
LET x = 1
LET y = 1
CALL add(x,y)
PRINT x,y
END

SUB add(x,y)
  LET x = x + 1
  LET y = y + 2
END SUB
```

What result is printed for x and y?

It is a bit misleading to say that variable names are passed to a subroutine. More precisely, variable names are not passed, but rather the memory location in the computer is passed. The variable name is simply a label that identifies the memory location. What are the values of x and y if **SUB add** in **Program global2** is written in the following form?

```
PROGRAM global2
LET x = 1
LET y = 1
CALL add(x,y)
PRINT x,y
END

SUB add(r,s)
  LET r = r + 1
  LET s = s + 2
END SUB
```

In the same spirit, we have to remember that the order as well as the number of the variables passed must be the same in each call to the subroutine and in the definition of the subroutine. What are the values of x and y if **SUB add** in **Program global3** is written as follows?

```
PROGRAM global3
LET x = 1
LET y = 1
CALL add(x,y)
PRINT x,y
END

SUB add(y,x)
  LET x = x + 1
  LET y = y + 2
END SUB
```

Local and global variables also exist in Pascal, but are defined in a somewhat different way. In contrast, ordinary BASIC does not have true subroutines.

Why do we care about subroutines? One of the important practical reasons is that they simplify programming. If we think of a program as a sequence of tasks, then many tasks appear again and again in different algorithms. Hence we can use previously written subroutines developed either by ourselves or by others. Since the subroutines are separate programs, we do not have to read through the listings and see if the same variable name has been used in different parts of our program. Another important reason is that the use of subroutines encourages the development of modular programs whose parts are as decoupled as possible so that a change in one part does not affect other parts. The separation of a program into parts lets us concentrate on one part at a time and makes it easier for us to follow the logic of the program and ensure that each part works as it should.

2.5 THE COFFEE COOLING PROGRAM

We now return to our cup of coffee and develop a computer program to obtain a numerical solution of Newton's law of cooling. In order to determine if our model of temperature cooling is reasonable, we give experimental data in Table 2.2 for the cooling of a real cup of coffee.

TABLE 2.2 Cooling of a cup of coffee in a ceramic mug. The temperature was recorded with an estimated accuracy of $0.1\,^\circ C$. The air temperature was $22.0\,^\circ C$.

time (min)	$T(^\circ C)$	time (min)	$T(^\circ C)$
0	83.0	8.0	64.7
1.0	77.7	9.0	63.4
2.0	75.1	10.0	62.1
3.0	73.0	11.0	61.0
4.0	71.1	12.0	59.9
5.0	69.4	13.0	58.7
6.0	67.8	14.0	57.8
7.0	66.4	15.0	56.6

Program cool, which implements the Euler algorithm for the numerical solution of Newton's law of cooling, is similar in structure to **Program example**. The only difference is that printing has been assigned to **SUB output** which is called from **SUB Euler**. Since **SUB output** contains only one line, this added subroutine might not seem necessary. However, our modular approach will be helpful when we later wish to plot rather than print our results.

```
PROGRAM cool                ! Euler approximation for coffee cooling problem
CALL initial(t,temperature,room_temp,r,dt,ncalc)
CALL Euler(t,temperature,room_temp,r,dt,ncalc)
END

SUB initial(t,temperature,room_temp,r,dt,ncalc)
    LET t = 0                   ! initial time
    LET temperature = 83        ! initial coffee temperature (C)
    LET room_temp = 22          ! room temperature (C)
    LET r = 0.1                 ! cooling constant (1/min)
    LET dt = 0.1                ! time step (min)
    LET tmax = 2                ! duration (min)
    LET ncalc = tmax/dt         ! total number of steps
END SUB
```

```
SUB Euler(t,temperature,room_temp,r,dt,ncalc)
   FOR icalc = 1 to ncalc      ! change calculated at beginning of interval
      LET change = -r*(temperature - room_temp)
      LET temperature = temperature + change*dt
      LET t = t + dt              ! time
      CALL output(t,temperature)
   NEXT icalc
END SUB

SUB output(t,temperature)
   PRINT t,temperature          ! print results
END SUB
```

PROBLEM 2.1 Coffee cooling program

a. After we have typed our program and removed all the syntax errors, how do we know whether or not the program correctly implements the desired algorithm? For example, you might have typed a minus sign rather than a plus sign. The minimum that we can do is to compare the results of our program to limiting cases for which an analytical solution or hand calculation is available. Use the Euler method and a calculator to obtain a numerical solution of Newton's law of cooling for the same parameters that are chosen in **Program cool**. Compare your hand calculations to the output of **Program cool** and *verify* your program in this case.

b. Modify **Program cool** using the **INPUT PROMPT** statement (see the True BASIC reference guide) so that the numerical values of the parameters r, $tmax$, and dt can be typed in from the keyboard.

c. Modify **Program cool** so that a heading for the tabular listing is printed above the results for the time and temperature.

d. Use a "nested" **FOR NEXT** loop so that results for the time and temperature are printed at convenient time intervals rather than after every time step.

Since the above programming problem might be new to you, we give a "solution" below. Note that **SUB Euler** has been modified so that it computes the iterated solution *ncalc* times between calls to **SUB output**. Of course our solution is not unique and should be used only as an example.

```
PROGRAM cooler                    ! modified program
CALL initial(t,temperature,room_temp,r,dt,ncalc,nprt)
CALL output(t,temperature)     ! print initial values
FOR iprt = 1 to nprt
  CALL Euler(t,temperature,room_temp,r,dt,ncalc)
  CALL output(t,temperature)   ! print results
NEXT iprt
END

SUB initial(t,temperature,room_temp,r,dt,ncalc,nprt)
  LET t = 0
  LET temperature = 83         ! initial coffee temperature (C)
  LET room_temp = 22           ! room temperature (C)
  INPUT prompt "cooling constant r = ": r     ! cooling constant
  INPUT prompt "duration = ": tmax
  INPUT prompt "time step dt = ": dt
  LET print_period = 0.5        ! time (min) between successive printing
  LET nprt =  tmax/print_period    ! number of times results are printed
  LET ncalc = print_period/dt       ! # of iterations between printing
  PRINT "time","temperature"
  PRINT                             ! skip line
END SUB

SUB Euler(t,temperature,room_temp,r,dt,ncalc)
  FOR icalc = 1 to ncalc
    LET change = -r*(temperature - room_temp)
    LET temperature = temperature + change*dt
  NEXT icalc
  LET t = t + dt*ncalc
END SUB

SUB output(t,temperature)
  PRINT t,temperature               ! print results
END SUB
```

PROBLEM 2.2 Analysis of the data

a. Since we have measured time in minutes, the units of the cooling constant r are min^{-1}. You might have noticed that the value $r = 0.1 \ \text{min}^{-1}$ used in **Program cool** gives a cooling curve $T(t)$ which does not correspond to the data given in Table 2.2. Use different values of r to find an approximate value of r which describes the "real world" results shown in Table 2.2. Make sure that your value of Δt is small enough to not affect your results for the time-dependence of the temperature. Consider the following questions. Is your value of r reasonable? Is Newton's law of cooling applicable to a cup of coffee? If r is much smaller or bigger than unity, what does that imply about our choice of units of time? Would r be larger or smaller, if we were to use a cup with special insulation?

b. The initial difference in temperature between the coffee and its surroundings is 61 °C. How long does it take for the coffee to cool so that the difference is $61/2 = 30.5$ °C? How long does it take the difference to become 61/4 and 61/8? First try to understand your results in simple terms without using the computer.

c. Use the value of r found in part (a) and make a graph showing the dependence of temperature on time. Plot the data given in Table 2.2 on the same graph and compare your results. Although we will learn in Sec. 2.7 how to write a computer program to plot data, it will still be a good idea to make preliminary plots by hand to obtain a "feel" for the nature of your data.

d. Suppose that the initial temperature of the coffee is 90 °C, but that the coffee can be sipped comfortably only when its temperature is below 75 °C. Assume that at 90 °C, the addition of milk cools the coffee by 5 °C. If you are in a hurry and want to wait the shortest possible time, should the milk be added first and the coffee be allowed to cool, or should you wait until the coffee has cooled to 80 °C before adding the milk? Although you might already know the answer, use your program to "simulate" the two cases. Choose a value of r which corresponds to a real cup of coffee. This type of "what if" simulation of a "dynamical system" is an important technique in policy analysis (see for example Roberts et al.).

2.6 ACCURACY AND STABILITY

Now that we have learned how to use the Euler method to find a numerical solution to a first-order differential equation, we need to develop some practical guidelines to help us estimate the accuracy of the method. Since we have replaced a differential equation by a difference equation, we know that our numerical solution cannot be identically equal to the "true" solution of the original differential equation. In general, the discrepancy between the two solutions is due to two causes. Computers do not store real numbers (e.g. numbers with decimal points and fractions) with infinite precision but instead store numbers to a maximum number of digits which is hardware and software dependent. Arithmetic operations such as addition and division which involve real numbers can introduce an additional error, called the *roundoff error.* For example, if we had a computer which only stored real numbers to two significant figures, the product 2.1 × 3.2 would be stored as 6.7. The significance of roundoff errors is that they accumulate with increasing amounts of calculation. Ideally we choose algorithms that do not significantly magnify the roundoff error, e.g. we avoid subtracting numbers which are the same order of magnitude.

The other source of the discrepancy between the true answer and the computed answer is the error which is characteristic of the choice of algorithm rather than the accuracy of the computer. This error is called the *truncation error* in some numerical analysis textbooks. Since these errors depend on your choice of algorithm, you should be motivated to learn more about numerical analysis and the estimation of truncation errors. However, there is no general prescription for the "best" method for obtaining numerical solutions of differential equations. We will find in later chapters that each method has advantages and disadvantages and the proper selection depends on the nature of the solution, which you might not know in advance, and on your objectives. How accurate must the answer be? Over how large an interval do you need the solution? What kind of computer are you using? How much computer time and personal time do you have?

In practice we determine the accuracy of our numerical solution by reducing the value of Δt until the numerical solution is unchanged at the desired level of accuracy. Of course, we have to be careful not to choose Δt too small, since too many steps would be required and the total computation time and roundoff error would increase.

In addition to accuracy, another important consideration is the stability of an algorithm. For example, it might happen that the numerical results are very good for short times, but diverge from the "true" solution for longer times. This divergence might occur if small errors in the algorithm are multiplied many times causing the error to grow geometrically. Such an algorithm is said to be *unstable* for the particular problem. We consider the accuracy and the stability of the Euler method in the following problem.

PROBLEM 2.3 Accuracy and stability of the Euler method

We can use the analytical solution of the differential equation (2.1) to study the accuracy of the Euler method. The analytical solution of (2.1) can be written in the form

$$T(t) = T_s - (T_s - T_0)e^{-rt} \quad . \tag{2.7}$$

Note that $T(t = 0) = T_s - (T_s - T_0) = T_0$, and $T(t \to \infty) = T_s$.

a. Use **Program cooler** to compute the temperature at $t = 1$ minute with $\Delta t = 0.1, 0.05, 0.025, 0.01$, and 0.005. Choose a value of r corresponding to a real cup of coffee. Make a table showing the difference between the exact solution (2.7) and your numerical solution as a function of Δt. Is the difference a decreasing function of Δt? If Δt is decreased by a factor of 2, how does the difference change? Plot the difference as a function of Δt. If your points fall approximately on a straight line, then the difference is proportional to Δt (for $\Delta t \ll 1$). A numerical method is called nth order, if the difference between the analytical and numerical solutions at a fixed value of t is proportional to $(\Delta t)^n$. What is the order of the Euler method?

b. What value of Δt is necessary for 0.1% accuracy at $t = 1$? What value of Δt is necessary for 0.1% accuracy at $t = 5$?

c. One way to determine the accuracy of a numerical solution is to repeat the calculation with a smaller step size and compare results. If the two computations agree to n decimal places, we can assume that the results are correct to that many places. Consider the differential equation

$$R\frac{dQ}{dt} = V - \frac{Q}{C} \tag{2.8}$$

with $Q = 0$ at $t = 0$. This equation represents the charging of a capacitor in an RC circuit with an applied voltage V. Measure t in seconds and choose $R = 2000$ ohms (Ω), $C = 10^{-6}$ farads (F), and $V = 10$ volts. Do you expect $Q(t)$ to increase with t? Does Q increase indefinitely or does $Q(t)$ reach a steady-state value? Write a simple program to solve (2.8) numerically using the Euler method. What value of Δt is necessary to obtain three decimal accuracy at $t = 0.005$ s?

d. What is the nature of your numerical solution to (2.8) for $\Delta t = 0.005$, 0.004, and 0.003? Does a small change in Δt lead to a large change in the computed value of Q? Is the Euler method stable for any value of Δt?

2.7 ELEMENTARY GRAPHICS

One of the advantages of microcomputers is their ability to generate graphics quickly and easily. Although a standard graphics language does not yet exist, the core graphics statements are similar on a variety of computers and an understanding of simple graphics routines on one computer will be sufficient to allow you to master another computer or another graphics language easily. In the following, we discuss the core graphics commands in True BASIC and develop a program to plot a function on the screen. The core graphics commands for several other languages and graphics packages are summarized in the FORTRAN and Pascal appendices at the end of Part I.

A graphics monitor is covered by a grid of "pixels." The number of pixels is hardware-dependent. One of the advantages of True BASIC is that the number of pixels is irrelevant. That is, the mapping of the absolute values of the coordinates to the device coordinates or pixels is done by True BASIC. The first step in using a graphics display with True BASIC is to specify the range of coordinates that are to be plotted. The statement

SET window xmin, xmax, ymin, ymax

determines the minimum and maximum x (horizontal) and y (vertical) coordinates and clears the screen. The statement

PLOT POINTS: x,y;

plots a point at (x, y) in the current window coordinates. Some of the "core" True BASIC graphics statements are summarized in Table 2.3. Several other commands will be introduced in later chapters as they are needed.

TABLE 2.3 Summary of "core" True BASIC graphics statements.

```
PLOT POINTS: x,y
PLOT LINES: x1,y1; x2,y2;
PLOT TEXT, at x,y: expr$
BOX LINES xmin,xmax,ymin,ymax
BOX ELLIPSE xmin,xmax,ymin,ymax
BOX AREA xmin,xmax,ymin,ymax
BOX CLEAR xmin,xmax,ymin,ymax
SET window xmin,xmax,ymin,ymax
SET COLOR color$
SET BACK color$
SET CURSOR line,column
CLEAR
FLOOD x,y
```

Run the following program to see how several of the graphics commands work. You might wish to add more **PAUSE** statements.

```
PROGRAM graphics
SET window 0,100,0,100
PLOT TEXT, at 35,90: "demonstration program"
LET xmin = 10
LET ymin = 10
LET xmax = 30
LET ymax = 30
FOR i = 1 to ymin
    PLOT POINTS: i,xmin
NEXT i
PAUSE 1                 ! one second pause
PLOT LINES: xmin,ymin; xmax,ymax
BOX LINES xmin,xmax,ymin,ymax
BOX ELLIPSE xmin,xmax,ymin,ymax
BOX AREA xmin,xmax,ymin,ymax
BOX CLEAR xmin,xmax,ymin,ymax
```

```
SET back "black"
CLEAR
SET color "white"
SET cursor 10,5          ! use character rather than window coordinates
PRINT "demonstration program"
BOX AREA xmin,xmax,ymin,ymax
BOX LINES 50,60,5,60
END
```

We now use several of the graphics commands to develop a program which plots a function on the screen. The structure of the main program is

```
PROGRAM plot                    ! example of plotting program
CALL minmax(xmin,xmax,ymin,ymax,title$)
CALL plot_axis(xmin,xmax,ymin,ymax,title$)
CALL plot_function(xmin,xmax)
END
```

The minimum and maximum values of the x and y axes are inputed from the keyboard in **SUB minmax**.

```
SUB minmax(xmin,xmax,ymin,ymax,title$)
  INPUT prompt "minimum value of horizontal variable? ": xmin
  INPUT prompt "maximum value of horizontal variable? ": xmax
  INPUT prompt "minimum value of vertical variable? ": ymin
  INPUT prompt "maximum value of vertical variable? ": ymax
  INPUT prompt "title of graph? ": title$
END SUB
```

SUB plot_axis draws the horizontal and vertical axes, adds "tick" or "hash" marks and labels the axes and graph. The optimum location and number of tick marks and labels depends on the resolution of your graphics screen. The numerical value corresponding to each tick mark is not given, since the physical size of the text characters might not match the scale of your plot. Note the use of the **PLOT TEXT** statement with the **PRINT using$** function and the **IF-THEN-ELSE** control structure.

```
SUB plot_axis(xmin,xmax,ymin,ymax,title$)
  LET ntick = 10              ! number of tick marks
  ! distance between tick marks on x-axis
  LET dx = (xmax - xmin)/ntick
  ! distance between tick marks on y-axis
  LET dy = (ymax - ymin)/ntick
  ! determine world or window coordinates
  SET window xmin - dx,xmax + dx,ymin - dy,ymax + dy
  ! determine location of axes
  IF xmin*xmax < 0 then
     LET x0 = 0
  ELSE
     LET x0 = xmin
  END IF
  IF ymin*ymax < 0 then
     LET y0 = 0
  ELSE
     LET y0 = ymin
  END IF
  ! draw axes
  PLOT LINES: x0,ymin; x0,ymax       ! vertical-axis
  PLOT LINES: xmin,y0; xmax,y0       ! horizontal axis
  ! determine length of tick marks
  LET Lx = 0.1*dy            ! length of vertical tick mark on x-axis
  LET Ly = 0.1*dx            ! length of horizontal tick mark on y-axis
  ! draw tick marks
  FOR itick = 0 to ntick
     LET col = xmin + itick*dx
     LET row = ymin + itick*dy
     PLOT LINES: col,y0 - Lx; col,y0 + Lx
     PLOT LINES: x0 - Ly,row; Ly + x0,row
  NEXT itick
  ! print title
  PLOT TEXT, at xmin + 7*dx,ymax: title$
  ! label maximum x and y values
  PLOT TEXT, at xmax - 0.5*Lx,y0: using$("###.#",xmax)
  PLOT TEXT, at x0 - 4*Ly,ymax + Ly: using$("###.#",ymax)
END SUB
```

The **PLOT** statement is used in **SUB plot_function** to plot the function $T(t)$ defined by (2.7). Since $T(t)$ is defined as an *external* function, the **DECLARE DEF** statement must be used in any subprogram which uses it.

```
SUB plot_function(xmin,xmax)
    DECLARE DEF f          ! external function f(t) used in subroutine
    FOR t = xmin to xmax step 0.01
        PLOT t,f(t);              ! abbreviated form of PLOT LINES: t,f(t);
    NEXT t
END SUB
```

The function $T(t)$ is defined in a separate subprogram; the main distinction between functions and subroutines is that functions involve a relatively small number of parameters and return a single value.

```
DEF f(t)                  ! begin definition
    LET r = 0.07
    LET TS = 22
    LET T0 = 83
    LET f = TS + (T0 - TS)*exp(-r*t)
END DEF                   ! end definition
```

PROBLEM 2.4 Cooling time

a. Incorporate the above subroutines into **Program cooler** so that the numerical solution for the time-dependence of the coffee temperature is plotted rather than printed. (An example of a program which plots numerical data is **Program Fall** in Chapter 3.)

b. Find the time it takes for the coffee to reach $1/e \approx 0.37$ of the difference between the initial coffee temperature and the room temperature. This time is called the *relaxation* or *cooling time.* Does the relaxation time depend on the initial temperature or the room temperature? Try different values of r and determine the qualitative dependence of the relaxation time on r.

2.8 PERSPECTIVE

Although this chapter is introductory in nature, you might feel, depending on your background, that you have been introduced to many new ideas and techniques. If you are not familiar with computer programming, the first use of a

computer and the introduction to the syntax of a new language might seem a
little bewildering. But take heart. There is not much more syntax to learn. If
you look at the program listings in a later chapter, you will probably find that
you recognize most of the syntax already.

REFERENCES AND SUGGESTIONS FOR ADDITIONAL READING

George B. Arfken, David F. Griffing, Donald C. Kelly and Joseph Priest,
University Physics, Academic Press (1984). Chapter 23 on heat transfer discusses
Newton's law of cooling.

Nancy Roberts, David Andersen, Ralph Deal, Michael Jaret, and William
Shaffer, *Introduction to Computer Simulation: The System Dynamics Approach,*
Addison-Wesley (1983). A book on computer simulation in the social sciences.
The numerical solution of the coupled nonlinear model equations are found using
the Euler algorithm.

It is impossible to list all the excellent books on numerical analysis, but some
introductory level books are listed here.

Forman S. Acton, *Numerical Methods That Work*, Harper & Row (1970).
An advanced but clearly written text.

L. V. Atkinson and P. J. Harley, *An Introduction to Numerical Methods with
Pascal*, Addison-Wesley (1983). A book which assumes a working knowledge of
Pascal and calculus, but no background in numerical analysis.

Samuel D. Conte and Carl de Boor, *Elementary Numerical Analysis: an
Algorithmic Approach,* McGraw-Hill (1972).

THE MOTION
OF
FALLING OBJECTS

3

We introduce a method for obtaining numerical solutions to Newton's equations of motion and discuss the qualitative and quantitative
behavior of bodies falling near the earth's surface.

3.1 BACKGROUND

A common example of motion is that of an object falling near the earth's surface. The simplest description of this motion ignores possible rotation and internal motions and describes an idealized object called a *particle,* i.e. an object without internal structure. Of course objects such as planets, rocks, baseballs and atoms are not "points." Nonetheless, their internal motion can be neglected and we can regard them as particles for many purposes.

Our initial discussion emphasizes one-dimensional motion with only one spatial coordinate needed to determine the position of a particle. We know that the instantaneous position $y(t)$, velocity $v(t)$, and acceleration $a(t)$ of a particle can be defined using the language of differential calculus:

$$v(t) = \frac{dy(t)}{dt} \tag{3.1}$$

and

$$a(t) = \frac{dv(t)}{dt} \ . \tag{3.2}$$

These quantities are known as *kinematical* quantities, since they describe the motion without regard to the cause of the motion.

Why do we need the concept of acceleration in kinematics? The answer can be found only *a posteriori.* Thanks to Newton, we know that the net force acting on a particle determines its acceleration. Newton's second law of motion tells us

$$a(t) = \frac{1}{m} F(y, v, t) \tag{3.3}$$

where F is the net *force* and m is the *inertial mass.* In general the force depends on position, velocity, and time. Note that Newton's law implies that the motion of a particle does not depend on d^2v/dt^2 or on any higher derivative of the velocity. It is a property of nature, not of mathematics, that we can find simple explanations for motion.

The description of motion of a particle requires the solution of two coupled first-order differential equations (3.1) and (3.3). Frequently (3.1) and (3.3) are combined to obtain a *second-order* differential equation for the position:

$$\frac{d^2y(t)}{dt^2} = \frac{F}{m} \ . \tag{3.4}$$

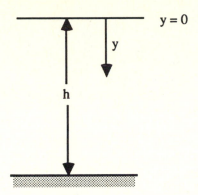

Fig. 3.1 A useful coordinate system for a body falling from an initial height h.

3.2 THE FORCE ON A FALLING OBJECT

In the absence of air resistance, all objects regardless of size, mass, or composition have the same acceleration at the same point near the earth's surface. This idealized motion in which air resistance is neglected is called "free fall." The acceleration of a freely falling object is commonly denoted by the symbol g and is directed towards the earth. Near the earth's surface, the magnitude of g is approximately $9.8\,m/s^2$. Let us adopt the coordinate system shown in Fig. 3.1 with the positive direction down. In this case $a = +g$ and the solution of (3.4) can be written as

$$v(t) = v_0 + gt \qquad (3.5a)$$

and

$$y(t) = y_0 + v_0 t + \frac{1}{2}gt^2 \qquad (3.5b)$$

where y_0 and v_0 are the initial position and velocity of the particle respectively. Note that two initial conditions are necessary to specify the motion.

For free fall near the earth's surface, the analytical solution (3.5) is so simple that further analysis is not necessary. However, it is not difficult to think of realistic modifications of the motion of objects in the earth's gravitational field which do not have simple analytical solutions. For example if we take into account the variation of the earth's gravity with the distance from the center of the earth,

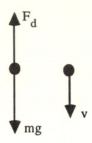

Fig. 3.2 The force diagram for a particle falling in air.

then the acceleration is not constant. According to Newton's law of gravitation, the force due to the earth on a particle of mass m is given by

$$F = \frac{GMm}{(R+y)^2} = \frac{gm}{(1+y/R)^2} \tag{3.6}$$

where y is measured from the earth's surface, R is the earth's radius, G is the gravitational constant, M is the mass of the earth and $g = GM/R^2$.

Another important modification of the free fall problem is the retarding drag force due to air resistance. The direction of the drag force must be opposite to the velocity of the object. We first discuss the motion of a falling particle. The direction of the drag force F_d is upward as shown in Fig. 3.2. If we use the coordinate system shown in Fig. 3.1, the total force F on the particle can be written as

$$F = F_g - F_d = mg - F_d \quad . \tag{3.7}$$

In general it is necessary to determine the velocity-dependence of F_d empirically over a limited range of conditions. One way to determine the form of $F_d(v)$ is to measure y as a function of t and to obtain the velocity and acceleration as a function of t. From this information it is possible to find the acceleration as a function of v and to extract $F_d(v)$. However, this method is not useful in general, since errors are introduced by taking the slopes needed to find the velocity and acceleration. A better method is to reverse the procedure, assume an explicit form of the v-dependence of $F_d(v)$, and use it to solve for $y(t)$. If the calculated $y(t)$ is consistent with the experimental values of $y(t)$, the assumed v-dependence of $F_d(v)$ is empirically justified.

The two common forms of the velocity-dependence of the magnitude of $F_d(v)$ are

$$F_d(v) = k_1 v \tag{3.8a}$$

and

$$F_d(v) = k_2 v^2 \tag{3.8b}$$

where the parameters k_1 and k_2 depend on the properties of the medium and the shape of the object. We stress that the forms (3.8) are not exact laws of physics, but instead are useful *phenomenological* expressions which yield approximate results for $F_d(v)$ over a limited range of v. Since $F_d(v)$ increases as v increases, there is a *limiting* or *terminal* speed at which $F_d = F_g$ and the acceleration equals zero. This speed can be found from (3.7) and (3.8) and is given by

$$v_1 = \frac{mg}{k_1} \qquad (3.9a)$$

or

$$v_2 = \left(\frac{mg}{k_2}\right)^{1/2} \qquad (3.9b)$$

for the linear and quadratic case. It is frequently convenient to measure velocities in terms of the terminal speed. We use (3.8) and (3.9) to write F_d in the linear and quadratic cases as

$$F_d = k_1 v_1 \left(\frac{v}{v_1}\right) = mg\left(\frac{v}{v_1}\right) \qquad (3.10a)$$

and

$$F_d = k_2 v_2{}^2 \left(\frac{v}{v_2}\right)^2 = mg\left(\frac{v}{v_2}\right)^2 \quad . \qquad (3.10b)$$

Hence we can write the net force on a falling object in the form

$$F_1(v) = mg\left(1 - \frac{v}{v_1}\right) \qquad (3.11a)$$

or

$$F_2(v) = mg\left(1 - \frac{v^2}{v_2{}^2}\right) \quad . \qquad (3.11b)$$

In order to determine if the effects of air resistance are important in the fall of ordinary objects, we consider the fall of a pebble of mass m= 10^{-2} kg. To a good approximation, the drag force is found to be proportional to v^2. For a pebble of radius 0.01 m, k_2 is found empirically to be $k_2 \approx 10^{-4}$kg/m. From (3.09b) we find the terminal speed is about 30 m/s. Since this speed would be achieved by a freely falling body in a vertical fall of approximately 50 m in a time of about 3 s, we expect that the effects of air resistance would be appreciable for times and distances much less than these. Hence many of the problems we encounter in elementary mechanics courses are not realistic.

3.3   NUMERICAL SOLUTION OF THE EQUATIONS OF MOTION

Since the analytical solution to the equation of motion (3.4) with the net force
(3.11b) is not trivial, we are motivated to apply numerical methods. The generalization of the Euler method to the solution of a second-order differential equation is straightforward. The first step is to write (3.4) as two coupled first-order
differential equations, (3.1) and (3.3). We let Δt be the time interval between
successive steps, so that the time t_n of the nth step is

$$t_n = t_0 + n\Delta t \quad . \tag{3.12}$$

We also let a_n, v_n, and y_n be the values of a, v and y at the nth step, e.g. $a_n = a_n(y_n, v_n, t_n)$. A straightforward generalization of the Euler method introduced
in Chapter 2 is

$$v_{n+1} = v_n + a_n\Delta t \tag{3.13a}$$

and

$$y_{n+1} = y_n + v_n\Delta t \quad . \tag{3.13b}$$

Note that v_{n+1}, the velocity at the end of an interval, is determined by a_n, the
rate of change of the velocity at the *beginning* of the interval. In the same spirit
y_{n+1}, the position at the end of an interval, is determined by v_n, the rate of
change of the position at the *beginning* of the interval.

   The algorithm we use to obtain a numerical solution of a differential equation
is not unique. For example, a simple variation of (3.13) is to determine y_{n+1} using
v_{n+1}, the velocity at the *end* of the interval rather than at the beginning. We
write this modified Euler method as

$$v_{n+1} = v_n + a_n\Delta t \tag{3.14a}$$

and

$$y_{n+1} = y_n + v_{n+1}\Delta t \quad . \tag{3.14b}$$

Since the algorithm represented by (3.14) has been investigated by Cromer (see
references), we will refer to (3.14) as the Euler-Cromer method. (Cromer refers
to (3.13) and (3.14) as the *first-point* and *last-point* approximations.) Is there
any *a priori* reason to prefer one method over the other?

3.4   ONE-DIMENSIONAL MOTION

A simple implementation of the Euler method for the motion of a freely falling
object is given in **Program fall**. The structure of the program is similar to **Program cooler**, but we have used a **DO ... LOOP** with the **WHILE** condition.
The general nature of **DO** loops can be seen by running this simple program.

```
PROGRAM do_loop
DO while i < 10
   LET i = i + 1
   PRINT i
LOOP
PAUSE 1
LET i = 0
DO
   LET i = i + 1
   PRINT i
LOOP until i = 10
END
```

A **WHILE** condition or **UNTIL** condition can appear in either the **DO** or the **LOOP** statement or in both. Is there any difference between the **WHILE** and **UNTIL** condition in **Program do_loop**?

```
PROGRAM fall                          ! freely falling particle
CALL initial(y,v,t,g,dt,height)       ! initial conditions and parameters
CALL print_parameters(dt,ncalc)       ! ncalc number of steps between printing
CALL print_table(y,v,g,t)             ! print initial values
DO
   CALL Euler(y,v,accel,t,g,dt,ncalc)       ! difference equation
   CALL print_table(y,v,accel,t)            ! print results after ncalc steps
LOOP UNTIL y > height
END

SUB initial(y,v,t,g,dt,height)
   LET t = 0                    ! initial time (sec.)
   LET y = 0                    ! initial displacement (m)
   LET height = 10              ! initial height of object above ground
   LET v = 0                    ! initial velocity
   INPUT prompt "timestep dt = ": dt
   LET g = 9.8                  ! (magnitude) of accel due to gravity
END SUB
```

The following subroutine determines several parameters and prints a heading for the table.

```
SUB print_parameters(dt,ncalc)
    LET print_period = 0.1              ! (sec.)
    LET ncalc = print_period/dt         ! number of steps between printing
    PRINT "time(s)","y(m)","velocity(m/s)","accel (m/(s*s))"
    PRINT
END SUB

SUB print_table(y,v,accel,t)           ! print  results in tabular form.
    PRINT t,y,v,accel
END SUB

SUB Euler(y,v,accel,t,g,dt,ncalc)
    FOR icalc = 1 to ncalc
        LET y = y + v*dt                ! use velocity at beginning of interval
        LET accel = g                   ! y positive downward
        LET v = v + accel*dt
    NEXT icalc
    LET t = t + dt*ncalc·
END SUB
```

It is instructive to see how **Program fall** can be modified so that the results can be given in different forms. For example, a simple way to "observe" the trajectory of the falling object is to replace **SUB print_parameters** and **SUB print_table** by the respective subroutines:

```
SUB plot_parameters(height,dt,ncalc)
    LET plot_period = 0.25
    LET ncalc = plot_period/dt
    SET window 0,20,height,-1
END SUB

SUB plot_trajectory(y)
    LET x = 10                          ! place line in middle of screen
    LET r = 0.1
    BOX AREA x - r,x + r,y - r,y + r      ! draw particle
END SUB
```

We might wish to make a graph of the position and velocity of the falling body as a function of time. In this case we can replace the output subroutines by **SUB graph_parameters** and **SUB graph** respectively.

```
SUB graph_parameters(height,t,dt,ncalc)
   LET plot_period = 0.05
   LET ncalc = plot_period/dt
   LET tmin = t
   LET tmax = 2
   LET ymax = height
   LET ymin = 0
   LET title1$ = "freely falling body"
   LET title2$ = "y versus t"
   CALL plot_axis(tmin,tmax,ymin,ymax,title1$,title2$)
END SUB

SUB graph(y,t)
   PLOT LINES: t,y;
END SUB
```

Note that **SUB graph_parameters** calls **SUB plot_axis** which we developed in Chapter 2. The only change we might wish to make is to pass two titles rather than one to **SUB plot_axis**. Although we do not need to list **SUB plot_axis** again, we do so for clarity.

```
SUB plot_axis(xmin,xmax,ymin,ymax,title1$,title2$)
   LET ntick = 10              ! number of tick marks
   LET dx = (xmax - xmin)/ntick    ! distance between tick marks on x-axis
   LET dy = (ymax - ymin)/ntick    ! distance between tick marks on y-axis
   SET window xmin - dx,xmax + dx,ymin - dy,ymax + dy
   IF xmin*xmax < 0 then
      LET x0 = 0
   ELSE
      LET x0 = xmin
   END IF
   IF ymin*ymax < 0 then
      LET y0 = 0
   ELSE
      LET y0 = ymin
   END IF
```

```
    PLOT LINES: x0,ymin; x0,ymax        ! vertical-axis
    PLOT LINES: xmin,y0; xmax,y0         ! horizontal axis
    ! determine length of tick marks
    LET Lx = 0.1*dy                      ! length of tick mark on x-axis
    LET Ly = 0.1*dx                      ! length of horizontal tick mark on y-axis
    FOR itick = 0 to ntick
        LET col = xmin + itick*dx
        LET row = ymin + itick*dy
        PLOT LINES: col,y0 - Lx; col,y0 + Lx
        PLOT LINES: x0 - Ly,row; Ly + x0,row
    NEXT itick
    ! x,y coordinate depends on title length
    PLOT TEXT, at xmin + 4*dx,ymax: title1$
    PLOT TEXT, at xmin + 4*dx,ymax - 1: title2$
    PLOT TEXT, at xmax - 0.5*Lx,y0: using$("###.#",xmax)
    PLOT TEXT, at x0 - 4*Ly,ymax + Ly: using$("###.#",ymax)
END SUB
```

In the following four problems, we use simple modifications of **Program fall** to study the vertical motion of simple objects with and without the effects of air resistance.

PROBLEM 3.1 Comparison of algorithms

a. Use **Program fall** to determine the time-dependence of the velocity and position of a freely falling body near the earth's surface. Assume the initial values $y = 0$, $height = 10$, and $v = 0$. (The parameter $height$ is the initial distance of the earth's surface from the origin.) The coordinate system used in **Program fall** is shown in Fig. 3.1. What is a suitable value of Δt? Compare your output to the exact results given in (3.5).

b. Modify **Program fall** to implement the Euler-Cromer method. (All that is necessary is the interchange of two lines in **SUB Euler**.) Is there any reason to choose one algorithm over the other? Think of a simple modification of either algorithm which yields exact results for the case of a freely falling body (no air resistance). Adopt the Euler or Euler-Cromer method for the remaining problems in this chapter.

c. Use **SUB plot_trajectory** to observe the position of the falling object at equal time intervals. Are the distances between the object at different times equal?

d. In order to compare $y(t)$ and $v(t)$ with their corresponding behavior in the presence of air resistance, use **SUB plot_graph** to plot y, v and a as functions of time.

Now that we have tested our programs in the absence of air resistance, we are ready to consider several more realistic problems. In Table 3.1, we show the result of measurements of the position of a falling styrofoam ball as a function of time. Are the effects of air resistance important?

TABLE 3.1 Results by Greenwood, Hanna, and Milton (see references) for the vertical fall of a styrofoam ball of mass 0.254 gm and radius 2.54 cm.

t (s)	position (m)
−0.132	0.0
0.0	0.075
0.1	0.260
0.2	0.525
0.3	0.870
0.4	1.27
0.5	1.73
0.6	2.23
0.7	2.77
0.8	3.35

PROBLEM 3.2 The fall of a styrofoam ball

Modify **Program fall** so that the net force is given by either (3.11a) or (3.11b). For each form of the force, determine the value of the terminal velocity which yields the best agreement between the computed values of $y(t)$ and experimental values shown in Table 3.1. Plot the two sets of computed values of $y(t)$ and the experimental values on the same graph and visually determine which form of $y(t)$ yields the best overall fit. What are the qualitative differences between the two theoretical forms of $y(t)$? Suggestion: Since the experimental values of y in Table 3.1 are not initially given at regular time intervals, you might wish to modify your program as follows:

```
PROGRAM styrofoam
CALL initial(y,v,t,g,vt2,dt,height)
CALL print_parameters(t,dt,n0,ncalc)
CALL print_table(y,v,g,t)              ! print initial conditions
CALL Euler(y,v,accel,t,g,vt2,dt,n0)
CALL print_table(y,v,accel,t)          ! print values at t = 0
DO
   CALL Euler(y,v,accel,t,g,vt2,dt,ncalc)
   CALL print_table(y,v,accel,t)
LOOP UNTIL y > height
END

SUB initial(y,v,t,g,vt2,dt,height)
   LET t = -0.132                       ! initial time
   LET y = 0! initial displacement (m)
   LET height = 4                       ! initial height of object above ground
   LET v = 0                            ! initial velocity
   INPUT prompt "time step = ": dt
   LET g = 9.8
   INPUT prompt "terminal velocity (m/s) = ": vterm
   LET vt2 = vterm*vterm
END SUB

SUB print_parameters(t,dt,n0,ncalc)
   LET print_period = 0.1               ! (sec.)
   LET ncalc = print_period/dt
   LET n0 = -t/dt
   PRINT "time(s)","y(m)","velocity(m/s)","accel (m/(s*s))"
   PRINT
END SUB
```

Note that **SUB Euler** has been called from the main program using two different values for the number of steps between the output of the results. **SUB Euler** is not listed since it is a simple generalization of the listing in **Program fall**.

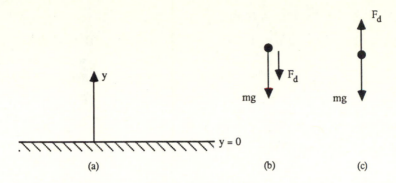

Fig. 3.3 (a) Coordinate system used in Problem 3.3 with y measured positive upwards from the ground. (b) The force diagram for upward motion. (c) The force diagram for downward motion.

PROBLEM 3.3 Effect of air resistance on the ascent and descent of a pebble

a. Let us verify the claim made in Sec. 3.2 that the effects of air resistance on a falling pebble can be appreciable. Compute the speed at which a pebble reaches the ground if it is dropped from rest at a height of 50 m. Compare this speed to that of a freely falling object under the same conditions. Assume that the drag force is proportional to v^2 and the terminal speed is 30 m/s.

b. Suppose an object is thrown vertically upward with an initial velocity v_0. If we neglect air resistance, we know that the maximum height reached by the object is $v_0^2/2g$, its velocity upon return to the earth equals v_0, the time of ascent equals the time of descent, and the total time in the air is $2v_0/g$. Before performing a numerical simulation, give a simple qualitative explanation of how you think these quantities will be affected by air resistance. Then perform a numerical simulation to determine if your qualitative answers are correct. Assume that $F_d \sim v^2$ with a terminal speed equal to 30 m/s. Suggestions: Choose the coordinate system shown in Fig. 3.3 with y positive upward. What is the net force for $v > 0$ and $v < 0$? You might find it convenient to use the sgn function, where $sgn(x)$ returns the sign of x. Or you can write the drag force in the form $F_d = -v * abs(v)$. One way to determine the maximum height of the pebble is to use the statement

IF v*vold < 0 then PRINT "maximum height = "; y

where $v = v_n$ and $vold = v_{n-1}$.

PROBLEM 3.4 Position-dependent force

If the force depends on position as in (3.6), a simple analytical solution for $y(t)$ does not exist. Modify **Program fall** to simulate the fall of a particle with the force law (3.6). Assume that a particle is dropped from a height h with zero initial velocity and compute its speed when it hits the ground. Determine the value of h for which this impact velocity differs by one percent from its value with a constant acceleration $g = 9.8\text{m/s}^2$. Take the radius of the earth to be $6.37 \times 10^6\text{m}$.

3.5 TWO-DIMENSIONAL TRAJECTORIES

You are probably familiar with two-dimensional trajectory problems neglecting air resistance. For example, if a ball is thrown in the air with an initial velocity v_0 at an angle θ_0 with respect to the ground, how far will the ball travel in the horizontal direction, what is its maximum height, and what is its time of flight? Suppose that a ball is released at a nonzero height h above the ground. What is the launch angle for the maximum range? Are your answers still applicable if air resistance is taken into account? We consider questions such as these in the following.

Consider an object of mass m with its initial velocity $\vec{v}_0$ directed at an angle θ_0 above the horizontal (see Fig. 3.4a). The particle is subjected to gravitational

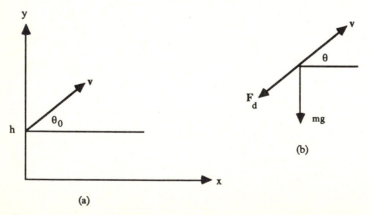

Fig. 3.4 (a) A ball is thrown from a height h at an launch angle θ_0 measured with respect to the horizontal. The initial velocity is $\vec{v}_0$. (b) The gravitational and drag forces on a particle.

and drag forces of magnitude mg and F_d, and the direction of the drag force is opposite to $\vec{v}$ (see Fig. 3.4b). Newton's equations of motion for the x and y components of the motion are written as

$$m\frac{dv_x}{dt} = -F_d \cos\theta \tag{3.15a}$$

$$m\frac{dv_y}{dt} = -mg - F_d \sin\theta \ . \tag{3.15b}$$

As an example, let us maximize the range of a round steel ball of radius $\approx$ 4 cm. A reasonable assumption for an object (e.g. a "shot") of this size and typical speed is that $F_d = k_2 v^2$. Since $v_x = v\cos\theta$ and $v_y = v\sin\theta$, we can rewrite (3.15) as

$$\frac{dv_x}{dt} = -Avv_x \tag{3.16a}$$

$$\frac{dv_y}{dt} = -g - Avv_y \tag{3.16b}$$

where $A = k_2/m$. Note that (3.16a) and (3.16b) for the change in v_x and v_y involve the magnitude of the velocity: $v^2 = v_x^2 + v_y^2$. Hence, we cannot calculate the vertical motion of a falling body without reference to the horizontal component.

PROBLEM 3.5 Trajectory of a shot

Modify **Program fall** so that the two-dimensional trajectory of a ball moving in air is computed and graphs of y as a function of x can be made. For example **SUB Euler** might be written as

```
SUB Euler(x,y,vx,vy,t,A,g,dt,ncalc)        ! Euler-Cromer method
   FOR icalc = 1 to ncalc
      LET v2 = vx*vx + vy*vy
      LET v = sqr(v2)
      LET ax = -A*v*vx
      LET ay = -g - A*v*vy
      LET vx = vx + ax*dt
      LET vy = vy + ay*dt
      LET x = x + vx*dt
      LET y = y + vy*dt
   NEXT icalc
   LET t = t + dt*ncalc
END SUB
```

a. As a check on your program, first neglect air resistance so that you can compare your results with known ones. For example, assume that a ball is thrown from ground level at an angle θ_0 above the horizontal with an initial velocity of $v_0 = 15$ m/s. Vary θ_0 and show that the maximum range occurs at $\theta_0 = \theta_m = 45°$. What is the maximum range, R_m, at this angle? Compare your numerical value to the analytical result $R_m = v_0^2/g$.

b. Now suppose that a ball ("shot") is thrown ("put") from a height h at an angle θ_0 above the horizontal with the same initial speed as in part (a). If you neglect air resistance, do you expect θ_m to be larger or smaller than 45°? Although this problem can be solved analytically, you can determine the numerical value of θ_m without changing your program. What is θ_m for $h = 2$m? By what percent is the range R changed if θ is varied by 2% from θ_m?

c. Now consider the effects of air resistance on the range and optimum angle of a shot put. For a typical shot put (mass ≈ 7 kg and cross-sectional area $\approx$ 0.01 m^2), the parameter k_2 defined by (3.8) is approximately 0.01. What are the units of k_2? It is convenient to first exaggerate the effects of air resistance, since we can determine the qualitative nature of the effects without being concerned about precise numbers. Compute the optimum angle for $h = 2$ m, $v_0 = 30$ m/s, and $A = k_2/m = 0.1$ and compare it to the value found in part (b). Is R more or less sensitive to changes in θ_0 from θ_m than in part (b)? Determine the optimum launch angle and the corresponding range for the more realistic value $A = 0.001$. A detailed discussion of the maximum range of the shot has been given by Lichtenberg and Wills (see references).

PROBLEM 3.6 Coupled motion

Consider the motion of two identical objects which start from a height h. One object is dropped vertically from rest and the other is thrown with a horizontal velocity v_0. Which object reaches the ground first?

a. Give physical reasons for your answer assuming air resistance can be neglected.

b. Assume that air resistance cannot be neglected and the drag force is proportional to v^2. Give physical reasons for your anticipated answer. Then perform numerical simulations using, for example, $A = k_2/m = 0.1$, $h = 10$ m, with $v_0 = 0$ and $v_0 = 30$ m/s. Are your qualitative results consistent with your anticipated answer? If they are not, the source of the discrepancy might be an error in your program. Or the discrepancy might be due to your failure to anticipate the effects of the coupling between the vertical and horizontal motion.

c. Suppose that the drag force is proportional to v rather than to v^2. Is your anticipated answer similar to that in part (b)? Do a numerical simulation to test your intuition.

3.6 OTHER APPLICATIONS

Applications of the ideas and methods that we have discussed are important in the physics of clouds. For example, in order to understand the behavior of falling water droplets, it is necessary to take into account drag resistance as well as droplet growth by condensation and other mechanisms. Because of the variety and complexity of the mechanisms, computer simulation plays an essential role.

Another area of interest is the trajectory of balls of various shapes through the air. Of particular interest to sports fans is the curve of balls in flight due to their rotation and the effect of air resistance on the range and speed of table tennis balls.

REFERENCES AND SUGGESTIONS FOR ADDITIONAL READING

William R. Bennett, *Scientific and Engineering Problem-Solving with the Computer,* Prentice-Hall (1976). One of the first and still one of the best books which incorporate computer problem solving. Many one and two-dimensional falling body problems are considered.

Byron L. Coulter and Carl G. Adler, "Can a body pass a body falling through the air?," *Am. J. Phys.* **47**, 841 (1979). The authors discuss the limiting conditions for which the drag force is linear or quadratic in the velocity.

Alan Cromer, "Stable solutions using the Euler approximation," *Am. J. Phys.* **49**, 455 (1981).

R. M. Eisberg, *Applied Mathematical Physics with Programmable Pocket Calculators,* McGraw-Hill (1976). Chapter 3 of this handy paperback is similar in spirit to the present discussion.

Richard P. Feynman, Robert B. Leighton and Matthew Sands, *The Feynman Lectures on Physics, Vol. 1*, Addison-Wesley (1963). Feynman discusses the numerical solution of Newton's equations in Chapter 9 in a way that only Feynman can.

A. P. French, *Newtonian Mechanics,* W. W. Norton & Company (1971). Chapter 7 has an excellent discussion of air resistance and does a detailed analysis of motion in the presence of drag resistance.

Margaret Greenwood, Charles Hanna and John Milton, "Air Resistance Acting on a Sphere: Numerical Analysis, Strobe Photographs, and Videotapes," *Phys. Teacher* **24**, 153 (1986). More experimental data and theoretical analysis are given for the fall of ping-pong and styrofoam balls.

K. S. Krane, "The falling raindrop: Variations on a theme of Newton," *Am. J. Phys.* **49**, 113 (1981). The author discusses the problem of mass accretion by a drop falling through a cloud of droplets.

D. B. Lichtenberg and J. G. Wills, "Maximizing the range of the shot put," *Am. J. Phys.* **46**, 546 (1978). Problem 3.5 is based in part on the discussion in this paper.

Rabindra Mehta, "Aerodynamics of Sports Balls" in *Ann. Rev. Fluid Mech.* **17**, 151 (1985).

R. R. Rogers, *A Short Course in Cloud Physics,* Pergamon Press (1976).

THE KEPLER PROBLEM

4

We apply Newton's laws of motion to planetary motion and emphasize some of the counter-intuitive consequences of Newton's laws.

4.1 INTRODUCTION

Planetary motion is of special significance since it played an important role in the conceptual history of the mechanical view of the universe. Few theories have affected Western civilization as much as Newton's laws of motion and gravitation which together related the motion of the heavens to the motion of terrestial objects.

Much of our knowledge of planetary motion is summarized by Kepler's laws which can be stated as:

1. Each planet moves in an elliptical orbit with the sun located at one of the foci of the ellipse.
2. The speed of a planet increases as its distance from the sun decreases such that the line from the sun to the planet sweeps out equal areas in equal times.
3. The ratio T^2/a^3 is the same for all planets that orbit the sun, where T is the period of the planet and a is the semi-major axis of the ellipse.

Kepler obtained these laws by a careful analysis of the observational data collected over many years by Tycho Brahe.

Note that Kepler's first and third laws are for the *shape* of the orbit rather than for the time-dependence of the position and velocity of a planet. Since it is not possible to obtain this time dependence in terms of elementary functions, we are motivated to discuss the numerical solution of the equations of motion of planets and satellites in orbit. In addition, we discuss the effects of perturbing forces on the nature of the orbit and consider problems which challenge our intuitive understanding of Newton's laws of motion.

4.2 THE EQUATIONS OF MOTION FOR PLANETARY MOTION

The motion of the sun and earth is an example of a *two-body problem.* We can reduce this problem to a one-body problem in one of two ways. The easiest way is to note that the mass of the sun is much greater than the mass of the earth. Hence we can assume that, to a good approximation, the sun is stationary and is a convenient choice of the origin of our coordinate system. If you are familar with the concept of a *reduced mass,* you know that this reduction is more general. That is, the motion of two objects of mass m and M whose total potential energy is a function only of their relative displacement can be reduced to an equivalent one-body problem involving the motion of an object of reduced mass μ given by

$$\mu = \frac{mM}{m+M} \quad . \tag{4.1}$$

Since the mass of the earth $m = 5.99 \times 10^{24}$ kg and the mass of the sun $M = 1.99 \times 10^{30}$ kg, we find that for most practical purposes, the reduced mass of the sun and the earth is that of the earth alone. Hence in the following we will consider only the problem of a single particle of mass m moving about a fixed center of force, which we take as the origin of the coordinate system.

Newton's universal law of gravitation states that a particle of mass M attracts another particle of mass m with a force

$$\vec{F} = -\frac{GMm}{r^3}\vec{r} \tag{4.2}$$

where the vector $\vec{r}$ is directed from M to m, and G is the gravitational constant which is determined experimentally to be

$$G = 6.67 \times 10^{-11} \frac{m^3}{kg \cdot s^2} \quad . \tag{4.3}$$

The negative sign in (4.2) implies that the gravitational force is attractive, i.e. it tends to decrease the separation r.

The force law (4.2) applies only to objects of negligible spatial extent. Newton delayed publication of his law of gravitation for 20 years while he invented integral calculus and showed that (4.2) also applies to any uniform sphere or spherical shell of matter if the distance r is measured from the center of each mass.

The gravitational force has two general properties: its magnitude depends only on the separation of the particles and its direction is along the line joining the particles. Such a force is called a *central force*. The assumption of a central force implies that the orbit of the earth is restricted to a plane (x-y), and the *angular momentum* $\vec{L}$ is conserved and lies in the third (z) direction. We write L_z in the form

$$L_z = (\vec{r} \times m\vec{v})_z = m(xv_y - yv_x) \tag{4.4}$$

where we have used the cross-product definition $\vec{L} = \vec{r} \times \vec{p}$ and $\vec{p} = m\vec{v}$. An additional constraint on the motion is that the total energy E given by

$$E = \frac{1}{2}mv^2 - \frac{GmM}{r} \tag{4.5}$$

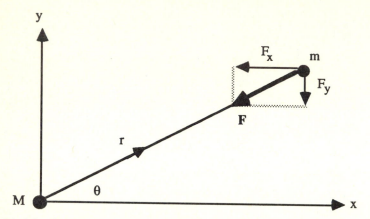

Fig. 4.1 A body of mass m moves under the influence of a central force F. Note that $cos\,\theta = x/r$ and $sin\,\theta = y/r$, providing useful relations for writing the equations of motion in component form suitable for numerical simulation.

is conserved. If we fix the coordinate system at mass M, the equation of motion is

$$m\frac{d^2\vec{r}}{dt^2} = -\frac{mMG}{r^3}\vec{r} \quad .$$

(4.6)

For the purpose of numerical simulation, it is convenient to write the force in Cartesian coordinates (see Fig. 4.1):

$$F_x = -\frac{GMm}{r^2}\,cos\,\theta = -\frac{GMm}{r^3}x$$

(4.7a)

$$F_y = -\frac{GMm}{r^2}\,sin\,\theta = -\frac{GMm}{r^3}y \quad .$$

(4.7b)

Hence the equations of motion in Cartesian coordinates are

$$\frac{d^2x}{dt^2} = -\frac{GM}{r^3}x$$

(4.8a)

$$\frac{d^2y}{dt^2} = -\frac{GM}{r^3}y$$

(4.8a)

where $r^2 = x^2 + y^2$. Equations (4.8a) and (4.8b) are examples of "coupled differential equations" since each differential equation contains both x and y.

4.3 CIRCULAR MOTION

Since many planetary orbits are nearly circular, it is useful to obtain the condition for a circular orbit. The magnitude of the acceleration $\vec{a}$ is related to the radius r of a circular orbit by

$$a = \frac{v^2}{r} \tag{4.9}$$

where v is the speed of the body. The acceleration is always directed towards the center and is due to the gravitational force. Hence we have

$$\frac{mv^2}{r} = \frac{mMG}{r^2} \tag{4.10}$$

or

$$v = (\frac{MG}{r})^{1/2} \quad . \tag{4.11}$$

The relation (4.11) between the radius and the speed is the general condition for a circular orbit.

We can also find the dependence of the period T on the radius of a circular orbit using the relation

$$T = \frac{2\pi r}{v} \tag{4.12}$$

in combination with (4.11) to obtain

$$T^2 = \frac{4\pi^2 r^3}{GM} \quad . \tag{4.13}$$

The relation (4.13) is a special case of Kepler's third law where the radius r corresponds to the semi-major axis of an ellipse.

4.4 ELLIPTICAL ORBITS

Since we know that the most general orbit is an ellipse, we summarize the description of an elliptical orbit. A simple geometrical characterization of an elliptical orbit is shown in Fig. 4.2. The two *foci* of an ellipse, F_1 and F_2, have the property that for any point P the distance $F_1 P + F_2 P$ is a constant. In general an ellipse has two perpendicular axes of unequal length. The longer axis is the major axis; half of this axis is the *semi-major axis a*. The shorter axis is the minor axis; the *semi-minor axis b* is half of this distance. It is common in astronomy to specify an elliptical orbit by a and the *eccentricity e* where e is the ratio of the distance

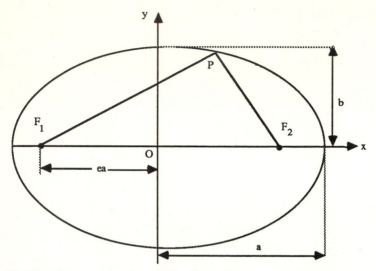

Fig. 4.2 The characterization of an ellipse in terms of the semi-major and semi-minor axes a and b. The eccentricity e is defined in the figure. The origin O in Cartesian coordinates is at the center of the ellipse.

between the foci to the length of the major axis. Since $F_1P + F_2P = 2a$, it is easy to show that (consider P at $x = 0, y = b$)

$$e = \sqrt{1 - \frac{b^2}{a^2}} \qquad (4.14)$$

with $0 < e < 1$. A special case is $b = a$ for which the ellipse reduces to a circle and $e = 0$. The magnitude of e for the earth's orbit is 0.0167.

4.5 ASTRONOMICAL UNITS

Since it is awkward at best to treat very small or very large numbers on the computer (e.g. G and M), it is convenient to choose a system of units in which the magnitude of the product GM is the order of unity. To describe the earth's motion, the convention is to choose the length of the earth's semi-major axis as the unit of length. This unit of length is called the *astronomical unit* (AU) and is

$$1\,AU = 1.496 \times 10^{11}\,m \quad . \qquad (4.15)$$

The unit of time is taken to be *one year* $= 3.15 \times 10^7 s$. In these units, $T = 1\, yr$ $a = 1\, AU$, and we can write

$$GM = \frac{4\pi^2 a^3}{T^2} = 4\pi^2 AU^3/yr^2 \quad . \tag{4.16}$$

4.6 PROGRAMMING NOTES

Since we will find that we do not have to introduce a more sophisticated algorithm to simulate the Kepler problem, the structure of our program to solve the coupled equations of motion (4.8) will be the same as in Chapter 3. Our main change will be to use an array variable to represent the two-dimensional position and velocity of the orbiting object. The definition of the dimension of an array and the passing of arrays to a subroutine is illustrated in **Program array**.

```
PROGRAM array              ! illustrate use of arrays
DIM x(10),r(3,3)           ! arrays defined in a DIM statement
CALL add(x,r)
FOR i = 1 to 10
    PRINT x(i);
NEXT i
PRINT
FOR i = 1 to 3
    FOR j = 1 to 3
        PRINT r(i,j);
    NEXT j
NEXT i
END
```

```
SUB add(x(),r(,))
  DIM y(-5 to 5)            ! arrays can be defined in main program or in subroutine
  FOR i = 1 to 10
    LET x(i) = i
  NEXT i
  FOR i = -5 to 5
    LET y(i) = i
    PRINT y(i);
  NEXT i
  FOR i = 1 to 3
    FOR j = 1 to 3
      LET r(i,j) = n
      LET n = n + 1
    NEXT j
  NEXT i
END SUB
```

We used the following characteristics of True BASIC:

1. Arrays are defined in a **DIM** statement and the number of elements of an array is given in parentheses. The variable x in the main program and the variable y in **SUB add** are examples of one-dimensional arrays; the variable r is an example of a two-dimensional array.

2. The lower and upper limit of each subscript in an array can be specified; the default lower limit is 1.

3. Arrays like other variables can be passed to a subroutine or function. Parentheses and commas are not used if an array is used as an *argument* in a **CALL** statement, for example

    CALL add(x,r)

    If the array is a *parameter*, then empty parentheses and commas are used to indicate the dimension of the array, for example,

    SUB add(x(),r(,))

4. Note that the entire array is not actually passed. Rather the address of the first element of the array is passed and hence there is no memory or speed penalty when arrays are passed to a subroutine.

Since it is instructive to observe an object in orbit, we wish to write a sub-routine which plots the trajectory of the orbiter. However, few screens are square and have the same number of pixels in the horizontal and vertical direction. Since we want a circular orbit to appear circular on the screen, we must correct for the *aspect ratio* of your screen. The following program draws a circle. If the shape does not look like a circle, make the appropriate correction in the **SET window** statement.

```
PROGRAM circle                      ! test aspect ratio of screen
LET r = 1                           ! radius of circle
! aspect_ratio is ratio of horizontal to vertical distances on screen
! aspect_ratio = 1.5 for Macintosh
INPUT prompt "aspect ratio = ": aspect_ratio
LET x = aspect_ratio*r
SET window -x,x,-r,r
BOX CIRCLE -r,r,-r,r
END
```

4.7   NUMERICAL SIMULATION OF THE ORBIT

In Chapter 3 we used the Euler and the Euler-Cromer algorithm interchangeably to simulate the motion of falling bodies. (You would have obtained better results by using the average velocity $\frac{1}{2}(v_n + v_{n+1})$ to obtain x_{n+1}.) In order to simulate the periodic motion of an elliptical orbit with a reasonable choice of time step, we will find that among the algorithms we have discussed, only the Euler-Cromer algorithm yields stable orbits over many revolutions.

Program planet uses three one-dimensional arrays of two elements each to represent the position, velocity, and acceleration of the orbiter. The use of an array allows us to write the equation of motion (4.8) in the symmetrical form

```
accel(i) = -GM*pos(i)/(r*r*r)
vel(i) = vel(i) + accel(i)*vel(i)
pos(i) = pos(i) + vel(i)*dt
```

where $pos(1)$ and $pos(2)$ represent the x and y-coordinates of the object re-spectively. Note that we have used separate subroutines to obtain the numerical values of the position and velocity, and to plot the orbit.

```
PROGRAM planet                    ! planetary motion
! use updated velocity to update position
DIM pos(2),vel(2)                 ! define the dimension of arrays
CALL initial(pos,vel,GM,dt,nplot,ncalc)
CALL output(pos)                  ! plot position of "earth"
FOR iplot = 1 to nplot
    CALL Euler(pos,vel,GM,dt,ncalc)
    CALL output(pos)
NEXT iplot
END

SUB initial(pos(),vel(),GM,dt,nplot,ncalc)
  LET GM = 4.0*pi*pi              ! astronomical units
  INPUT prompt "time step = ": dt
  INPUT prompt "duration = ": tmax ! (yrs)
  INPUT prompt "plot period = ": plot_period          ! (yrs)
  LET ncalc = plot_period/dt            ! # of iterations between plots
  LET nplot = tmax/plot_period
  INPUT prompt "initial x position = ": pos(1)
  LET pos(2) = 0                  ! initial y-position
  LET vel(1) = 0                  ! initial x-velocity
  INPUT prompt "initial y-velocity = ": vel(2)
  LET r = 2*pos(1)          ! assumed maximum value of semi-major axis
  ! screen not square
  ! aspect ratio = (horizontal distance)/(vertical distance)
  LET aspect_ratio = 1.5          ! value for Macintosh
  LET x = aspect_ratio*r
  SET window -x,x,-r,r
  LET radius = 0.1                ! radius of "sun"
  BOX CIRCLE -radius,radius,-radius,radius          ! "sun" at origin
  FLOOD 0,0                       ! paint sun in foreground color
END SUB
```

```
SUB Euler(pos(),vel(),GM,dt,ncalc)
  DIM accel(2)
  FOR icalc = 1 to ncalc
     LET r = sqr(pos(1)*pos(1) + pos(2)*pos(2))
     FOR i = 1 to 2
        LET accel(i) = -GM*pos(i)/(r*r*r)
        LET vel(i) = vel(i) + accel(i)*dt
        LET pos(i) = pos(i) + vel(i)*dt
     NEXT i
  NEXT icalc
END SUB

SUB output(pos())                        ! plot orbit
  PLOT POINTS: pos(1),pos(2)
END SUB
```

PROBLEM 4.1 Verification of Program planet for circular orbits

a. Verify **Program planet** by considering the special case of a circular orbit. As an example choose (in astronomical units) $x_0 = 1$, $y_0 = 0$ and $v_x(t = 0) = 0$. Use the relation (4.11) to find the numerical value of $v_y(t = 0)$ which yields a circular orbit. Choose a value of Δt such that to a good approximation the total energy E is conserved. (Note that it is sufficient to calculate E/m.) Is your value of Δt small enough to yield an orbit reproducible over many periods?

b. Run **Program planet** for different sets of values of initial conditions, x_0 and $v_y(t = 0)$, consistent with the condition for a circular orbit. Set $y_0 = 0$ and $v_x(t = 0) = 0$. For each orbit, measure the radius and the period and verify Kepler's third law. Think of a simple condition which allows you to find the numerical value of the period and use this condition in a separate subroutine.

c. Show that the Euler method does not yield stable orbits for the same choice of Δt as in parts (a) and (b). Is it sufficient to simply choose a smaller Δt or is the Euler method not stable for this dynamical system? Use the average velocity $\frac{1}{2}(v_n + v_{n+1})$ to obtain x_{n+1}. Are the results any better?

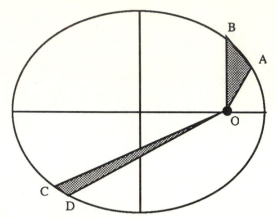

Fig. 4.3 Illustration of Kepler's second law of equal areas in equal
times.

PROBLEM 4.2 Verification of Kepler's third law for elliptical orbits

a. Set $y_0 = 0$ and $v_x(t = 0) = 0$. By trial and error find several choices of x_0
and $v_y(t = 0)$ which yield convenient elliptical orbits. Determine the total
energy, angular momentum, semi-major and semi-minor axes, eccentricity,
and period for each orbit. What is the significance of the sign of the total
energy? If you have the program compute the semi-major axis, eccentricity,
and period directly, write this part of the program as a separate subroutine.
Use your data for the period and the semi-major axis to verify Kepler's third
law. See Appendix 4A for a discussion of the use of log-log plots to obtain
simple power-law relationships.

b. You probably have noticed that the Euler-Cromer algorithm with a fixed
value of Δt breaks down if the "planet" is too close to the sun. How are you
able to visually confirm the breakdown of the method? What is the cause
of the failure of the method? Think of a simple modification of the program
which can improve your numerical results.

PROBLEM 4.3 Verification of Kepler's second law

a. Choose initial conditions such that a convenient elliptical orbit is obtained. Since the distance between adjacent "points" of an orbit is a measure
of the speed of the planet, first determine qualitatively the variation of the
planet's speed. Where is the speed a maximum (minimum)?

b. Choose points A, B, C and D on the orbit as shown in Fig. 4.3. These points may be located anywhere on the orbit, but it is best if A and B are near one end of the major axis and C and D are near the other end. Measure the shaded areas OAB and OCD. (One way is to place the orbit over graph paper and count the squares inside each region.) Measure the times t_{AB} and t_{CD} for the planet to travel from A to B and C to D and form the ratio OAB/t_{AB} and OCD/t_{CD}. Compare your results to the predictions of Kepler's second law.

PROBLEM 4.4 Non-inverse square forces

a. Let us consider the dynamical effects of a small change in the attractive inverse-square force law, e.g. $Km/r^{2+\delta}$, where $\delta = 0.05$. For convenience choose the numerical value of the constant K to be $4\pi^2$ as before. Consider the initial conditions $x_0 = 1$, $v_y(t = 0) = 5$ (with $y_0 = 0$ and $v_x(t = 0) = 0$ as usual). You will find that the orbit of the planet does not retrace itself. Verify that this result is not due to your choice of Δt. Does the planet spiral away from or into the sun? One way to describe the path is as an elliptical orbit which slowly rotates or *precesses* in the same sense as the motion of the planet. A convenient measure of the precession is the angle between successive orientations of the semi-major axis of the ellipse. This angle is the rate of precession per revolution. Estimate the magnitude of this angle for your choice of orbit parameters and δ. What is the effect of decreasing the semi-major axis? What is the effect of increasing δ?

b. Suppose that the attractive gravitational force law depends on the inverse-cube of the distance, e.g. Km/r^3. What are the units of K? Choose the numerical value $K = 4\pi^2$. Consider the initial condition $x_0 = 1$, $y_0 = 0$, $v_x(t = 0) = 0$ and determine analytically the numerical value of $v_y(t = 0)$ necessary for a circular orbit. How small must Δt be in order that the Euler-Cromer algorithm yield a circular orbit over several periods? How does this value of Δt compare with its value for the inverse-square force law?

c. Vary $v_y(t = 0)$ by approximately 2% from the circular orbit condition which you determined in part (b). What is the nature of the new orbit? What is the sign of the total energy? Is the orbit bound? Is it closed?

PROBLEM 4.5 Effect of drag resistance on satellite orbit

Consider a satellite in orbit about the earth. In this case it is convenient to measure distance in terms of the radius of the earth $R = 6.37 \times 10^6$ m. Time is measured in units of hours. In these earth units (EU) the numerical value of the gravitational constant G is

$$G = 6.67 \times 10^{-11} \frac{m^3}{kg \cdot s^2} \left(\frac{1\,EU}{6.37 \times 10^6\,m} \right)^3 (3.6 \times 10^3 \frac{s}{h})^2$$

$$= 3.34 \times 10^{-24} \frac{EU^3}{kg \cdot h^2} \quad . \tag{4.17}$$

Since the force on the satellite is proportional to Gm (m is the mass of the earth), we need to evaluate the numerical value of the product Gm in earth units. We obtain

$$Gm = 3.34 \times 10^{-24} \frac{EU^3}{kg \cdot h^2} \times 5.99 \times 10^{24}\,kg$$

$$= 20.0\,EU^3/h^2 \quad . \tag{4.18}$$

Modify **Program planet** to incorporate the effects of drag resistance on the motion of an orbiting earth satellite. Choose initial conditions such that a circular orbit would be obtained in the absence of drag resistance and allow at least one revolution before "switching on" the drag resistance. Assume the drag force is proportional to the square of the speed of the satellite. In order to be able to observe the effects of air resistance in a reasonable time, also assume that the magnitude of the drag force is approximately one-tenth the magnitude of the gravitational force. Describe the qualitative change in the orbit due to drag resistance. How do the total energy and speed of the satellite change with time?

4.8 PERTURBATIONS

We now challenge your intuitive understanding of Newton's laws of motion by considering perturbations on the standard Kepler problem. In each case answer the questions before doing the numerical simulation.

PROBLEM 4.6 Radial perturbations

a. Suppose a small radial "kick" or impulse is applied to a satellite in a circular orbit about the earth (see Fig. 4.4a.) How will the orbit change?

b. How does the change in the orbit depend on the strength of the kick and its duration?

c. After you have answered parts (a) and (b), perform the simulation (see **Program key**) and determine the new orbit. Choose earth units so that the numerical value of the product Gm is given by (4.18). Is the orbit *stable*, e.g. does a small impulse lead to a small change in the orbit? Does the orbit retrace itself indefinitely if no further perturbations are applied?

d. Determine if the angular momentum and total energy are changed by a radial perturbation.

PROBLEM 4.7 Tangential perturbations

a. Suppose a small tangential "kick" or impulse is applied to a satellite in a circular orbit about the earth (see Fig. 4.4b). How will the orbit change?

b. How does the change in the orbit depend on the strength of the kick and its duration?

c. After you have answered parts (a) and (b), perform the simulation and determine the new orbit. Is the orbit stable?

d. Determine if the angular momentum and total energy are changed by a tangential perturbation.

e. Determine the stability of an analogous inverse-cube force law to radial or tangential perturbations.

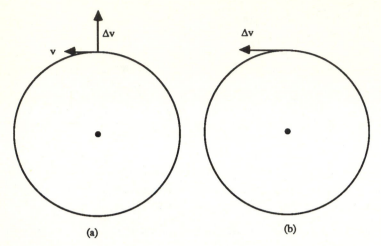

(a)   (b)

Fig. 4.4 (a) An impulse applied in the radial (vertical) direction. (b) An impulse applied in the tangential (horizontal) direction.

A simple way to apply an external force at a desired time is to use the **key input** statement. An example of its use is given in **Program key**. Run the program and determine the effect of pressing the letter k or K from the keyboard.

```
PROGRAM key
FOR i = 1 to 10
    IF key input then GET KEY kick          ! key input true if key pressed
        IF kick = ord("k") or kick = ord("K") then
            PRINT kick
        ELSE
        PRINT "no kick"
    END IF
    PAUSE 1
    LET kick = 0
NEXT i
END
```

The **key input** statement returns the logical value true if any key has been pressed since the last input was read from the keyboard. The **GET KEY** statement stores the value of the key pressed and is used in **Program key** to determine which key has been pressed. The **ord** function returns the value or ASCII code number of its argument. What are the "values" of lower case 'k' and upper case 'K'?

A modified version of **SUB Euler** which allows us to apply a vertical or horizontal kick is shown in the following. The magnitude of the "kick" was chosen for a circular orbit of radius 1 and a time step of 0.01.

```
SUB Euler(pos(),vel(),Gm,dt,ncalc)              ! impulsive perturbation
  DIM accel(2),impulse(2)
  FOR icalc = 1 to ncalc
    LET impulse(1) = 0
    LET impulse(2) = 0
    LET kick = 0
    LET r = sqr(pos(1)*pos(1) + pos(2)*pos(2))
    IF key input then GET KEY kick
    IF (kick = ord("k")) or (kick = ord("K")) then
      LET magnitude = Gm/(r*r)               ! magnitude of force per unit mass
      LET magnitude = 100*magnitude          ! magnitude of "kick"
      LET impulse(2) = magnitude*dt          ! vertical impulse per unit mass
    END IF
    FOR i = 1 to 2
      LET accel(i) = -Gm*pos(i)/(r*r*r) + impulse(i)
      LET vel(i) = vel(i) + accel(i)*dt
      LET pos(i) = pos(i) + vel(i)*dt
    NEXT i
  NEXT icalc
END SUB
```

In this version of **SUB Euler** the impulse is applied in the vertical direction. Hence if we wish to apply a radial (tangential) impulse, we have to apply it when the orbiter is as shown in Fig. 4.4a (Fig. 4.4b). In the more general case, the impulse can be written either as

```
LET impulse(i) = magnitude*pos(i)/r          ! radial impulse
```

or

```
LET impulse(1) = -magnitude*pos(2)/r         ! tangential impulse
LET impulse(2) = magnitude*pos(1)/r
```

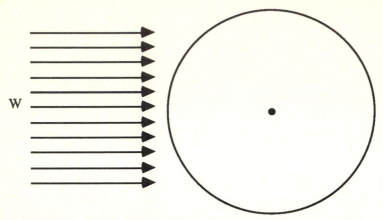

Fig. 4.5 What is the change in the orbit due to a "solar wind"?

Use either form of the **Euler** subroutine to simulate the effects of the perturbations in Problems 4.6 and 4.7.

*PROBLEM 4.8 Effect of a "solar wind"

Assume that the satellite is affected not only by the earth's gravitational force but also by a weak uniform "solar wind" force of magnitude W acting in the horizontal direction (see Fig. 4.5). The equations of motion can be written as

$$\frac{d^2x}{dt^2} = -\frac{GMx}{r^3} + W \qquad\qquad (4.19a)$$

$$\frac{d^2y}{dt^2} = -\frac{GMy}{r^3} \quad . \qquad\qquad (4.19b)$$

Choose initial conditions so that a circular orbit would be obtained for $W = 0$. Then choose a value of W whose magnitude is about 3% of the acceleration due to the gravitational field and simulate the orbit numerically. How does the orbit change? (See Luehrmann for further discussion of this problem.)

4.9 VELOCITY SPACE

In the above cases, your intuition might have been incorrect. For example, in Problems (4.6) and (4.7), you might have thought that the orbit would elongate in the direction of the kick. In fact the orbit does elongate, but in a direction *perpendicular* to the kick. Do not worry, you are in good company! Few students have a good qualitative understanding of Newton's law of motion (cf McCloskey). One qualitative way to state Newton's second law is

Forces act on the paths of particles by changing velocity not position.

If we fail to take into account this fact, we may encounter physical situations that appear counter-intuitive.

Since force acts to change velocity directly, it is reasonable to consider both velocity and position on an equal basis. In fact both variables are treated in such a manner in advanced formulations of classical mechanics and in quantum mechanics.

Let us now "discover" some properties of orbits in "velocity" space in the same manner as we have done for orbits in "position" space. Modify your program so that the path in velocity space of the earth is plotted. That is, plot $\{v_x, v_y\}$ in the same way you plotted $\{x, y\}$. The path in velocity space is a series of successive values of the object's velocity vector. If the position space orbit is an ellipse, what is the shape of the orbit in velocity space? We consider such questions in the context of the bound motion of a particle in an inverse-square force. A detailed discussion of velocity space orbits is given by Abelson et al.

PROBLEM 4.9 Properties of velocity space orbits

a. Verify that the velocity space orbit is a circle (even if the orbit in position space is an ellipse). Does the center of this circle coincide with the origin $\{v_x, v_y\} = \{0, 0\}$ in velocity space? Consider both elliptical and circular orbits in position space. It is a good idea to choose the same initial conditions that you considered in Problems 4.1 and 4.2.

b. Let $\vec{u}$ denote the radius vector of a point on the velocity circle, and $\vec{w}$ denote the vector from the origin in velocity space to the center of the velocity circle (see Fig. 4.6). Then the velocity of the particle can be written as

$$\vec{v} = \vec{u} + \vec{w} \quad . \tag{4.20}$$

Compute u and verify that its magnitude is given by

$$u = GMm/L \tag{4.21}$$

where L is the magnitude of the angular momentum. Note that L is proportional to m so that it is not necessary to know the magnitude of m.

c. Verify that at each moment in time, the planet's position vector $\vec{r}$ is perpendicular to $\vec{u}$. Explain why this relation holds.

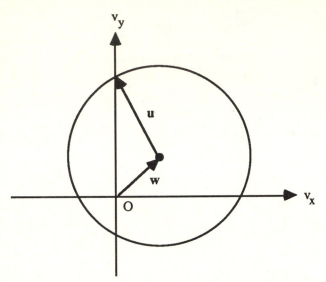

Fig. 4.6 The orbit of a particle in velocity space. The vector $\vec{w}$ points
from the origin in velocity space to the center of the circular orbit.
The vector $\vec{u}$ points from the center of the orbit to the point $\{v_x, v_y\}$.

PROBLEM 4.10 Perturbations in velocity space

How does the velocity space orbit change when an impulsive kick is applied
in the tangential direction? In the radial direction? How does the magnitude
and direction of $\vec{w}$ change? From the observed change in the velocity orbit
and the above considerations, explain the observed change of the orbit in
position space.

*PROBLEM 4.11 Orbits in the solar wind

Determine the change in the velocity space orbit when the solar wind (4.19) is
applied. How does the total angular momentum and energy change? Explain
in simple terms the previously observed change in the position space orbit.

4.10   A MINI-SOLAR SYSTEM

So far our numerical study of planetary orbits has been restricted to two-body
central forces. However, the solar system is not a two-body system since all the

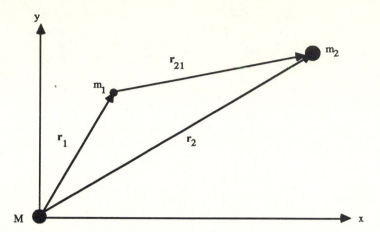

Fig. 4.7 The coordinate system used in (4.22). Planets of mass m_1 and m_2 orbit a "sun" of mass M.

planets exert gravitational forces on one another. Although the interplanetary forces are small in magnitude in comparison to the gravitational force of the sun, they can produce measurable effects. For example, the existence of the planet Neptune was conjectured on the basis of a discrepancy between the experimentally measured orbit of Uranus and the predicted orbit calculated from the known forces.

The presence of other planets implies that the total force on a planet is no longer a central force. Furthermore, since the orbits of the planets are not exactly in the same plane, an analysis of the solar system must be extended to three dimensions if accurate calculations are required. For the sake of simplicity, we will consider a model of a two-dimensional solar system with two planets in orbit about a sun.

The equations of motion of two planets of mass m_1 and mass m_2 can be written in vector form as (see Fig. 4.7)

$$m_1 \frac{d^2 \vec{r}_1}{dt^2} = -\frac{m_1 M G}{r_1{}^3}\vec{r}_1 + \frac{m_1 m_2 G}{r_{21}{}^3}\vec{r}_{21} \qquad (4.22a)$$

and

$$m_2 \frac{d^2 \vec{r}_2}{dt^2} = \frac{m_2 M G}{r_2{}^3}\vec{r}_2 - \frac{m_1 m_2 G}{r_{21}{}^3}\vec{r}_{21} \qquad (4.22b)$$

where $\vec{r}_1$ and $\vec{r}_2$ are directed from the sun to planets 1 and 2, and $\vec{r}_{21} = \vec{r}_2 - \vec{r}_1$ is the vector from planet 1 to planet 2. Although no analytic solution exists for (4.22), its numerical solution can be obtained by a straightforward extension of our previous method. In **Program planet2**, the position, velocity, and acceleration of the two planets are given in two-dimensional arrays where the first argument is the planet number and the second argument is the x or y component of the corresponding vector. We choose astronomical units so that the product GM is given by (4.16). For illustrative purposes, we adopt the numerical values $m_1/M = 0.001$ and $m_2/M = 0.01$.

```
PROGRAM planet2                  ! d = 2 solar system with major and minor planet
DIM pos(2,2),vel(2,2)
CALL initial(pos,vel,GM,dt,ncalc)
CALL output(pos)
DO until key input
   CALL Euler(pos,vel,GM,dt,ncalc)
   CALL output(pos)
LOOP
END

SUB initial(pos(,),vel(,),GM,dt,ncalc)
  LET GM = 4.0*pi*pi                      ! astronomical units
  LET dt = 0.001                          ! time step (yrs)
  LET plot_period = 0.02! yrs
  LET ncalc = plot_period/dt
  ! planet one
  LET pos(1,1) = 1                        ! initial x position of planet 1
  LET pos(1,2) = 0                        ! initial y position of planet 1
  LET vel(1,1) = 0                        ! initial x velocity of planet 1
  LET vel(1,2) = sqr(GM/pos(1,1))         ! initial y velocity of planet 1
  ! planet two
  LET pos(2,1) = (4)^(1/3)                ! initial x position of planet 2
  LET pos(2,2) = 0                        ! initial y position of planet 2
  LET vel(2,1) = 0                        ! initial x velocity of planet 2
  LET vel(2,2) = sqr(GM/pos(2,1))         ! initial y velocity of planet 2
  LET r = 2*pos(2,1)
  LET aspect_ratio = 1.5
  LET x = aspect_ratio*r
  SET window -x,x,-r,r
  LET radius = 0.1
  BOX CIRCLE -radius,radius,-radius,radius          ! sun at origin
  FLOOD 0,0
END SUB
```

```
SUB Euler(pos(,),vel(,),GM,dt,ncalc)
  DIM a(2,2),r(2)
  FOR icalc = 1 to ncalc
      ! compute distance dr between planets 1 and 2
      LET dx = pos(2,1) - pos(1,1)
      LET dy = pos(2,2) - pos(1,2)
      LET dr = sqr(dx*dx + dy*dy)        ! distance between planets 1 and 2
      LET accel = GM/(dr*dr*dr)
      LET a(1,1) = -0.01*accel*dx        ! accel of planet 1 due to planet 2
      LET a(1,2) = -0.01*accel*dy
      LET a(2,1) = -0.001*a(1,1)         ! accel of planet 2 due to planet 1
      LET a(2,2) = -0.001*a(1,2)
      FOR iplanet = 1 to 2                            ! sum over planets
         LET dist2 = pos(iplanet,1)*pos(iplanet,1)
         LET dist2 = dist2 + pos(iplanet,2)*pos(iplanet,2)
         ! distance of planet from sun from sun
         LET r(iplanet) = sqr(dist2)
         FOR i = 1 to 2                  ! sum over components
           LET r3 = r(iplanet)*r(iplanet)*r(iplanet)
           LET accel = -GM*pos(iplanet,i)/r3
           LET accel = accel + a(iplanet,i)
           LET vel(iplanet,i) = vel(iplanet,i) + accel*dt
           LET pos(iplanet,i) = pos(iplanet,i) + vel(iplanet,i)*dt
         NEXT i
      NEXT iplanet
  NEXT icalc
END SUB


SUB output(pos(,))                        ! plot orbits
    PLOT POINTS: pos(1,1),pos(1,2)        ! planet one
    PLOT POINTS: pos(2,1),pos(2,2)        ! planet two
END SUB
```

*PROBLEM 4.12 Planetary perturbations

a. Use **Program planet2** with the initial conditions given in the program. What would be the shape of the orbits and the periods of the two planets if they did not mutually interact? What is the qualitative effect of their mutual interaction? Why is one planet affected more by the mutual interaction than the other? Describe the shape of the two orbits. Are the angular momentum and total energy of planet one conserved? Is the total energy and angular momentum of the two planets conserved? If you are interested, you might wish to use real astronomical data for the earth and Jupiter and determine if Jupiter has any effect on the earth's orbit.

b. Another interesting dynamical system is the motion of a planet orbiting about two fixed stars of equal mass. In this case there are no closed orbits but the orbits can be classified as stable or unstable. Stable orbits may be open loops which encircle both stars, figure eights, or Kepler-like orbits which encircle only one star. Unstable orbits will eventually collide with one of the stars.

REFERENCES AND SUGGESTIONS FOR ADDITIONAL READING

Harold Abelson, Andrea diSessa and Lee Rudolph, "Velocity Space and the Geometry of Planetary Orbits," *Am. J. Phys.* **43**, 579 (1975). See also Andrea diSessa, "Orbit: A mini-environment for exploring orbital mechanics," in 0. Lecarme and R. Lewis, eds, *Computers in Education*, 359, North-Holland (1975). Detailed geometrical rather than calculus based arguments on the origin of closed orbits for inverse-square forces are presented. Are geometrical arguments easier to understand than algebraic arguments?

Ralph Baierlein, *Newtonian Dynamics,* McGraw-Hill (1983). An intermediate level text on mechanics. Of particular interest are the discussions on the stability of circular orbits and the effects of an oblate sun.

Alan Cromer, "Stable solutions using the Euler approximation," *Am. J. Phys.* **49**, 455 (1981). The author shows that a minor modification of the usual Euler approximation yields stable solutions for oscillatory systems including planetary motion and the harmonic oscillator.

Alan Cromer, "Computer-Simulated Physics Experiments," EduTech, Northeastern University (1980). A laboratory manual written for use with the Apple II+ computer.

Robert M. Eisberg and Lawrence S. Lerner, *Physics*, Vol. 1, McGraw-Hill (1981). An introductory level text with numerical applications to planetary motion.

A. P. French, *Newtonian Mechanics,* W.W. Norton & Company (1971). An introductory level text with more than a cursory treatment of planetary motion.

Herbert Goldstein, *Classical Mechanics,* 2nd ed., Addison-Wesley (1980). Chapter 3 has an excellent discussion of the Kepler problem and the conditions for a closed orbit.

Arthur W. Luehrmann, "Orbits in the Solar Wind—a Mini-Research Problem," *Am. J. Phys.* **42**, 361 (1974). Luehrmann emphasizes the desirability of student problems requiring inductive rather than deductive reasoning.

Michael McCloskey, "Intuitive Physics," *Sci. Amer.* **249**, 122 (April, 1983). A discussion of the "non-intuitive" nature of Newton's laws.

APPENDIX 4A LOG-LOG PLOTS

In Problem 4.2, we obtained "data" for the period and the semi-major axis of several elliptical orbits. Representative data for T and a are given in Table 4.1. In general we wish to analyze data such as that shown in the table to determine if the measured variables satisfy some particular mathematical relationship. In the following we analyze the data in Table 4.1 and discuss how such relationships might be found in simple cases.

Suppose we wish to test whether two variables y and x satisfy some particular functional relationship $y = f(x)$. In order to simplify the analysis, we will ignore possible errors in the measurements of y and x. (A discussion of fitting data with errors is given in Appendix 11A.) The simplest relationship between y and x is linear, i.e. $y = mx + b$. The existence of such a relationship can be seen by plotting y versus x on simple graph paper. It is a good idea to always make such a plot first, unless the values of y or x vary by many orders of magnitude.

From Table 4.1 we see that T is not a linear function of a. Depending on the nature of the problem, it might be reasonable to assume the general form

$$y(x) = Ae^{rx} \tag{4.23}$$

or

$$y(x) = Ax^r \tag{4.24}$$

where A and r are unknown parameters. If we assume the form (4.23), we can take the natural logarithm of both sides to find $ln\, y = ln\, A + rx$. Note that if

TABLE 4.1 Data for the period T and semi-major axis a from Problem 4.2. The time step used was $\Delta t = 0.01$. The estimated error is ± 0.02 for both T and a.

T	a
0.50	0.62
0.63	0.73
2.18	1.18
3.44	2.28
8.95	4.31

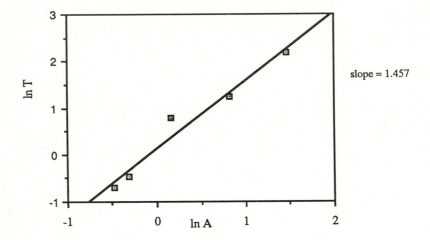

Fig. 4.8 Plot of $\ln T$ versus $\ln a$ using the data in Table 4.1. The slope is approximately 1.46.

(4.23) applies, a plot of $\ln y$ versus x would be a straight line with slope r and intercept $\ln A$. The traditional way to plot such a relationship is to use semi-log graph paper with the vertical axis ruled logarithmically and the horizontal axis ruled in the usual linear manner. An alternative procedure is to plot $\ln y$ versus x on regular graph paper.

If we wish to try to fit our data to the form (4.24), we can take the natural logarithm of both sides and obtain $\ln y = \ln A + r \ln x$. In this case a plot of y versus x on log-log paper yields the slope r, which is the quantity of interest. Of course we can also plot $\ln y$ versus $\ln x$ on linear graph paper.

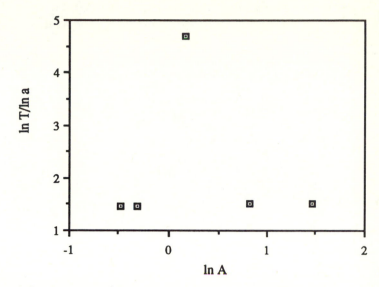

Fig. 4.9 Plot of the ratio *ln T/ ln a* versus *ln a*. Does it appear that we were a little sloppy in taking our data?

We illustrate a simple analysis of the data in Table 4.1. In Fig. 4.8, *ln T* is plotted versus *ln a*. Inspection of the plot indicates that a linear relationship between *ln T* and *ln a* is reasonable. In Chapter 11, we will discuss the "least squares" method for fitting a straight line through a number of data points. However, with a little practice you can do a visual analysis which is nearly as good. The measured slope is found to be approximately 1.46, a value which is consistent with the theoretical prediction of 1.5.

The direct plot of *ln T* versus *ln a* in Fig. 4.8 gives us an overall picture of the nature of the relationship between T and a. However, now that we are confident that a linear relationship has been established, a plot of the ratio *ln T/ ln a* against *ln a* as shown in Fig. 4.9 is much more sensitive to discrepancies and errors.

Of course not all functional dependencies are simple power-laws or exponentials. Clearly some theoretical input is necessary to guide the analysis of the data.

REFERENCES

G. L. Squires, *Practical Physics,* 3rd ed., Cambridge University Press (1985). An excellent text on the design of experiments and the analysis of data.

OSCILLATORY MOTION

5

We explore the qualitative behavior of linear and non-linear oscillatory systems in the context of mechanics and electronics.

5.1 SIMPLE HARMONIC OSCILLATOR

There are many physical systems which undergo regular, repeating motion. Motion which repeats itself at definite intervals, e.g. the motion of the earth about the sun, is said to be *periodic* or *harmonic*. If an object undergoes periodic motion between two limits over the same path, we call the motion *oscillatory*. Examples of oscillatory motion which are familiar to us from our everyday experience include the pendulum in a grandfather clock and a plucked guitar string. Less obvious examples are microscopic phenomena such as the the oscillations of the atoms in crystalline solids. Many nonmechanical examples can be taken from electromagnetic and atomic phenomena.

To illustrate the important concepts associated with simple oscillatory phenomena, consider a body of mass m connected to the free end of a spring. The body slides on a frictionless, horizontal surface (see Fig. 5.1). We specify the position of the body by x and take $x = 0$ to be the *equilibrium* position of the body, i.e. the position when the spring is relaxed. If the body is moved from $x = 0$ and then released, the body oscillates along a horizontal line. We know that if the spring is not compressed or stretched too far from $x = 0$, the force on the body at position x is linearly related to x:

$$F = -kx \quad .$$

$$(5.1)$$

The *force constant k* is a measure of the stiffness of the spring. The negative sign in (5.1) implies that the force acts to restore the body to its equilibrium position. Newton's equation of motion of the body can be written as

$$\frac{d^2x}{dt^2} = -\omega_0^2 x$$

$$(5.2)$$

where the quantity ω_0 is defined by

$$\omega_0^2 = \frac{k}{m} \quad .$$

$$(5.3)$$

The equation of motion (5.2) is an example of a *linear* differential equation since it involves only first powers of x and its derivatives. The dynamical behavior described by (5.2) is called *simple harmonic motion* and can be solved analytically in terms of sine and cosine functions. Since the form of the solution will help us introduce several terms needed to discuss oscillatory motion, we include the solution here. One form of the solution is

$$x(t) = A \cos(\omega_0 t + \delta)$$

$$(5.4)$$

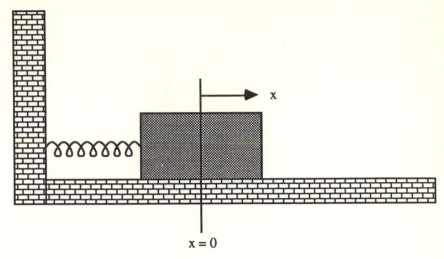

x = 0

Fig. 5.1 An example of a one-dimensional simple harmonic oscillator.
The block slides horizontally on the frictionless surface.

where A and δ are constants and the argument of the cosine is in radians. It
is straightforward to check by substitution that (5.4) is a solution of (5.2). The
constants A and δ are called the *amplitude* and the initial *phase* and may be
determined by the initial conditions for x and the velocity $v = dx/dt$.

Since the cosine is a periodic function with period 2π, we know that $x(t)$ in
(5.4) is also periodic. We define the *period* T as the smallest time for which the
motion repeats itself, i.e.

$$x(t + T) = x(t) \quad . \tag{5.5}$$

Since $\omega_0 T$ corresponds to one *cycle*, we have

$$T = \frac{2\pi}{\omega_0} = \frac{2\pi}{\sqrt{k/m}} \quad . \tag{5.6}$$

The *frequency* ν of the motion is the number of cycles per second and is given
by $\nu = 1/T$. Note that T depends on the ratio k/m and not on A and δ. Hence
the period of simple harmonic motion is independent of the amplitude of the
motion.

Although the position and velocity of the oscillator are continuously changing, the total energy E remains constant and is given by

$$E = \frac{1}{2}mv^2 + \frac{1}{2}kx^2 \quad . \tag{5.7}$$

The two terms in (5.7) can be identified with the kinetic and potential energies.

5.2   NUMERICAL SIMULATION OF THE HARMONIC OSCILLATOR

The now familiar Euler-Cromer algorithm is particularly useful for the simulation of oscillatory motion. A summary of some of the common "higher order" numerical methods is given in Appendix 5A.

Program sho computes the time-dependence of the position and velocity for a simple harmonic oscillator using the Euler-Cromer algorithm. The results for the position *pos* and velocity *vel* are printed on the screen until the program is ended when any key is pressed. Examples of the use of the **tab** function and **PRINT using** functions are given in **SUB initial** and **SUB output** respectively.

```
PROGRAM sho                              ! simple harmonic oscillator
CALL initial(pos,vel,w2,dt,ncalc)
DO until key input
    CALL output(pos,vel,t)
    CALL Euler(pos,vel,w2,dt,ncalc)
    LET t = t + ncalc*dt
LOOP
END

SUB initial(pos,vel,w2,dt,ncalc)
  INPUT prompt "initial position = ": pos      ! meters
  LET vel = 0                                  ! initial velocity (m/s)
  INPUT prompt "ratio of k/m = ": w2           ! natural (angular) frequency
  INPUT prompt "time step (sec) = ": dt
  LET print_period = 0.05
  LET ncalc = print_period/dt
  PRINT tab(7);"time";tab(17);"position";tab(28);"velocity"
  PRINT                                        ! skip line
END SUB

SUB Euler(pos,vel,w2,dt,ncalc)                 ! Euler-Cromer algorithm
  FOR icalc = 1 to ncalc
    LET accel = -w2*pos
    LET vel = vel + accel*dt
    LET pos = pos + vel*dt
  NEXT icalc
END SUB
```

```
SUB output(pos,vel,t)
  ! - prints number with leading space or minus sign
  ! % prints leading zeroes as '0'
  PRINT using "——%.####": t,pos,vel
END SUB
```

We first verify that the Euler-Cromer algorithm can be applied to the dynamical motion of the simple harmonic oscillator using a reasonable choice of Δt. Since we know the analytical solution in this case, one criterion for the choice of Δt is that our computed solutions must be consistent with the analytical results (5.4). However, we need a more general criterion which does not depend on the existence of an analytical solution. We will find in the following problem that a necessary criterion is that the total energy be conserved.

PROBLEM 5.1 Energy conservation and the selection of algorithms

a. Modify **Program sho** so that E_n, the total energy per unit mass, is computed at each time step t_n. Compute the time-dependence of the difference $\Delta_n = (E_n - E_0)/E_0$ for at least one complete cycle and plot Δ_n as a function of the time t_n. (E_0 is the initial total energy.) Is the difference Δ_n uniformly small throughout the cycle? For simplicity choose $x_0 = 1$, $v_0 = 0$ and $\omega_0{}^2 = k/m = 9$ for your initial runs. What are the units of k and the ratio k/m in SI units?

b. Use the Euler method to compute Δ_n over one cycle and describe the qualitative difference between the time-dependence of Δ_n using the Euler and the Euler-Cromer methods. Which method is more consistent with the requirement of conservation of energy?

c. For fixed Δt, which method yields better results for the position in comparison to the analytical solution (5.4)? Is the conservation of energy requirement consistent with the relative accuracy of the computed positions? Adopt the Euler or the Euler-Cromer method for the remaining problems in this chapter.

d. Choose a reasonable numerical value of Δt for $\omega_0{}^2 = 9$ and for $\omega_0{}^2 = 90$. How do the values of Δt correspond to the relative values of the period in the two cases?

*e. Use one or more of the "higher order" algorithms discussed in Appendix 5A to simulate the simple harmonic oscillator. Is one of these algorithms more suitable than the Euler-Cromer method?

PROBLEM 5.2 Analysis of simple harmonic motion

a. Modify **Program sho** so that the position and velocity of the oscillator are plotted as a function of the time t. Describe the qualitative behavior of the position and velocity.

b. Compute the numerical values of the period T for different values of ω_0. What is your procedure for computing T? Assume that T is proportional to $(k/m)^\alpha$ and estimate the exponent α by making a log-log plot of T versus k/m (see Appendix 4A).

c. Compute the amplitude A and the total energy E for the initial conditions $x_0 = 4$, $v_0 = 0$, and $x_0 = 0$, $v_0 = 4$; choose $\omega_0{}^2 = 4$ in both cases. What quantity determines the value of the amplitude A?

d. Plot the time-dependence of the potential energy and the kinetic energy through one complete cycle. Where in the cycle is the kinetic energy a maximum?

e. Compute the average value of the kinetic energy and the potential energy during a complete cycle. Is there a relation between the two averages?

f. Compute $x(t)$ for different values of A and show that the shape of $x(t)$ is independent of A, i.e. $x(t)/A$ is a *universal* function of t for a fixed value of k/m. In what units should the time be measured in order that $x(t)/A$ be independent of A and k/m?

*g. We know that the state of motion of the one-dimensional oscillator is completely specified as a function of time if the two quantities $x(t)$ and $v(t)$ are given. These quantities may be considered to be the coordinates of a point in a two-dimensional space, called *phase space*. As the time increases, the point $\{x, v\}$ moves along a trajectory in phase space. Modify your program so that v is plotted as a function of x. Choose v and x as the vertical and horizontal axes respectively. Set $\omega_0{}^2 = 9$ and compute the phase trajectories for the different initial conditions $\{x_0 = 1, v_0 = 0\}$, $\{x_0 = 0, v_0 = 1\}$ and $\{x_0 = 4, v_0 = 0\}$. Do you find a different phase path for each initial condition? What physical quantity distinguishes the phase paths? What is the shape of the phase paths? Is this shape similar for all paths? Is the motion of a representative point $\{x, v\}$ always in the clockwise or counterclockwise direction?

5.3 THE SIMPLE PENDULUM

Another common example of a mechanical system which exhibits oscillatory motion is the "simple" pendulum (see Fig. 5.2). A simple pendulum is an idealized system consisting of a particle or "bob" of mass m attached to the lower end of a rigid rod of length L and negligible mass; the upper end of the rod pivots without friction. If the bob is pulled to one side from its equilibrium position and released, the pendulum swings in a vertical plane.

Since the bob is constrained to move along the arc of a circle of radius L about the center O, the bob's position is specified by the arc length or by the angle θ (see Fig. 5.2). The linear velocity and acceleration of the bob as measured along the arc are given by

$$v = L\frac{d\theta}{dt} \tag{5.8}$$

$$a = L\frac{d^2\theta}{dt^2} \quad . \tag{5.9}$$

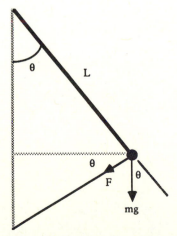

Fig. 5.2 Force diagram for a simple pendulum. The angle θ is measured from the vertical and is positive if the mass is to the right of the vertical and negative if it is to the left.

In the absence of friction, two forces act on the body: the force mg vertically downward and the force of the rod. The latter force is outward from the center if $|\theta| < \pi/2$. Since the rod does not exert a force along the arc, we need to consider only the component of mg along the arc. From Fig. 5.2, it can be seen that this component is $mg \sin \theta$ in the direction of decreasing θ. Hence the equation of motion becomes

$$mL\frac{d^2\theta}{dt^2} = -mg \sin \theta \tag{5.10}$$

or

$$\frac{d^2\theta}{dt^2} = -\frac{g}{L} \sin \theta \quad . \tag{5.11}$$

Equation (5.11) is an example of a non-linear equation since $\sin \theta$ rather than θ appears. Most non-linear equations do not have analytical solutions in terms of well known functions and (5.11) is no exception. However, if the pendulum is undergoing oscillations of sufficiently small amplitude, then $\sin \theta \approx \theta$ and (5.11) reduces to

$$\frac{d^2\theta}{dt^2} \approx -\frac{g}{L}\theta \tag{5.12}$$

for $\theta \ll 1$. (Remember that θ is measured in radians.)

Part of the fun in studying physics comes from realizing that equations which appear in different areas (and different fields) are often identical. Hence the study of a phenomenon in one area may permit us to apply our knowledge to another area. A simple example of this "crossover" effect can be seen from a comparison of (5.2) and (5.12). If we associate x with θ, we see that the two equations are identical in form, and we can immediately conclude that for $\theta \ll 1$, the period of a simple pendulum is given by

$$T = 2\pi\sqrt{L/g} \quad . \tag{5.13}$$

One way to understand the motion of a pendulum with large oscillations is to solve (5.11) numerically. Since we know that a numerical solution must be consistent with conservation of total energy, we derive its form here. The potential energy can be found from the following considerations. If the rod is deflected by the angle θ, then the bob is raised by the distance $h = L - L\cos \theta$ (see Fig. 5.2). Hence the potential energy of the bob in the gravitational field of the earth can be expressed as

$$U = mgh = mgL(1 - \cos \theta) \tag{5.14}$$

where the zero of the potential energy corresponds to $\theta = 0$. Since the kinetic energy of the pendulum is $\frac{1}{2}mv^2 = \frac{1}{2}mL^2(d\theta/dt)^2$, the total energy E is

$$E = \frac{1}{2}mL^2(\frac{d\theta}{dt})^2 + mgL(1 - \cos \theta) \quad . \tag{5.15}$$

PROBLEM 5.3 Large angle oscillations of a simple pendulum

a. Use **Program sho** to simulate small amplitude oscillations of the simple pendulum. Since $sin\,\theta \approx \theta$, no changes are necessary. However, it is desirable to let $x \to \theta$, $v \to \omega = d\theta/dt$ and $k/m \to g/L$. In this context, the quantity ω is the angular velocity of the pendulum. What are the units of the ratio g/L? Choose $g/L = 9$ and the initial conditions $\theta(t = 0) = 0.1$, $\omega(t = 0) = 0$ and determine the period.

b. Modify your program to simulate the large amplitude oscillations of the simple pendulum by using (5.11). Set $g/L = 9$ and choose Δt so that the numerical integration procedure generates a stable solution, i.e. a solution which does not diverge with time from the "true" solution. Check the stability of the solution by monitoring the total energy and ensuring that it does not drift from its initial value.

c. Set $\omega(t = 0) = 0$ and make plots of $\theta(t)$ and $\omega(t)$ for the initial conditions $\theta(t = 0) = 0.1, 0.2, 0.4, 0.8$ and 1.0. (Remember that θ is measured in radians and is restricted to $|\theta| < \pi/2$.) Describe the qualitative behavior of θ and ω. What is the period T and amplitude θ_m in each case? Plot T versus θ_m and discuss the qualitative dependence of the period on the amplitude. How do your results for T compare in the linear and non-linear cases, e.g. which period is larger? Explain the relative values of T in physical terms.

*__d.__ Obtain several phase space plots for the simple pendulum for different values of the total energy. Are the phase space paths closed? Does the shape of the path depend on the total energy?

5.4   PROGRAMMING NOTES

We introduce in this section several new programming statements for the output of results. So far we have printed the results of our computations on a computer screen in tabular or graphical form. On most computers this screen output can then be "dumped" to a printer by "printing the screen". However, frequently it is convenient to print the results directly on a printer. True BASIC treats the screen, keyboard, printer, and the disk drives as peripheral "devices" which are accessed by the computer using a path called a data channel. Before a device can be accessed, a channel to that device must be opened. The keyboard and display are assigned to channel #0 and are always open. Other channels are defined in an **OPEN** statement. For example, to access the printer we can use

> OPEN #1: printer

where the channel number is arbitrary. We then can output the value of the variable *pos* to the printer by using

> PRINT #1: pos

The last step in the sequence is to close the channel number:

> CLOSE #1

Program print accesses a printer, prints a result, and closes the printer. Note that a channel number can be passed as a parameter to a subroutine.

```
PROGRAM print
CALL initial(#1,x)
CALL add(x)
CALL output(#1,x)
END

SUB initial(#1,x)
  OPEN #1: printer
  LET x = 150
END SUB

SUB add(x)
  LET x = x + 200
END SUB

SUB output(#1,x)
  PRINT #1, using "####.##": x
  CLOSE #1
END SUB
```

In order to make animated pictures, True BASIC allows screen images to be stored as a string variable and redisplayed without the need for further calculation. The following True BASIC program illustrates the use of the **BOX KEEP**, **BOX CLEAR**, and **BOX SHOW** statements to create the illusion of motion across the screen.

```
PROGRAM animation
SET window 1,10,1,10
BOX AREA 1,2,1,2                    ! draw shape
BOX KEEP 1,2,1,2 in box$           ! store shape in string variable box$
FOR i = 1 to 9 step 0.05
    BOX CLEAR i,i+1,1,2            ! erase shape
    BOX SHOW box$ at i + 0.05,1    ! redraw shape at different location
NEXT i
END
```

In order to gain insight into the qualitative differences between the linear and non-linear restoring forces, we can "observe" a linear and non-linear pendulum under the same conditions. **SUB animation** given in **Program pendula** makes a "motion picture" of a linear and non-linear pendulum in two different windows. The "pendula" are represented by circles which are drawn on the screen at a position proportional to their angular displacement. The previous position of the pendula is erased and the circles "move" across the screen horizontally.

```
PROGRAM pendula                     ! animation of linear and non-linear pendula
CALL initial(#1,#2,x1,v1,x2,v2,w2,dt,ball$,r)
DO until key input
    CALL linear(x1,v1,w2,dt,x1old)      ! Euler-Cromer algorithm
    CALL nonlinear(x2,v2,w2,dt,x2old)
    CALL animation(#1,x1,x1old,ball$,r)
    CALL animation(#2,x2,x2old,ball$,r)
LOOP
CLOSE #1
CLOSE #2
END
```

```
SUB initial(#1,#2,x1,v1,x2,v2,w2,dt,ball$,r)
    INPUT prompt "time step = ": dt
    LET x1 = 0.5                         ! initial position (radians) of linear oscillator
    LET x2 = 0.5                         ! initial position of non-linear oscillator
    LET v1 = 0                           ! initial angular velocity (linear oscillator)
    LET v2 = 0                           ! non-linear oscillator
    LET w2 = 9                           ! g/L ratio
    LET xmax = x1                        ! size of window
    LET aspect_ratio = 1.5*2             ! corrected for use of only half of screen
    LET vmax = xmax
    LET hmax = aspect_ratio*xmax

    OPEN #1: screen 0,1,0,0.5            ! bottom half of screen
    SET window -hmax,hmax,-vmax,vmax
    PRINT "linear oscillator"
    ! draw circle
    LET r = 0.1                          ! radius of circle
    BOX CIRCLE x1 - r,x1 + r,- r,r
    ! store circle in string variable ball$
    BOX KEEP x1 - r, x1 + r,-r,r in ball$
    OPEN #2: screen 0,1,0.5,1            ! top half of screen
    SET window -hmax,hmax,-vmax,vmax
    PRINT "non-linear oscillator"
    BOX CIRCLE x2 - r,x2 + r,- r,r
END SUB

SUB animation(#9,theta,old_theta,ball$,r)
    WINDOW #9
    LET x = old_theta
    BOX CLEAR x - r, x +  r,- r,r        ! erase old circle
    LET x = theta
    BOX SHOW ball$ at x - r,-r           ! draw new circle
END SUB
```

SUB **linear** and SUB **nonlinear** are not listed since they are similar to SUB **Euler** in **Program sho**. The only difference is that the previous position of the oscillators, $x1old$ and $x2old$, must be passed to the main program and to SUB **animation**.

*PROBLEM 5.4 Animation of the linear and non-linear oscillator

a. Describe the qualitative nature of the motion of the pendula. Where do they move relatively quickly or slowly?

b. Describe the qualitative features of the relative motion of the linear and non-linear pendulum.

c. Write a program to make the observations more interesting visually by replacing the circle by a more realistic looking pendulum.

5.5 DAMPED OSCILLATORY MOTION

We know from experience that most oscillatory motion in nature gradually decreases until the displacement becomes zero; such motion is said to be *damped*. As an example of a damped harmonic oscillator, consider the motion of the block in Fig. 5.1 when a horizontal drag force is included. For small velocities, it is a reasonable approximation to assume that the drag force is proportional to the first power of the velocity. In this case the equation of motion can be written as

$$\frac{d^2x}{dt^2} = -\omega_0{}^2 x - \gamma\frac{dx}{dt} \tag{5.16}$$

where the *damping coefficient* γ is a measure of the magnitude of the drag term. Note that the drag force in (5.16) opposes the motion. What is the behavior of $x(t)$ if the linear restoring term in (5.16) is neglected? We simulate the behavior of the damped harmonic oscillator in Problem 5.5.

PROBLEM 5.5 Damped harmonic oscillator

a. Incorporate the effects of damping into your program and plot the time-dependence of the position and velocity of the harmonic oscillator. For simplicity make all runs for $\omega_0{}^2 = 9$ and $x_0 = 1$, $v_0 = 0$.

b. Choose $\gamma = 0.5$ and plot $x(t)$. Define the period of the motion as the time between successive maxima of $x(t)$. Compute the period and corresponding angular frequency and compare their values to the undamped case. Is the period (frequency) longer or shorter? Make additional runs for $\gamma = 1, 2$, and 3. Does the period (frequency) increase or decrease with greater damping?

c. Define the amplitude as the maximum value of x during one cycle. Compute the *relaxation time* τ, the time it takes for the amplitude of an oscillation to change from its maximum value to $1/e \approx 0.37$ of its maximum value. Show that the value of τ is constant throughout the motion. Compute τ for the values of γ considered in part (b) and discuss the qualitative dependence of τ on γ.

d. Plot the total energy as a function of time for several of the values of γ considered in part (b). If the decrease in energy is not monotonic, explain the cause of the time-dependence.

e. Compute the average value of the kinetic energy, the potential energy, and the total energy over a complete cycle. Plot these averages as a function of the number of cycles. Due to the presence of damping, these averages decrease with the number of cycles. Is the decrease uniform? Characterize the time-dependence of these averages in terms of τ for $\gamma = 0.5$ and $\gamma = 1$.

f. Compute the time-dependence of $x(t)$ and $v(t)$ for $\gamma = 4$, 5, 6, 7, and 8. Is the motion oscillatory for all γ? Choose a useful operational definition of equilibrium, e.g. $|x| < 0.0001$. How quickly does $x(t)$ decay to equilibrium? For fixed ω_0, the oscillator is said to be *critically damped* at the smallest value of γ for which the decay to equilibrium is monotonic. For what value of γ does critical damping occur for $\omega_0 = 3$ and $\omega_0 = 2$? For each value of ω_0, compute the value of γ for which the system approaches equilibrium most quickly.

*g. Construct the phase space diagram for cases $\omega_0 = 3$ and $\gamma = 0.5$, 2, 4, 6, and 8. Are the qualitative features of the phase space plot independent of γ? If not, discuss the qualitative differences.

5.6 LINEAR RESPONSE TO EXTERNAL FORCES

How can we determine the period of a pendulum which is not already in motion? The obvious way is to disturb the system, for example to displace the bob and observe its motion. We will find in the following that the nature of the *response* of the system to the perturbation tells us something about the nature of the system in the absence of the perturbation.

Consider the *driven* damped linear oscillator with an external force $F(t)$ in addition to the linear restoring force and linear damping force. The equation of motion can now be written as

$$\frac{d^2x}{dt^2} = -\omega_0{}^2x - \gamma v + \frac{1}{m}F(t) \quad . \tag{5.17}$$

It is customary to interpret the "response" of the system in terms of the displacement x rather than the velocity v.

The time-dependence of $F(t)$ in (5.17) is arbitrary. Since many forces are harmonic, we first consider the form

$$\frac{1}{m}F(t) = A_0 \, cos \, \omega t \tag{5.18}$$

where ω is the angular frequency of the driving force. We consider in Problem 5.6 the response of the damped linear oscillator to the harmonic force.

PROBLEM 5.6 Steady state behavior of a driven damped linear oscillator

a. Modify **Program sho** so that an external force of the form (5.18) is included. Introduce this force as an external function whose form can be easily modified without changing the main program. For example we can write **SUB Euler** in the form:

```
SUB Euler(pos,vel,nat_freq2,gamma,ang_freq,t,dt,ncalc)
   DECLARE DEF f                       ! external force
   FOR icalc = 1 to ncalc
      LET t = t + dt                   ! time (sec)
      LET accel = -nat_freq2*pos       ! linear restoring force
      LET accel = accel - gamma*vel    ! damping term
      LET accel = accel + f(t,ang_freq) ! external force
      LET vel = vel + accel*dt
      LET pos = pos + vel*dt
   NEXT icalc
END SUB
```

The parameter nat_freq2 in **SUB Euler** is the ratio k/m. Both nat_freq2 and the angular frequency ang_freq of the external force are defined in **SUB initial**. The external force is defined as an external function:

```
DEF f(t,w)
   LET A0 = 1               ! amplitude of external force divided by mass
   LET f = A0*cos(w*t)
END DEF
```

b. Set $\omega_0 = 3$, $\gamma = 0.5$, $A_0 = 1$, and $\omega = 2$ for all the runs in parts (b)–(e) unless otherwise stated. We know from Problem 5.5b that for these values of ω_0 and γ, the dynamical behavior of the system in the absence of an external force is that of a lightly damped oscillator. Plot $x(t)$ versus t with the initial condition $\{x_0 = 1, v_0 = 0\}$. How does the qualitative behavior of $x(t)$ differ from the unperturbed case? What is the period and angular frequency of $x(t)$ after several oscillations have occurred? Obtain a similar plot for $x(t)$ with $\{x_0 = 0, v_0 = 1\}$. What is the period and angular frequency of $x(t)$ after several oscillations have occurred? Does $x(t)$ approach a limiting behavior which is independent of the initial conditions? Does the short-time behavior of $x(t)$ depend on the initial conditions? Identify a *transient* part of $x(t)$ which depends on the initial conditions and decays in time, and a *steady state* part which dominates at longer times and which is independent of the initial conditions.

c. Compute $x(t)$ for $\omega = 1$ and $\omega = 4$. What is the period and angular frequency of the steady state motion in each case?

d. Compute $x(t)$ for $\omega_0 = 4$; otherwise choose the same parameters as in part (b). What is the angular frequency of the steady state motion? On the basis of your results in parts (b)–(d), explain which parameters determine the frequency of the steady state behavior.

e. Verify that the steady state behavior of $x(t)$ is given by

$$x(t) = A(\omega)\cos(\omega t + \delta) \tag{5.19}$$

where δ is the phase difference between the applied force and the steady state motion. Compute δ for $\omega_0 = 3$, $\gamma = 0.5$, and $\omega = 0$, 1.0, 2.0, 2.2, 2.4, 2.6, 2.8, 3.0, 3.2, and 3.4. Repeat the computation for $\gamma = 1.5$ and plot δ versus ω for the two values of γ. Discuss the qualitative ω-dependence of $\delta(\omega)$ in the two values of γ.

PROBLEM 5.7 The response of a damped linear oscillator

a. The long-term behavior of a driven harmonic oscillator depends on the frequency of the driving force. One measure of this behavior is the maximum steady state displacement $A(\omega)$. The following additional statements in **SUB Euler** allow $A(\omega)$ to be computed directly. Be sure to pass the variable *amplitude* to the main program.

```
IF pos > amplitude then
    LET amplitude = pos
    PRINT t, "amplitude = "; amplitude
END IF
```

Adopt the initial condition $\{x_0 = 0, v_0 = 0\}$. Compute $A(\omega)$ for $\omega = 0, 1.0$, $2.0, 2.2, 2.4, 2.6, 2.8, 3.0, 3.2$, and 3.4 with $\omega_0 = 3$ and $\gamma = 0.5$. Plot $A(\omega)$ versus ω and describe the qualitative behavior of $A(\omega)$. If $A(\omega)$ has a maximum, determine the resonance angular frequency ω_m, which is the frequency at the maximum of A. Is the value of ω_m close to the natural angular frequency ω_0? Estimate the numerical value of ω_m and make a quantitative comparison of its value to ω_0 and the frequency of the damped linear oscillator in the absence of an external force (see Problem 5.5b).

b. Compute A_m, the value of the amplitude at $\omega = \omega_m$, and the ratio $\Delta\omega/\omega_m$, where $\Delta\omega$ is the "width" of the resonance. Define $\Delta\omega$ as the frequency interval between points on the amplitude resonance curve which are $1/\sqrt{2} \approx 0.707$ of A_m. Set $\omega_0 = 3$ and consider $\gamma = 0.1, 0.5, 1.0$, and 2.0. Describe the qualitative dependence of A_m and $\Delta\omega/\omega_m$ on γ. The quantity $\Delta\omega/\omega_m$ is proportional to $1/Q$, where Q is the "quality" factor of the oscillator.

c. Describe the qualitative behavior of the steady state amplitude $A(\omega)$ near $\omega = 0$ and $\omega \gg \omega_0$. Why is $A(\omega = 0) > A(\omega)$ for small ω? Why does $A(\omega) \to 0$ for $\omega \gg \omega_0$?

*d. So far we have found the resonant frequency ω_m from the condition for a resonance of the steady state amplitude. Compute the mean kinetic energy over one cycle once steady state conditions have been reached. Does the mean kinetic energy resonate at the same frequency as the amplitude? Set $\omega_0 = 3$, $\gamma = 0.5$, and $A = 1$.

For many types of problems, the sinusoidal driving force considered in Problems 5.6 and 5.7 is not realistic. Another example of an external force can be found by observing someone pushing a child on a swing. Since the force is nonzero only for short intervals of time, this type of force is said to be *impulsive*. In the following problem, we consider the response of a damped linear oscillator to such a force.

*PROBLEM 5.8 The response to non-sinusoidal external forces

a. For simplicity assume that a swing can be modeled by a linear restoring force and a linear damping term. Modify **Program sho** to include an external periodic impulse. For simplicity let the duration of the push be equal to a time step Δt. Since the effect of an impulse is to change the velocity, we include the effects of the external impulse in **SUB Euler** as

```
LET ntime = int(t/dt)              ! # of time steps
LET vel = vel + accel*dt + impulse(ntime,dt)
```

We write the impulse as an external function using the **mod** function.

```
DEF impulse(ncount,dt)
    LET Im = 1.0                    ! magnitude of impulse
    LET ang_freq = 2.8             ! angular frequency of external force
    LET T = 2*pi/ang_freq           ! period of external force
    LET nperiod = int(T/dt)        ! corresponding # of time steps
    IF mod(ncount,nperiod) < 1 then
        LET impulse = Im
    ELSE
        LET impulse = 0
    END IF
END DEF
```

In order to save computation time, it would be better to define the external angular frequency and the parameter *nperiod* in **SUB initial** and to pass the latter to **DEF impulse**.

b. Determine the steady state amplitude $A(\omega)$ for various values of the applied angular frequency $\omega = 2\pi/T$ at which the impulse is non-zero. T is the time between "pushes". Are your results consistent with your experience in pushing a swing and with the comparable results of Problem 5.7?

c. Consider the amplitude response to the "half-wave" external force consisting of the positive part of a cosine function (see Fig. 5.3). Compute the steady state amplitude $A(\omega)$ for a damped linear oscillator with $\omega_0 = 3$ and $\gamma = 0.5$ and $\omega = 1.0$, 1.3, 1.4, 1.5, 1.6, 2.5, 3.0, and 3.5. At what angular frequencies does $A(\omega)$ have relative maxima? Can you observe any evidence

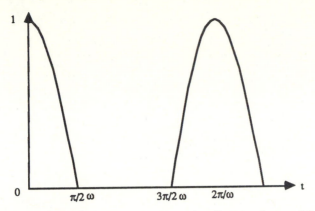

Fig. 5.3 A half-wave driving force corresponding to the positive part of a cosine function.

that the half-wave cosine driving force is equivalent to a sum of cosine functions of different frequencies? For example, does $A(\omega)$ have more than one resonance?

5.7   THE PRINCIPLE OF SUPERPOSITION

So far we have considered the response of our system to a single external force. In the next problem, we determine the response of a damped linear oscillator to an external force which is the sum of harmonic terms.

PROBLEM 5.9 The principle of superposition

a. Set $\omega_0 = 3$, $\gamma = 0.5$, and $\omega = 2$ and compute $x(t)$ for the external harmonic force $F_1(t) = \cos \omega t$ and $F_2(t) = 2 \cos \omega t$. Denote the corresponding values of x as $x_1(t)$ and $x_2(t)$. How do the steady state results for $x_2(t)$ compare to the steady state results for $x_1(t)$? What do you expect to find for $F(t) = 4 \cos \omega t$? Do the transient parts of $x(t)$ for the different external forces satisfy the same relation as the steady state parts?

b. Compute the steady state response $x(t)$ for $\omega_0 = 3$ and $\gamma = 0.5$ to the external function

$$\frac{1}{m}F(t) = \frac{1}{\pi} + \frac{1}{2} \cos \omega t + \frac{2}{3\pi} \cos 2\omega t - \frac{2}{15\pi} \cos 4\omega t \qquad (5.20)$$

with $\omega = 1.0$. Compare the behavior of $x(t)$ to the comparable results for $x(t)$ for the half-wave cosine function considered in Problem 5.8c.

c. Plot the function $F(t)$ defined in (5.20) versus t for $\omega = 2$. How does $F(t)$ compare to the half-wave cosine function (see Fig. 5.3). Use your results to conjecture a *principle of superposition* for the solutions to linear equations.

In Problem 5.9 we found that the response of the damped harmonic oscillator to an external driving force is linear. For example, if the magnitude of the external force is doubled, then the magnitude of the steady state motion is also doubled. This behavior is a consequence of the linear nature of the equation of motion. We now investigate the response of a non-linear oscillator, e.g. one for which the restoring force is proportional to $\sin\theta$ rather than to θ.

PROBLEM 5.10 The response of a non-linear oscillator

Modify your program from Problem 5.9 to simulate a non-linear pendulum with an external harmonic force and a linear drag term. Set $\omega_0{}^2 = g/L = 9$, $\gamma = 0.5$, and $\omega = 2$. Determine the steady state amplitude $A(\omega)$ as a function of the magnitude A of the driving force for $A = 0.5$, 1, 2, and 4. Is the response linear for small A? Is the response linear for larger A? Is the superposition principle applicable to non-linear systems?

5.8   ELECTRICAL CIRCUIT OSCILLATIONS

We now discuss several electrical analogues of the mechanical systems we have considered. Although the equations of motion are identical in form, it is convenient to consider electrical circuits separately since the notation and the nature of the questions are somewhat different.

The starting point for electrical circuit theory is Kirchhoff's loop rule which states that the sum of the voltage drops around a closed path of an electrical circuit is zero. This law is a consequence of conservation of energy, since a voltage drop represents the amount of energy which is lost or gained when a unit charge passes through a circuit element. The relationships for the voltage drops across each circuit element are summarized in Table 5.1.

Imagine an electrical circuit with an alternating voltage source $V_s(t)$ attached in series to a resistor, inductor, and capacitor (see Fig. 5.4). The corresponding loop equation is

$$V_L + V_R + V_C = V_s(t) \quad . \tag{5.21}$$

TABLE 5.1 The voltage drops across the basic electrical circuit elements. Q is the charge (coulombs) on one plate of the capacitor and I is the current (amperes).

element	voltage drop	units
resistor	$V_R = IR$	resistance R, ohms (Ω)
capacitor	$V_C = \frac{Q}{C}$	capacitance C, farads (F)
inductor	$V_L = L\frac{dI}{dt}$	inductance L, henries (H)

The voltage source term V_s in (5.21) is the *emf* and is measured in units of volts. If we substitute the relationships shown in Table 5.1, we find

$$L\frac{d^2Q}{dt^2} + R\frac{dQ}{dt} + \frac{Q}{C} = V_s(t) \qquad (5.22)$$

where we have used the definition of current $I = dQ/dt$. We see that (5.22) for the series RLC circuit is identical in form to the damped harmonic oscillator (5.17). The analogies between ideal electrical circuits and mechanical systems are summarized in Table 5.2.

Although we are already familiar with (5.22), we first consider the dynamical behavior of an RC circuit described by

$$RI(t) = R\frac{dQ}{dt} = V_s(t) - \frac{Q}{C} \quad . \qquad (5.23)$$

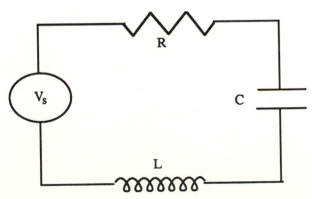

Fig. 5.4 A simple series RLC circuit with a voltage source V_s.

TABLE 5.2 Analogies between electrical
parameters and mechanical parameters.

Electric circuit	Mechanical system
charge Q	displacement x
current $I = \frac{dQ}{dt}$	velocity $v = \frac{dx}{dt}$
voltage drop	force
inductance L	mass m
inverse capacitance $\frac{1}{C}$	spring constant k
resistance R	damping γ

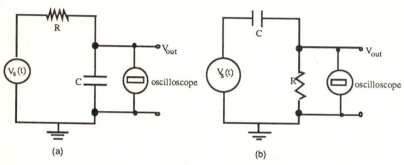

(a)   (b)

Fig. 5.5 Examples of RC circuits used as low and high pass filters.
Which circuit is which?

Since the current I has units of charge per unit time, the product RC must
have units of time, i.e. seconds. Two RC circuits corresponding to (5.23) are
shown in Fig. 5.5. Although the loop equation (5.23) is identical regardless of
the order of placement of the capacitor and resistor in Fig. 5.5, the output voltage
measured by the oscilloscope in Fig. 5.5 will be different. We will see in Problem
5.11 that these circuits act as *filters* which pass voltage components of certain
frequencies while rejecting others.

The most important advantage of a computer simulation of an electrical
circuit is that the measurement of a voltage drop across a circuit element does
not affect the properties of the circuit—an electronics technician's dream! In fact
digital computers are often used to optimize the design of circuits for special
applications. **Program rc** simulates an RC circuit with an alternating current
(ac) voltage source of the form $V_{in}(t) = V_0 \cos \omega t$. The time-dependences of the
voltage source and the voltage drop across the resistor are shown in separate
windows. **SUB screen** calls **SUB plot_axis** which was developed in Chapter 2.

The only change that needs to be made in the latter subroutine is in the format statements:

    PLOT TEXT, at xmax - 0.5*Ly,y0: using$("#.###",xmax)

Since **Program rc** makes extensive use of windows, it must be extensively modified to be written in other programming languages.

```
PROGRAM rc
CALL initial(R,tau,V0,w,tmax,dt)
CALL screen(#1,#2,V0,tmax)
CALL scope(#1,#2,R,tau,V0,w,tmax,dt)
CLOSE #1
CLOSE #2
END

SUB initial(R,tau,V0,w,tmax,dt)
   LET V0 = 1                          ! amplitude of external voltage
   INPUT prompt "external voltage frequency (hertz) = ":f
   LET w = 2*pi*f                      ! angular frequency
   INPUT prompt "resistance (ohms) = ":R
   INPUT prompt "capacitance (farads) = ":C
   INPUT prompt "time step dt = ": dt
   LET tau = R*C                       ! relaxation time
   LET T = 1/f                         ! period of external frequency
   IF T > tau then
      LET tmax = 2*T
   ELSE
      LET tmax = 2*tau
   END IF
END SUB

SUB screen(#1,#2,V0,tmax)
   OPEN #1: screen 0,1,0,0.5
   LET tmin = 0
   LET Vmin = -V0
   LET title$ = "source voltage"
   CALL plot_axis(tmin,tmax,Vmin,V0,title$)
   OPEN #2: screen 0,1,.5,1
   LET title$ = "resistor voltage drop"
   CALL plot_axis(tmin,tmax,Vmin,V0,title$)
END SUB
```

```
SUB scope(#1,#2,R,tau,V0,w,tmax,dt)
   ! compute voltage drops and plot results
   DECLARE DEF V
   LET Q = 0
   DO while t <= tmax
      LET t = t + dt
      LET I = V(V0,w,t)/R - Q/tau
      LET Q = Q + I*dt
      CALL source_voltage(#1,V0,w,t)
      CALL output_voltage(#2,I,R,t)
   LOOP
END SUB

DEF V(V0,w,t) = V0*cos(w*t)

SUB source_voltage(#1,V0,w,t)
   DECLARE DEF V
   WINDOW #1
   PLOT LINES: t,V(V0,w,t);
END SUB

SUB output_voltage(#2,I,R,t)          ! voltage drop across the resistor
   WINDOW #2
   PLOT LINES: t,I*R;
END SUB
```

PROBLEM 5.11 Simple filter circuits

a. Use **Program rc** with $R = 1000\,\Omega$ and $C = 1.0\mu F(10^{-6}\,farads)$. Find the steady state amplitude of the voltage drops across the resistor and the capacitor as a function of the angular frequency w of the source or "input" voltage $V_{in} = V_0\cos wt$. (The program needs to be modified to plot the voltage drop across the capacitor.) Consider the frequencies $f = 10, 50, 100, 160, 200, 500, 1000, 5000$, and $10000\,Hz$. Choose Δt to be at least 0.0001 sec. for $f = 10\,Hz$. What is a reasonable value of Δt for $f = 10000\,Hz$? Is the initial condition important?

b. The output voltage depends on where the "oscilloscope" is connected. What is the output voltage of the oscilloscope in Fig. 5.5a? Plot the ratio of the amplitude of the output voltage to the amplitude of the input voltage as a function of ω. Use a logarithmic scale for ω. (Remember that $\omega = 2\pi f$.) What range of frequencies is passed? Does this circuit act as a high pass or low pass filter? Answer the same questions for the oscilloscope in Fig. 5.5b. Use your results to explain the operation of a high and low pass filter. Compute the value of the "cutoff frequency" for which the amplitude of the output voltage drops to $1/\sqrt{2}$ (half-power) of the input value. How is the cutoff frequency related to RC?

c. Plot the voltage drops across the capacitor and resistor as a function of time. The phase difference ϕ between each voltage drop and the source voltage can be found by finding the time t_m between the corresponding maxima of the voltages. Since ϕ is usually expressed in radians, we have the relation $\phi/2\pi = t_m/T$, where T is the period of the oscillation. What is the phase difference ϕ_C between the capacitor and the voltage source and the phase difference ϕ_R between the resistor and the voltage source? Do these phase differences depend on ω? Does the current lead or lag the voltage, i.e. does the maxima of $V_R(t)$ come before or after the maxima of $V_{in}(t)$? What is the phase difference between the capacitor and the resistor? Does the latter difference depend on ω?

d. Modify **Program rc** to find the steady state response of an LR circuit with a source voltage $V_{in}(t) = V_0 \cos \omega t$. Let $R = 100\,\Omega$, $L = 2 \times 10^{-3} H$. Since $L/R = 2 \times 10^{-5}$ sec, it is convenient to measure the time and frequency in units of $T_0 = L/R$. We write $\tau = t/T_0$, $\tilde{\omega} = \omega T_0$ and write the equation of motion of an LR circuit as

$$I(\tau) + \frac{dI(\tau)}{d\tau} = \frac{V_0}{R} \cos \tilde{\omega}\tau \quad . \tag{5.24}$$

What is a reasonable value of the step size $\Delta\tau$? Compute the steady state amplitude of the voltage drops across the inductor and the resistor for the input frequencies $f = 10, 20, 30, 35, 50, 100$, and $200\,Hz$. Use these results to explain how an LR circuit can be used as a low pass or high pass filter. Plot the voltage drops across the inductor and resistor as a function of time and determine the phase differences ϕ_R and ϕ_L between the resistor and the voltage source and the inductor and the voltage source. Do these phase differences depend on ω? Does the current lead or lag the voltage? What is the phase difference between the inductor and the resistor? Does the latter difference depend on ω?

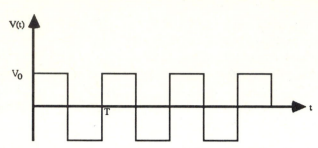

Fig. 5.6 Square wave voltage with period T and amplitude V_0.

PROBLEM 5.12 Square wave response of an RC circuit

a. Modify **Program rc** so that the voltage source is a periodic square wave as shown in Fig. 5.6. Use a 1.0 μF capacitor and a 3000 Ω resistor. Plot the computed voltage drop across the capacitor as a function of time. Make sure the period of the square wave is large enough so that the capacitor is fully charged during one half-cycle. What is the approximate time-dependence of $V_C(t)$ while the capacitor is charging (discharging)?

b. Change the input voltage to a "TTL" (transistor-transistor logic) pulse as shown in Fig. 5.7. Such a train of pulses is used as a clock in digital circuits. What is the difference between your results for $V_C(t)$ with the TTL pulses and the periodic square wave?

We now consider the steady state behavior of the series RLC circuit shown in Fig. 5.4 and represented by (5.22). The response of an electrical circuit is the current rather than the charge on the capacitor. By analogy with the mechanical system, we already know much about the behavior of driven RLC circuits. Nonetheless, we will find in the following two problems several interesting features of ac electrical circuits.

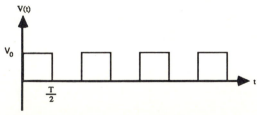

Fig. 5.7 TTL pulses with period T and amplitude V_0.

PROBLEM 5.13 Response of an RLC circuit

a. Consider an RLC series circuit with $R = 100\,\Omega$, $C = 3.0\,\mu F$, and $L = 2\,mH$. Modify **Program sho** or **Program rc** to simulate an RLC circuit and compute the voltage drops across the three circuit elements. Assume an ac voltage source of the form $V(t) = V_0 \cos \omega t$. Plot the current I as a function of time and determine the maximum steady state current I_m from the plot for different values of ω. Obtain the *resonance curve* by plotting $I_m(\omega)$ as a function of ω and compute the value of ω at which the resonance curve is a maximum. This value of ω is the *resonant frequency.*

b. The sharpness of the resonance curve of an ac circuit is related to the quality factor or Q value. Q should not be confused with the charge on the capacitor! The sharper the resonance, the larger the Q. Circuits having high Q (and thus a sharp resonance) are useful for tuning circuits in a radio so that only one station is heard at a time. We define $Q = \omega_0/\Delta\omega$, where the width $\Delta\omega$ is the frequency interval between points on the resonance curve $I_m(\omega)$ which are 0.707 of I_m at its maximum. Compute Q for the values of R, L, and C given in part (a). Change the value of R by 10% and compute the corresponding percentage change in Q. What are the corresponding changes in Q if L or C is changed by 10%? A discussion of Q in the context of a mechanical system was given in Problem 5.7b. Note that the definitions of Q vary slightly but all the definitions have the same qualitative interpretation.

c. Compute the time-dependence of the voltage drops across each circuit element for approximately fifteen frequencies ranging from 1/10 to 10 times the resonant frequency. Plot the time-dependence of the voltage drops so that you can make measurements on them later.

d. The ratio of the amplitude of the sinusoidal source voltage to the amplitude of the current is called the *impedance Z* of the circuit, i.e. $V_m = I_m Z$. This definition of Z is a generalization of the resistance which is defined by the relation $V = IR$ for dc (direct current) circuits. Use the plots of part (c) to determine I_m and V_m for different frequencies and verify that the impedance is given by

$$Z = \sqrt{R^2 + (\omega L - 1/\omega C)^2} \quad . \tag{5.25}$$

For what value of ω is Z a minimum? Note that the relation $V = IZ$ holds only for the maximum values of I and V and not for I and V at any time.

e. Compute the phase difference ϕ_R between the voltage drop across the resistor and the voltage source. Consider $\omega \ll \omega_0$, $\omega = \omega_0$ and $\omega \gg \omega_0$. Does the current lead or lag the voltage in each case, i.e. does the current reach a maxima before or after the voltage? Also compute the phase differences ϕ_L and ϕ_C and describe their dependence on ω. Do the relative phase differences between V_C, V_R, and V_L depend on ω?

f. Compute the amplitude of the voltage drops across the inductor and the capacitor at the resonant frequency. How do these voltage drops compare to the voltage drop across the resistor and to the source voltage? Also compare the relative phases of V_C and V_I at resonance. Explain how an RLC circuit can be used to amplify the input voltage.

REFERENCES AND SUGGESTIONS FOR ADDITIONAL READING

Alfred Bork and Andres Zellweger, "Least action via computer," *Am. J. Phys.* **37**, 386 (1969). Newton's laws are not the only possible formulation of classical mechanics.

A. Douglas Davis, *Classical Mechanics*, Academic Press (1986). The author gives a "crash" course in conversational BASIC and Pascal and simple numerical solutions of Newton's equations of motion. Much emphasis is given to the harmonic oscillator problem.

Richard P. Feynman, Robert B. Leighton, and Matthew Sands, *The Feynman Lectures on Physics*, Vol. 1, Addison-Wesley (1963). Chapters 21, 23, 24, and 25 are devoted to various aspects of harmonic motion.

Charles Kittel, Walter D. Knight, and Malvin A. Ruderman, *Mechanics*, 2 ed. revised by A. Carl Helmholz and Burton J. Moyer, McGraw-Hill (1973).

Jerry B. Marion, *Classical Dynamics*, Academic Press (1970). Excellent discussion of linear and non-linear oscillators.

M. F. McInerney, "Computer-aided experiments with the damped harmonic oscillator," *Am. J. Phys.* **53**, 991 (1985).

J. C. Sprott, *Introduction to Modern Electronics*, John Wiley & Sons (1981). The first five chapters treat the topics discussed in Sec. 5.7.

S. C. Zilio, "Measurement and analysis of large-angle pendulum motion," *Am. J. Phys.* **50**, 450 (1982).

APPENDIX 5A NUMERICAL INTEGRATION OF NEWTON'S EQUATION OF MOTION

We summarize several of the common finite difference methods for Newton's equations of motion with continuous force functions. It is important to remember that the success of a numerical method is determined not only by how well it approximates the derivative at each step, but also by how well the method approximates the constants of the motion, e.g. the total energy. The variety of algorithms currently in use is evidence that no single method is superior under all conditions.

To simplify the notation, we consider the motion of a particle in one dimension and write Newton's equations of motion in the form

$$\frac{dv}{dt} = a \tag{5.30a}$$

and

$$\frac{dx}{dt} = v \quad . \tag{5.30b}$$

The object of all finite difference methods is to determine the values of x_{n+1}, v_{n+1} (a point in "phase space") at time $t_{n+1} = t_n + \Delta t$. We have already seen that Δt must be chosen so that the integration method generates a stable solution. One way to check the stability of the solution is to monitor the total energy and ensure that it does not drift from its initial value if the total energy is conserved. A value of Δt which is too large will result in nonconservation of total energy and unstable solutions for x_{n+1} and v_{n+1}, i.e. numerical solutions whose departure from the true solution increases with time.

The nature of many of the algorithms can be understood by expanding $v_{n+1} \equiv v(t_n + \Delta t)$ and $x_{n+1} \equiv x(t_n + \Delta t)$ in a Taylor series. We write

$$v_{n+1} = v_n + a_n \Delta t + O[(\Delta t)^2] \tag{5.31a}$$

and

$$x_{n+1} = x_n + v_n \Delta t + \frac{1}{2} a_n (\Delta t)^2 + O[(\Delta t)^3] \quad . \tag{5.31b}$$

The familiar Euler method is equivalent to retaining the $O(\Delta t)$ terms in (5.31):

$$v_{n+1} = v_n + a_n \Delta t \tag{5.32a}$$

and

$$x_{n+1} = x_n + v_n \Delta t \quad . \tag{5.32b}$$

Since we retained the order Δt terms in (5.32), the "local" error (the error in one step) is order $(\Delta t)^2$. However, there is an accumulation of errors from step to step so that the "global" error, the total error over the time of interest, is expected to be order Δt. This latter estimate is reasonable since the number of steps into which the total time is divided is proportional to $1/\Delta t$. Hence the order of the global error is reduced by a factor of $(\Delta t)^{-1}$ relative to the local error. Since a method is conventionally called nth order if its local error is order $(\Delta t)^{n+1}$, the Euler method is an example of a *first-order* method.

The Euler method is asymmetrical since it advances the solution by a step size Δt, but uses information about the derivative only at the beginning of the interval. We have already found that the accuracy of the Euler method is limited and that frequently its solutions are not stable. Fortunately the use of sophisticated algorithms is not usually necessary. For example we found that a simple modification of (5.32), developed by Cromer and others, yields solutions which are stable for oscillatory systems. For completeness, we repeat the Euler-Cromer algorithm or "last-point" approximation here:

$$v_{n+1} = v_n + a_n \Delta t \tag{5.33a}$$

and

$$x_{n+1} = x_n + v_{n+1} \Delta t \quad . \tag{5.33b}$$

Perhaps the most obvious way to improve the Euler method is to use the mean velocity during the interval to obtain the new position. The corresponding *midpoint* method can be written as

$$v_{n+1} = v_n + a_n \Delta t \tag{5.34a}$$

and

$$x_{n+1} = x_n + \frac{1}{2}(v_{n+1} + v_n)\Delta t \quad . \tag{5.34b}$$

Note that if we substitute (5.34a) for v_{n+1} into (5.34b), we obtain

$$x_{n+1} = x_n + v_n \Delta t + \frac{1}{2}a_n \Delta t^2 \quad . \tag{5.35}$$

Hence the midpoint method yields second-order accuracy for the position and first-order accuracy for the velocity. Although the midpoint approximation yields exact results for constant acceleration, in general it does not yield substantially better results than the Euler method. In fact both methods are equally poor, since the errors increase with each step.

The half-step method is a higher-order method which has an error that is bounded. The average velocity during an interval is taken to be the velocity in the middle of the interval. The half-step method can be written as

$$v_{n+\frac{1}{2}} = v_{n-\frac{1}{2}} + a_n \Delta t \tag{5.36a}$$

and

$$x_{n+1} = x_n + v_{n+\frac{1}{2}}\Delta t \quad . \tag{5.36b}$$

Note that the half-step method is not "self-starting", i.e. (5.36) does not allow the calculation of $v_{\frac{1}{2}}$. This problem can be overcome by adopting the procedure

$$v_{\frac{1}{2}} = v_0 + \frac{1}{2}a_0\Delta t \quad . \tag{5.36c}$$

Since (5.36) can be iterated indefinitely, the half-step method is a common textbook method (see for example Feynman et al. and Eisberg and Lerner).

One of the most common "drift-free" higher-order algorithms is attributed to Verlet. We write the Taylor series expansion for x_{n-1} in a form similar to (5.31):

$$x_{n-1} = x_n - v_n\Delta t + \frac{1}{2}a_n(\Delta t)^2. \tag{5.37}$$

If we add the forward and reverse forms, (5.31) and (5.37) respectively, we obtain

$$x_{n+1} + x_{n-1} = 2x_n + a_n(\Delta t)^2 + O[(\Delta t)^4] \tag{5.38}$$

or

$$x_{n+1} = 2x_n - x_{n-1} + a_n(\Delta t)^2 \quad . \tag{5.39a}$$

Similarly the subtraction of the Taylor series for x_{n+1} and x_{n-1} yields

$$v_n = \frac{x_{n+1} - x_{n-1}}{2\Delta t} \quad . \tag{5.39b}$$

Note that the global error associated with the *Verlet algorithm* (5.39) is third-order for the position and second-order for the velocity. However, the velocity plays no part in the integration of the equations of motion. In the numerical analysis literature, the Verlet algorithm is known as the "explicit central difference method."

One disadvantage of the Verlet algorithm is that, since it is not self-starting, another algorithm must be used to obtain the first few phase points. An additional problem is that the new velocity is found in (5.39b) by finding the difference between two quantities of the same order of magnitude. As we discussed in Chapter 2, such an operation results in a loss of numerical precision and may give rise to a serious round-off error.

A less well known but mathematically equivalent version of the Verlet algorithm is the form:

$$x_{n+1} = x_n + v_n\Delta t + \frac{1}{2}a_n(\Delta t)^2 \tag{5.40a}$$

and

$$v_{n+1} = v_n + \frac{1}{2}(a_{n+1} + a_n)\Delta t \quad . \tag{5.40b}$$

We see that (5.40), known as the *velocity* form of the Verlet algorithm, is self-starting and minimizes round-off errors. We can "derive" (5.40) from (5.39) by the following considerations. We first add and subtract $(1/2)x_{n+1}$ from both sides of (5.39a) and write

$$x_{n+1} = x_n + \frac{1}{2}(x_{n+1} - x_{n-1}) - \frac{1}{2}x_{n-1} + \frac{1}{2}x_{n-1} + x_n + a_n(\Delta t)^2$$

$$= x_n + v_n\Delta t - \frac{1}{2}(x_{n+1} - 2x_n + x_{n-1}) + a_n(\Delta t)^2 \tag{5.41}$$

where we have used (5.39b). From (5.39a) we find a_n is given in the Verlet method by

$$a_n = \frac{x_{n+1} - 2x_n + x_{n-1}}{(\Delta t)^2} \quad . \tag{5.42}$$

It is easy to see that the substitution of (5.42) into (5.41) yields (5.40a). In the same spirit, we rewrite (5.39b) in terms of v_{n+1}:

$$v_{n+1} = \frac{x_{n+2} - x_n}{2\Delta t} \quad . \tag{5.43}$$

The first step is to rewrite (5.39a) in terms of x_{n+2} and substitute this result into (5.43). We find

$$v_{n+1} = \frac{x_{n+1} + v_{n+1}\Delta t + \frac{1}{2}a_{n+1}(\Delta t)^2 - x_n}{\Delta t} \quad . \tag{5.44}$$

Then using (5.39a) for x_{n+1}, we repeat this procedure and substitute x_{n+1} in (5.44); after some algebra we obtain the desired result (5.40b).

Another useful algorithm which avoids the round-off error of the original Verlet algorithm is due to Beeman and Schofield. We write the *Beeman* algorithm in the form:

$$x_{n+1} = x_n + v_n\Delta t + \frac{1}{6}(4a_n - a_{n-1})(\Delta t)^2 \tag{5.45a}$$

and

$$v_{n+1} = v_n + \frac{1}{6}(2a_{n+1} + 5a_n - a_{n-1})\Delta t \quad . \tag{5.45b}$$

Note that (5.45) does not calculate particle trajectories more accurately than the Verlet algorithm. Rather its advantage is that in general it does a better job of maintaining energy conservation. However, the Beeman algorithm is not self-starting. Beeman's algorithm and the velocity form of Verlet's algorithm are used in **Program Beeman** (see Problem 5.15).

We conclude with a summary of two methods which are commonly discussed in textbooks on numerical analysis. An example of the *predictor -corrector* method is given in the following. First we *predict* the value of the new position:

$$predictor : \bar{x}_{n+1} = x_{n-1} + 2v_n \Delta t \quad . \tag{5.46a}$$

The predicted value of the position allows us to predict the acceleration $\bar{a}_{n+1}$. Then using $\bar{a}_{n+1}$, we obtain the *corrected* values of v_{n+1} and x_{n+1}:

$$corrected : v_{n+1} = v_n + \frac{1}{2}(\bar{a}_{n+1} + a_n)\Delta t$$

$$x_{n+1} = x_n + \frac{1}{2}(v_{n+1} + v_n)\Delta t \quad . \tag{5.46b}$$

The corrected value of x_{n+1} is used to obtain a new predicted value of a_{n+1}, and hence a new predicted value of v_{n+1} and x_{n+1}. This process is repeated until the predicted and corrected values of x_{n+1} differ by less than a desired value. The method can be generalized to higher-order to involve not only a relation between x_{n+1}, x_n, and v_n, but also values of v_{n-1} and v_{n-2}. Note that the predictor-corrector method is not self-starting.

In order to explain the *Runge-Kutta* method, we first consider the solution of the first-order differential equation

$$\frac{dy}{dx} = f(x, y) \quad . \tag{5.47}$$

The *second-order* Runge-Kutta solution of (5.47) can be written using standard notation as:

$$k_1 = f(x_n, y_n)\Delta x$$

$$k_2 = f(x_n + \frac{1}{2}\Delta x, y_n + \frac{1}{2}k_1)\Delta x$$

$$y_{n+1} = y_n + k_2 + O[(\Delta x)^3] \quad . \tag{5.48}$$

The interpretation of (5.48) is as follows. The Euler method assumes that the slope $f(x_n, y_n)$ at the point (x_n, y_n) can be used to extrapolate to the next point, i.e. $y_{n+1} \doteq y_n + f(x_n, y_n)\Delta x$. However, a plausible way to make a better estimate of the slope is to use the Euler method to extrapolate to a point *halfway* across the interval and then to use the midpoint derivative across the full width of the interval. Hence the Runge-Kutta estimate for the slope is $f(x_n + \frac{1}{2}\Delta x, y^*)$, where $y^* = y_n + \frac{1}{2}f(x_n, y_n)\Delta x$ (see (5.48)).

The application of the second-order Runge-Kutta method to Newton's equation of motion (5.30) yields

$$k_{1,x} = v_n \Delta t$$
$$k_{1,v} = a_n \Delta t$$
$$k_{2,x} = (v_n + \frac{1}{2}k_{1,v})\Delta t \tag{5.49}$$
$$k_{2,v} = a(x_n + \frac{1}{2}k_{1,x})\Delta t$$
$$x_{n+1} = x_n + k_{2,x}$$
$$v_{n+1} = v_n + k_{2,v} \quad .$$

Since Runge-Kutta methods are self-starting, they are frequently used to obtain the first few iterations for a non self-starting algorithm.

As we have emphasized, it is not necessary to assume that one algorithm is superior to another, even if a textbook such as ours claims it is. Advances in computer technology now allow us to experiment readily with different algorithms on different dynamical systems. The following problem will give you some experience in comparing algorithms.

PROBLEM 5.15 Comparison of algorithms

a. Consider a particle of unit mass moving in a Morse potential

$$V(x) = e^{-2x} - 2e^{-x} \tag{5.50}$$

with total energy $E = \frac{1}{2}p^2 + V(x) < 0$. The force on the particle is given by

$$F(x) = -\frac{dV}{dx} = 2e^{-x}[e^{-x} - 1] \quad . \tag{5.51}$$

Plot $V(x)$ and $F(x)$ versus x. Where is $V(x)$ a minimum? What is the total energy for the initial condition $x_0 = 2$ and $v_0 = 0$? What type of motion do you expect?

b. Use **Program Beeman** to compare the Euler-Cromer, velocity Verlet and the Beeman algorithms by computing $x(t)$, $v(t)$ and E_n, where E_n is the total energy after the nth step. One measure of the error is the difference $\Delta E = <E> - E_0$, where E_0 is the initial energy and $<E>$ is the mean energy given by

$$<E> = \frac{1}{n+1}\sum_{i=0}^{n} E_i \quad . \tag{5.52}$$

Another measure of the error is the quantity δE defined by

$$\delta E = \sqrt{<E^2> - <E>^2} \tag{5.53}$$

where

$$<E^2> = \frac{1}{n+1} \sum_{i=0}^{n} E_i^2 \quad . \tag{5.54}$$

Calculate ΔE and δE for $\Delta t = 0.2$ and 0.1. If a method is second-order, this relative change in Δt should decrease the global truncation error by a factor of approximately 4. The absence of such a decrease would indicate that roundoff errors might be important. In order to see the effects of round-off errors, increase the precision of your calculation by either using double precision variables in FORTRAN or using a computer which has a greater accuracy. If the period is periodic, compute the period.

c. Compare your results for $x(t)$ to the analytical result

$$x(t) = ln(\alpha \cos \omega t + \beta \sin \omega t - E_0^{-1}) \tag{5.55}$$

with

$$\alpha = exp(x_0) + E_0^{-1}$$
$$\beta = \omega^{-1} v_0 \, exp(x_0)$$
$$\omega = (2|E_0|)^{1/2} \quad .$$

d. Repeat the computations of part (a) with the initial conditions $x_0 = 3$ and $v_0 = 1$. Is the motion periodic? Which algorithm is most suitable in this case?

Program Beeman simulates the Morse oscillator using the Beeman algorithm. Since this algorithm is not self-starting, the velocity form of the Verlet algorithm is used to generate x_1, v_1 and a_1.

```
PROGRAM Beeman                 ! simulation of the Morse oscillator
CALL initial(x,v,aold,dt,dt2,nmax)
CALL energy(x,v,ecum,e2cum)     ! compute initial energy
CALL Verlet(x,v,a,aold,dt,dt2)
CALL energy(x,v,ecum,e2cum)
LET n = 1
DO while n < nmax
  LET n = n + 1                ! number of steps
  CALL Beeman(x,v,a,aold,dt,dt2)
  ! compute total energy after every time step
  CALL energy(x,v,ecum,e2cum)
LOOP
CALL output(ecum,e2cum,n)
END

SUB initial(x,v,aold,dt,dt2,nmax)
  DECLARE DEF f                ! force defined as external function
  LET x = 2
  LET v = 0
  LET aold = f(x)
  INPUT prompt "time step (sec) = ":dt
  LET dt2 = dt*dt
  INPUT prompt "duration = ":tmax
  LET nmax = tmax/dt
END SUB

SUB Verlet(x,v,a,aold,dt,dt2)
  DECLARE DEF f
  LET x = x + v*dt + 0.5*aold*dt2
  LET a = f(x)
  LET v = v + 0.5*(a + aold)*dt
  LET aold = a
END SUB
```

```
SUB Beeman(x,v,a,aold,dt,dt2)
  DECLARE DEF f
  LET x = x + v*dt + (4*a - aold)*dt2/6
  LET anew = f(x)                 ! value at n+1 step
  LET v = v + (2*anew + 5*a - aold)*dt/6
  LET aold = a                    ! value at n - 1
  LET a = anew                    ! value at n
END SUB

DEF f(x)
  LET e = exp(-x)
  LET f = 2*e*(e - 1)
END DEF

SUB energy(x,v,ecum,e2cum)
  LET KE = 0.5*v*v
  LET e = exp(-x)
  LET PE = e*(e - 2)
  LET etot = KE + PE
  LET ecum = ecum + etot
  LET e2cum = e2cum + etot*etot
END SUB

SUB output(ecum,e2cum,n)
  LET n = n + 1                   ! count initial value
  LET ebar = ecum/n
  PRINT "average energy = ";ebar
  LET sigma2 = e2cum/n - ebar*ebar
  PRINT "sigma = "; sqr(sigma2)
END SUB
```

REFERENCES

F. S. Acton, *Numerical Methods That Work,* Harper and Row (1970), Chapter 5.

R. P. Feynman, R. B. Leighton, M. Sands, *The Feynman Lectures in Physics, Vol. 1*, Addison-Wesley (1963). See Chapter 9.

W. H. Press, B. P. Flannery, S. A. Teukolsky, W. T. Vetterling, *Numerical Recipes*, Cambridge University Press (1986). Chapter 15 discusses the integration of ordinary differential equations.

THE DYNAMICS OF MANY PARTICLE SYSTEMS

6

We simulate the dynamical behavior of many particle systems and observe their qualitative features. Some of the basic ideas of equilibrium statistical mechanics and kinetic theory are introduced.

6.1   INTRODUCTION

Thus far we have studied the dynamical behavior of systems with only a few particles. However many systems in nature such as gases, liquids and solids contain many mutually interacting particles. To illustrate, consider two cups of coffee prepared under similar conditions. Each cup contains roughly 10^{23}–10^{25} molecules which, to a good approximation, move according to the laws of classical physics. Although the intermolecular forces produce a complicated trajectory for each molecule, the observable properties of the coffee in each glass are indistinguishable and are relatively easy to describe. For example, we know that the temperature of the coffee remaining in a cup achieves the temperature of the room and no longer changes with time. How is the temperature of the coffee related to the trajectories of the individual molecules? Why is the temperature of coffee independent of time even though the trajectories of the individual molecules are continually changing?

The example of a cup of coffee presents a challenge: How can we understand the observable behavior of a complex many particle system beginning from the known intermolecular interactions? The most direct approach is to meet this challenge head-on by a computer simulation of the many particle problem itself. We might imagine solving on some future supercomputer the microscopic equations of motion for 10^{25} mutually interacting particles. Indeed this approach, known as the *molecular dynamics* method, has been applied to "small" many particle systems of typically several hundred to several thousand particles and has yielded much insight into the observable behavior of gases, liquids, and solids. However, a detailed knowledge of the trajectories of 10^4 or even 10^{25} particles is not helpful unless we know the right questions to ask. What are the essential characteristics and regularities exhibited by many particle systems? What are the useful parameters needed to describe such systems? Questions such as these are addressed by statistical mechanics and many of the ideas of statistical mechanics are discussed in this chapter. However, the only background required for this chapter is a knowledge of the numerical solution of Newton's laws, which we have already discussed, and an exposure to kinetic theory.

6.2   THE INTERMOLECULAR POTENTIAL

Our first goal is to specify the *model* system we wish to simulate. Since we wish to understand the qualitative properties of many particle systems, we make the simplifying assumptions that the dynamics can be treated classically and that the molecules are spherical and chemically inert. We also assume that the force between any two molecules depends only on the distance between them. In this case the total potential energy U is a sum of two-particle interactions:

$$U = V(r_{12}) + V(r_{13}) + \ldots + V(r_{23}) + \ldots$$

$$= \sum_{i<j=1}^{N} V(r_{ij}) \tag{6.1}$$

where $V(r_{ij})$ depends only on the magnitude of the distance $\vec{r}_{ij}$ between particles i and j. The pairwise interaction form (6.1) is appropriate for "simple" liquids such as liquid argon.

The form of $V(r)$ for electrically neutral atoms can be constructed, in principle, by a detailed first principles quantum mechanical calculation. Such a calculation is very difficult, and it is usually sufficient to choose a simple phenomenological form for $V(r)$. The most important features of $V(r)$ for simple liquids are a strong repulsion for small r and a weak attraction at large separations. The repulsion for small r is a consequence of the exclusion principle. That is, if the electron clouds of two atoms overlap, some of the electrons must gain kinetic energy in order to be in different quantum states. The net effect is a repulsion between the electrons, known as *core repulsion*. The dominant weak attraction at larger r is due to the mutual polarization of each atom; the resultant attractive force is called the *van der Waals* force.

One of the most useful phenomenological forms of $V(r)$ is the Lennard-Jones potential

$$V(r) = 4\epsilon[(\frac{\sigma}{r})^{12} - (\frac{\sigma}{r})^{6}] \quad . \tag{6.2}$$

A plot of the Lennard-Jones potential is shown in Fig. 6.1. Although the r^{-6} dependence in (6.2) is in accordance with theory, the r^{-12} dependence is chosen for convenience only. The Lennard-Jones potential is parameterized by a "length" σ and an "energy" ϵ. Note that at $r = \sigma, V(r) = 0$. The parameter ϵ is the depth of the potential at the minimum of $V(r)$; the minimum occurs at a separation $r = 2^{1/6}\sigma$. Note that the potential is "short-range" and $V(r)$ is essentially zero for $r > 2.5\sigma$.

It is convenient to express lengths, energy, and mass in units of σ, ϵ, and m, where m is the mass of the particles. We measure velocities in units of $(\epsilon/m)^{\frac{1}{2}}$ and the time in units of $\tau = (m\sigma^2\epsilon)^{\frac{1}{2}}$. The parameters ϵ and σ of the Lennard-Jones potential for liquid argon are $\epsilon/k_B = 119.8\,K$ and $\sigma = 3.405\,\mathring{A}$. The mass m of an argon atom is $6.69 \times 10^{-23}\,gm$ and hence $\tau = 1.82 \times 10^{-12}$ sec. To avoid confusion, we denote all dimensionless or reduced quantities with an asterisk. For example, the reduced density in two dimensions is given by $\rho^* = \rho/\sigma^2$.

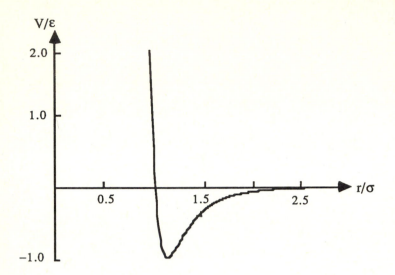

Fig. 6.1 Plot of the Lennard-Jones potential. Note that r is measured in units of σ and $V(r)$ is measured in units of ϵ.

6.3 THE NUMERICAL ALGORITHM

Now that we have a well-defined model of a many particle system, we need to introduce a numerical integration method for calculating the trajectories of each particle. We have found in our earlier simulations of Newton's equations of motion that the stability of the numerical solution can be checked by monitoring the total energy and ensuring that it does not drift from its initial value. As might be expected, the Euler and Euler-Cromer algorithms cannot maintain conservation of energy for the times of interest in molecular dynamics simulations. Fortunately, we do not usually have to adopt an elaborate algorithm. An algorithm which is especially attractive for its intuitive appeal is given by

$$x_{n+1} = x_n + v_n \Delta t + \frac{1}{2} a_n (\Delta t)^2 \qquad (6.3a)$$

$$v_{n+1} = v_n + \frac{1}{2}(a_{n+1} + a_n)\Delta t. \qquad (6.3b)$$

To simplify the notation, we have written the algorithm for only one component of the particle's motion. The algorithm represented by (6.3) is known as the *velocity form* of the *Verlet algorithm* and is discussed in Appendix 5A. An equivalent but different form of the Verlet algorithm is commonly used in the molecular dynamics literature. Since the new position x_{n+1} is computed using the acceleration a_n as well as the velocity v_n, the Verlet algorithm is "higher-order" in Δt than the Euler and Euler-Cromer algorithms. The new position is used to find the new acceleration a_{n+1} which is used together with a_n to obtain the new velocity v_{n+1}.

6.4 BOUNDARY CONDITIONS

A useful simulation must incorporate all the relevant features of the physical system of interest. Remember that the ultimate goal of our simulations is to obtain estimates for the behavior of macroscopic systems—systems of the order of $N \approx 10^{23}$–10^{25} particles. Consider a spherical bowl of water. The fraction of water molecules near the walls is proportional to the surface to volume ratio, $(4\pi R^2)/(4\pi R^3/3)$. Since $N = \rho(4/3\pi R^3)$ where ρ is the density, the fraction of particles near the walls is proportional to $N^{2/3}/N = N^{-1/3}$, a vanishing small fraction for $N \approx 10^{23}$. In comparison, the number of particles which can be studied in molecular dynamics simulations is typically 10^2–10^4, and the fraction of particles near the walls is not small. Consequently we cannot do a simulation of a macroscopic system by placing the particles in a container with rigid walls. In addition, if a particle is reflected off a rigid wall, its position and hence its potential energy of interaction is changed without any change in its kinetic energy. Hence the presence of rigid walls would imply that the total energy of the system is conserved.

One way to minimize surface effects and to simulate more closely the properties of a macroscopic system is to use *periodic boundary conditions.* The implementation of periodic boundary conditions for short-range interactions such as the Lennard-Jones potential is familiar to all video game players. First consider a one-dimensional "box" of N particles constrained to move on a line segment of length L. The ends of the line segment serve as the "walls." The use of periodic boundary conditions is equivalent to wrapping the line around to form a circle (see Fig. 6.2). Note that since the separation between particles is the distance measured along the arc, the maximum separation is $L/2$.

In two dimensions we can imagine a box with opposite edges joined so that the box becomes the surface of a torus (the shape of a doughnut). Thus, if a particle crosses a face of the box, it is reinserted at the opposite face. Note that

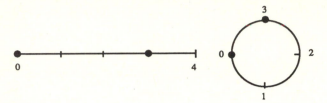

Fig. 6.2 (a) Two particles at $x = 0$ and $x = 3$ on a line of length $L = 4$; the separation between the particles is 3. (b) The line of part (a) is transformed to a circle; the smallest separation of the two particles on the circle equals 1.

the maximum separation between particles in the x and y directions is $L/2$ rather than L.

An alternative but equivalent point of view is illustrated in Fig. 6.3. Suppose particles 1 and 2 are in the central cell. The cell is surrounded by periodically repeating replicas of itself; each image cell contains the two particles in the same relative positions. When a particle enters or leaves one face of the central cell, the move is accompanied by an image of that particle leaving or entering a neighboring cell through the opposite face. The use of periodic boundary conditions implies that particle 1 interacts with particle 2 in the central cell and with all the periodic replicas of particle 2. However for short-range interactions, we can adopt the *minimum image* convention. This convention implies that particle 1 in the central cell interacts only with the nearest image of particle 2; the interaction is set equal to zero if the separation of the image is greater than $L/2$ (see Fig. 6.3). Since this convention implies that we can visualize the central cell as a torus, this use of periodic boundary conditions together with the minimum image convention should more accurately be referred to as *toroidal* boundary conditions. However, we defer to common usage and refer to these conditions as periodic boundary conditions. Note that the use of periodic boundary conditions implies that every point in the box is equivalent.

6.5 A MOLECULAR DYNAMICS PROGRAM

We are now ready to develop a molecular dynamics program to follow the trajectories of the particles on a screen. We consider a two-dimensional system, since

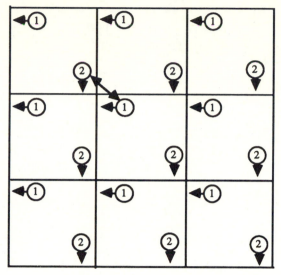

Fig. 6.3 Example of periodic boundary conditions in two dimensions. Note that particle 1 is about to leave the left face of the central cell and to enter the central cell through the right face. The minimum image distance convention implies that the separation between particles 1 and 2 is given by the bold line.

it is easier to visualize the results and the computations are not as cpu intensive. The structure of **Program md** is given by

```
PROGRAM md
DIM x(30),y(30)
DIM vx(30),vy(30),ax(30),ay(30)
CALL initial(x,y,vx,vy,N,Lx,Ly,dt,dt2,nsnap)
CALL screen(x,y,N,Lx,Ly,ball$,r)
CALL accel(x,y,ax,ay,N,Lx,Ly,pe0)
DO
    FOR isnap = 1 to nsnap              ! # of time steps between snapshots
        CALL Verlet(x,y,vx,vy,ax,ay,N,Lx,Ly,dt,dt2,virial,xflux,yflux,pe,ke)
    NEXT isnap
    LET itime = itime + nsnap           ! number of time steps
    CALL snapshot(x,y,N,Lx,Ly,ball$,r)            ! draw positions on screen
    CALL output(N,Lx,Ly,virial,xflux,yflux,pe,ke,nsnap,itime)
LOOP until key input
END
```

Note that the x- and y-components of the positions, velocities and accelerations are represented by arrays. Lx and Ly are the horizontal and vertical lengths of the rectangular container. The quantities ke and pe are cumulative sums for the kinetic energy and potential energy; the quantities $xflux$, $yflux$, and $virial$ will be used to determine the pressure. The nature of these quantities will be discussed in the following.

Since the system is deterministic, the nature of the motion is determined by the initial conditions. An appropriate choice of the initial conditions is more difficult than it might first seem. For example, how do we choose the initial configuration (a set of positions and velocities) to correspond to a fluid at the desired temperature? We postpone discussion of such questions until Sec. 6.6 and instead first consider the nature of the evolution of the system from arbitrary initial states.

One choice of initial conditions is to place the particles on a rectangular grid and to choose the x- and y-components of the velocities at random. Most programming languages include a function which generates a sequence of "random numbers" in the interval $[0,1]$. Since a digital computer is deterministic, it cannot compute truly random number sequences. However, a computer can generate numbers in no obvious sequence, and for now, the distinction is irrelevant. A discussion of random number sequences is given in Chapter 11. In True BASIC, we can use the **rnd** function to generate a random number in the range $0 \leq rnd < 1$. A random value of v_x in the interval $[-vmax, vmax]$ is generated by the statement

```
LET vx(i) = vmax*(2*rnd - 1)
```

The number of particles, the linear dimensions of the system, and the initial positions and velocities of the particles are specified in **SUB initial**. Note that Lx and Ly are measured in terms of σ, the Lennard-Jones parameter. Since the velocities are chosen at random, we need to correct for the possibility that the initial total momentum in the x or y direction might be nonzero. The grid in **SUB initial** is chosen so that $N = 12$ particles are initially placed on the left-half of the box.

```
SUB initial(x(),y(),vx(),vy(),N,Lx,Ly,dt,dt2,nsnap)
    LET N = 12                     ! number of particles
    INPUT prompt "Lx and Ly = ": Lx, Ly
    INPUT prompt "time step = ": dt
    LET dt2 = dt*dt
    LET nsnap = 5                  ! # of time steps between snapshots
    INPUT prompt "maximum initial speed = " : vmax
    LET pos_row = Ly/3
    LET pos_col = Lx/8             ! configuration for Fig. 6.4
    FOR row = 1 to 3
        FOR col = 1 to 4
            LET i = i + 1
            LET x(i) = pos_col*(col - 0.5)
            LET y(i) = pos_row*(row - 0.5)
            ! choose random  velocities
            LET vx(i) = vmax*(2*rnd - 1)
            LET vy(i) = vmax*(2*rnd - 1)
        NEXT col
    NEXT row
    FOR i = 1 to N
        LET vxcum = vxcum + vx(i)        ! total center of mass velocity (momentum)
        LET vycum = vycum + vy(i)
    NEXT i
    LET vxcum = vxcum/N
    LET vycum = vycum/N
    FOR i = 1 to N
        LET vx(i) = vx(i) - vxcum
        LET vy(i) = vy(i) - vycum
    NEXT i
END SUB
```

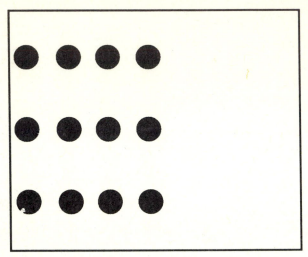

Fig. 6.4 Initial conditions used in Problem 6.1 using the parameters
shown in **SUB initial**.

In **SUB screen** we define the parameters needed for the visual display of
the N particles. We show the particles as solid circles rather than as "points."
The solid circles are saved in the variable *ball$*.

```
SUB screen(x(),y(),N,Lx,Ly,ball$,r)
    LET mx = 0.1*Lx                       ! margin sizes
    LET my = 0.1*Ly
    LET aspect_ratio = 1.5
    LET mx = aspect_ratio*mx
    LET Sx = aspect_ratio*Lx
    LET Sy = Ly
    SET window -mx,Sx+mx,-my,Sy+my
    BOX LINES 0,Lx,0,Ly
    LET r = 0.2                           ! draw ball to represent particle
    BOX CIRCLE x(1)-r,x(1)+r,y(1)-r,y(1)+r
    FLOOD x(1),y(1)
    BOX KEEP x(1)-r,x(1)+r,y(1)-r,y(1)+r in ball$
    FOR i = 1 to N
        BOX SHOW ball$ at x(i)-r,y(i)-r
    NEXT i
END SUB
```

We next implement Verlet's algorithm for the numerical solution of Newton's equations of motion. Note that the velocity is partially updated using the old acceleration. Then **SUB accel** is called to determine the acceleration using the new position and the velocity is updated again. **SUB Verlet** calls **SUB periodic** which in turn ensures that only particles in the central cell are considered.

```
SUB Verlet(x(),y(),vx(),vy(),ax(),ay(),N,Lx,Ly,dt,dt2,virial,xflux,yflux,pe,ke)
    FOR i = 1 to N
        LET xnew = x(i) + vx(i)*dt + 0.5*ax(i)*dt2
        LET ynew = y(i) + vy(i)*dt + 0.5*ay(i)*dt2
        ! return particle to central cell if necessary
        CALL periodic(xnew,ynew,Lx,Ly)
        LET x(i) = xnew
        LET y(i) = ynew
    NEXT i
    FOR i = 1 to N
        ! partially update velocity using old acceleration
        LET vx(i) = vx(i) + 0.5*ax(i)*dt
        LET vy(i) = vy(i) + 0.5*ay(i)*dt
    NEXT i
    CALL accel(x,y,ax,ay,N,Lx,Ly,pe)                  ! compute new acceleration
    FOR i = 1 to N              ! partially update velocity using new acceleration
        LET vx(i) = vx(i) + 0.5*ax(i)*dt
        LET vy(i) = vy(i) + 0.5*ay(i)*dt
    NEXT i
END SUB
```

SUB accel uses Newton's third law to find the total force on each particle. (Recall that the mass of a particle is unity in our units.) **SUB separation** is called to ensure that the separation between particles is no greater than $Lx/2$ in the x direction and $Ly/2$ in the y direction.

```
SUB accel(x(),y(),ax(),ay(),N,Lx,Ly,pe)
   FOR i = 1 to N
      LET ax(i) = 0
      LET ay(i) = 0
   NEXT i
   FOR i = 1 to (N - 1)                    ! compute total force on particle i
      FOR j = (i + 1) to N
         LET dx = x(i) - x(j)
         LET dy = y(i) - y(j)
         CALL separation(dx,dy,Lx,Ly)
         LET r = sqr(dx*dx + dy*dy)
         CALL f(r,force,potential)
         LET ax(i) = ax(i) + force*dx
         LET ay(i) = ay(i) + force*dy
         LET ax(j) = ax(j) - force*dx      ! Newton's third law
         LET ay(j) = ay(j) - force*dy
      NEXT j
   NEXT i
END SUB

SUB separation(dx,dy,Lx,Ly)
   ! sgn function returns sign of argument
   IF abs(dx) > .5*Lx then LET dx = dx - sgn(dx)*Lx
   IF abs(dy) > .5*Ly then LET dy = dy - sgn(dy)*Ly
END SUB

SUB periodic(xtemp,ytemp,Lx,Ly)
   IF xtemp < 0 then LET xtemp = xtemp + Lx
   IF xtemp > Lx then LET xtemp = xtemp - Lx
   IF ytemp < 0 then LET ytemp = ytemp + Ly
   IF ytemp > Ly then LET ytemp = ytemp - Ly
END SUB
```

The potential and the force are computed in **SUB f**.

```
SUB f(r,force,potential)
    LET ri = 1/r
    LET ri3 = ri*ri*ri
    LET ri6 = ri3*ri3
    LET g = 24*ri*ri6*(2*ri6 - 1)
    LET force = g/r        ! 1/r factor compensated by factor of dx,dy for Fx, Fy
    LET potential = 4*ri6*(ri6 - 1)
END SUB
```

The positions of the particles are displayed in **SUB snapshot**. The frequency at which the positions of the particles should be redrawn on the screen depends on Δt.

```
SUB snapshot(x(),y(),N,Lx,Ly,ball$,r)
    CLEAR
    FOR i = 1 to N
        BOX SHOW ball$ at x(i) - r,y(i) - r
    NEXT i
    BOX LINES 0,Lx,0,Ly
END SUB
```

PROBLEM 6.1 Approach to equilibrium of a dilute gas

a. Consider $N = 12$ particles interacting via the Lennard-Jones potential in a box of linear dimensions $Lx = Ly = 8$. For this choice of N and $L, \rho^* = 12/64 \approx 0.19$. Suppose that the particles are initially constrained to be in the left half of the box and are placed on a rectangular grid as shown in Fig. 6.4. At $t = 0$, the constraint is removed and the particles move freely throughout the entire box. Use $vmax = 1.0$, the maximum initial speed of the particles, and $\Delta t = 0.02$. The optimum choice of parameters such as $nsnap$, the number of time steps between "snapshots" of the particles, depends on the computational speed of your computer and the speed and resolution of your graphics display. Remember that drawing graphical images is relatively time consuming on most personal computers. Observe a sufficient number of snapshots for the particles to move significantly from their initial positions. (It will take on the order of 100–200 time steps.) Does the system become more or less random?

b. From the visual snapshots of the trajectories of the particles, estimate the time for the system to reach equilibrium. What is your qualitative criterion for "equilibrium"?

c. Compute $n(t)$, the number of particles in the left half of the box. Plot $n(t)$ as a function of time. What is the qualitative behavior of $n(t)$? What is the mean number of particles on the left side?

*d. Record the positions and velocities of all the particles at a time t at which $n(t) \sim 6$. (Print the positions and the velocities $vx(i)$ and $vy(i)$ or use **SUB save_config** listed before Problem 6.4.) Then consider the time-reversed process, i.e. the motion that would occur if the direction of time were reversed. This process is equivalent to letting $\vec{v} \rightarrow -\vec{v}$ for all particles. Use **Program md** with the initial conditions $vx(i) \rightarrow -vx(i)$ and $vy(i) \rightarrow -vy(i)$ and describe the qualitative dependence of $n(t)$. What is the state of the system at $t = 0$?

PROBLEM 6.2 Special initial conditions

a. Consider the initial conditions corresponding to $N = 11$, $Lx = Ly = 10$, $x(i) = Lx/2$, $y(i) = (i - 0.5) * Ly/N$, $vx(i) = 1$, and $vy(i) = 0$ (see Fig. 6.5). Eliminate the statements in **SUB initial** which ensure that the total average momentum is zero. Does the system eventually reach equilibrium? Why or why not?

b. Change the direction of the velocity of particle 4 such that $vx(4) = 0.9$ and $vy(4) = sqr(1 - vx(4)*vx(4))$. Does the system eventually reach equilibrium? Explain why "almost" all initial states lead to the same qualitative behavior.

The snapshots generated in Problem 6.1 show the system in its greatest possible detail. From this *microscopic* viewpoint, the snapshots appear rather complex since the positions of the particles are different in each snapshot. However, if we are not interested in the trajectory of each individual particle, we see that the system can be specified more simply. That is, the macroscopic state or *macrostate* of the system can be described in part by determining the number of particles in any part of the box. Your observations of the temporal behavior of the number of particles in the left half of the box should be consistent with the two general conclusions:

Fig. 6.5 Example of a "special" initial condition; the arrows represent
the magnitude and the direction of each particle's velocity.

1. After the removal of an internal constraint, an isolated system changes in
   time from a "less random" to a "more random" state.
2. The final macroscopic state is characterized by relatively small fluctuations
   about a mean which is independent of time.

A many particle system whose macroscopic state is independent of time is
said to be in *equilibrium*. A process is said to be *irreversible* if the time-reversed
process $(t \rightarrow -t)$ is highly improbable. For example if we spill a cup of coffee
(never near a computer), we know that the coffee will flow from the cup. In
principle the time-reversed process is possible but extremely unlikely. Note that
there is nothing intrinsic in the laws of motion which gives time a preferred
direction (see Problem 6.1d).

Our description of the approach to equilibrium has been qualitative. That
is, the constant motion of the particles almost always results in a uniform distribution which fills the entire box. One macroscopic measure of the "randomness"
of a many particle system is the entropy, a quantity we will discuss in Chapter
14.

Before we continue, it would be prudent to monitor the total energy and
verify our claim that the Verlet algorithm maintains conservation of energy with
a reasonable choice of Δt.

PROBLEM 6.3 Verlet's algorithm and conservation of energy

Use **Program md** with $N = 12$, $vmax = 0.2$, $Lx = Ly = 8$. Place the
particles on a rectangular grid which fills the box and choose the velocities at
random. Determine the value of Δt necessary to conserve the total energy to

within 5% for 200 time steps. (Most research applications conserve the energy to within 1% or better.) Are the kinetic and potential energy conserved separately? Suggestions: In **SUB Verlet** add the following statement in the appropriate place to compute the kinetic energy:

```
LET ke = ke + 0.5*(vx(i)*vx(i) + vy(i)*vy(i)
```

In **SUB accel** add the following statement to compute the potential energy:

```
LET pe = pe + potential
```

SUB output is called from the main program and computes the mean kinetic and potential energies after every snapshot.

```
SUB output(N,Lx,Ly,virial,pe,ke,nsnap,itime)
   ! accumulated values of ke and pe computed nsnap times
   LET ke = ke/nsnap
   LET pe = pe/nsnap
   LET E = (ke + pe)/N              ! total energy per particle
   SET cursor 1,1
   PRINT "energy per particle = "; E
   SET cursor 1,50
   PRINT "ke = "; ke
   SET cursor 2,50
   PRINT "pe = "; pe
   SET CURSOR 4,50
   PRINT "time = "; itime
   LET ke = 0                       ! reinitialize variables
   LET pe = 0
END SUB
```

6.6   MEASUREMENT OF MACROSCOPIC QUANTITIES

We have characterized the macrostate of the gas by the number of particles in the left half of the box. We know that we can also characterize an equilibrium macrostate by other parameters, such as the absolute temperature T, the mean pressure P, as well as the volume and total energy.

The kinetic definition of the temperature follows from the equipartition theorem: each quadratic term in the energy of a classical system in equilibrium at temperature T has a mean value equal to $\frac{1}{2}k_BT$, where k_B is Boltzmann's constant. Thus we can define the temperature T of the system in d spatial dimensions by the relation

$$\frac{d}{2}Nk_BT = \sum \frac{1}{2} <mv_i^2>$$ (6.4)

where the sum is over the N particles in the system and the d-components of the velocity. The bracket $<...>$ denotes a time average. Equation (6.4) is an example of the relation of a macroscopic quantity, the temperature, to a time average over the trajectories of the particles. Note that the relation (6.4) holds only if the motion of the center of mass of the system is zero—we do not want the motion of the center of mass of the container to change the temperature! In SI units T is measured in degrees kelvin (K) and $k_B = 1.38 \times 10^{-23} J/K$. In the following we will measure the temperature in terms of ϵ/k_B.

Another thermal quantity is the *heat capacity* at constant volume $C_V = (\partial E/\partial T)_V$, where E is the total energy. C_V is a measure of the amount of heat needed to produce a change in the temperature. Since the heat capacity depends on the size of the system, it is convenient to define the *specific heat* per particle, $c_V = C_V/N$. The easiest way to obtain c_V is to determine the mean potential energy at neighboring temperatures T and $T+\Delta T$; c_V is related to the temperature dependence of the potential energy plus the specific heat associated with the kinetic energy, $(d/2)k_B$.

In order to determine the mean pressure, suppose for the moment that the particles are in a container with rigid walls. We know that the collisions of particles with the walls of the container cause a mean net force to be exerted on each element of the wall. The mean force per unit area is the pressure P of the gas. The pressure can be found by relating the force in the horizontal direction to the rate of change of the corresponding component of the linear momentum of the particles hitting the wall.

We can use a similar argument to obtain the mean pressure in the absence of the walls. Since the pressure is uniform at equilibrium, we can relate the pressure to the net transfer of momentum across an element of area anywhere in the system. Consider an element of area dA and let $\vec{S}_+$ be the mean momentum crossing the surface per unit time from left to right and let $\vec{S}_-$ be the mean momentum crossing the surface per unit time from right to left. Then the mean force $\vec{F}$ is

$$\vec{F} = \vec{S}_+ - \vec{S}_-$$ (6.5)

and the mean pressure is given by

$$P = \frac{dF_n}{dA}$$ (6.6)

where F_n is the component of the force normal to the element of area. (For two dimensions the pressure is the rate of momentum flow through a unit line segment instead of through a unit area.) What is the appropriate measure of pressure for the Lennard-Jones potential?

One way to implement this method for determining the mean pressure is to imagine four imaginary surfaces at the "edges" of the unit cell. Then we can modify **SUB periodic** to determine the momentum transfer during one time step.

```
SUB periodic(xnew,ynew,px,py,Lx,Ly,xflux,yflux)
    ! modified subroutine to find flux
    ! define px = vx(i) and py = vy(i) in SUB Verlet
    IF xnew < 0 then
        LET xnew = xnew + Lx
        LET xflux = xflux - px                ! momentum transfer
    END IF
    IF xnew > Lx then
        LET xnew = xnew - Lx
        LET xflux = xflux + px
    END IF
    IF ynew < 0 then
        LET ynew = ynew + Ly
        LET yflux = yflux - py
    END IF
    IF ynew > Ly then
        LET ynew = ynew - L
        LET yflux = yflux + py
    END IF
END SUB
```

The mean pressure can be found by adding the following statements to **SUB output**:

```
LET pressure = ( (xflux/(2*Lx)) + (yflux/(2*Ly)) )/(dt*nsnap)     ! flux method
LET xflux = 0                ! reinitialize variables and pass them to main program
LET yflux = 0
```

An alternative way of calculating the pressure is from the virial theorem:

$$PV = Nk_BT + \frac{1}{d} <\sum_{i}^{N} \vec{r}_i \cdot \vec{F}_i> \qquad (6.7)$$

where $\vec{r}_i$ is the position of the ith particle, $\vec{F}_i$ is the total force on particle i due to all the other particles, and the sum is over all N particles. A derivation of (6.7) is given in Appendix 6A. To compute the pressure using the virial, we add the following statement to **SUB Verlet**:

```
LET virial = virial + x(i)*ax(i) + y(i)*ay(i)
```

To compute the mean pressure, we add the following statements to **SUB output**:

```
LET pvirial = (N*T)/(Lx*Ly) + 0.5*virial/(Lx*Ly*nsnap)
LET virial = 0
```

We have now seen two examples, (6.4) and (6.7), of the relation of macroscopic quantities to time averages of functions of the coordinates and velocities of the particles in the system. In equilibrium these averages are independent of time. In Chapters 15 and 16 we will consider a second type of averaging— an average over statistical ensembles. The relation between the two methods of averaging is discussed briefly in Chapter 15.

In many molecular dynamics simulations the process of equilibration can account for a substantial fraction of the total computer time. In general, the most practical choice of initial conditions is an "equilibrium" configuration from a previous run which is at a temperature and density close to the desired temperature. The following subroutine saves the last configuration of a run and can be included as the last subroutine called in **Program md**.

```
SUB save_config(x(),y(),vx(),vy(),N,Lx,Ly)
    INPUT prompt "name of file for last configuration = ": file$
    OPEN #1: name file$, access output, create new
    PRINT #1: N, ",", Lx, ",", Ly
    FOR i = 1 to N
        PRINT #1: x(i), ",", y(i)
        PRINT #1: vx(i), ",", vy(i)
    NEXT i
    CLOSE #1
END SUB
```

The following statements can be added to **SUB initial** so that a prior equilibrium configuration can be used as the initial configuration of a new run.

```
INPUT prompt "new configuration (y/n)?": new$
IF new$ = "n" or IF new$ = "N" then
    INPUT prompt "filename? ": file$
    OPEN #1: name file$, access input
    INPUT #1: N,Lx,Ly
    FOR i = 1 to N
        INPUT #1: x(i),y(i)
        INPUT #1: vx(i),vy(i)
    NEXT i
    CLOSE #1
ELSE
! choose initial conditions as before
END IF
```

It is necessary to start a molecular dynamics simulation with the system in an arbitrary configuration only once. Subsequent calculations for different states can be started by modifying the conditions existing at the end of a prior calculation. Changes in the temperature of the system at constant density are discussed in Problem 6.6.

PROBLEM 6.4 Qualitative nature of a liquid and a gas

a. Use the following data and read statements to obtain your initial configuration for all parts of this problem. The **READ** statement reads data items from **DATA** statements and assigns their values to the corresponding variables. Each **READ** statement reads another item of the **DATA** statements in order. Write a short program which uses the **READ** and **DATA** statements and convince yourself that you understand how these statements work.

```
DATA 0.4,0.8,3.1,0.9,5.2,1.3,5.4,5.9,0.4,2.3,1.6,2.1,3.9,1.6,5.3,2.3
DATA 5.4,4.5,2.3,4.1,3.7,4.0,4.9,3.3,0.8,4.4,2.8,5.3,4.3,0.6,4.4,4.6
    FOR i = 1 to N
        READ x(i),y(i)
        LET x(i) = rscale*x(i)
        LET y(i) = rscale*y(i)
        LET vx(i) = 0
        LET vy(i) = 0
    NEXT i
```

Choose $N = 16, Lx = Ly = 6, rscale = 1$, and $\Delta t = 0.02$. What is the reduced density? Choose $nsnap = 20$ and run the simulation for at least 200 time steps. What is the initial temperature of the system? What is the nature of your snapshots? How long does it take for the system to reach equilibrium? What is your criterion for equilibrium? Compute the total energy, temperature, and pressure for the system. Do not include the non-equilibrium configurations in your averages.

b. In part (a) the total energy was found to be negative. What is the implication of the sign of the total energy? Repeat the simulation with the same initial conditions ($rscale = 1$), but with $Lx = Ly = 30$. Is the total energy the same as in part (a)? If not, why not? Describe the nature of your snapshots. Do the particles fill the box uniformly on a time scale on the order of 200 steps or do they tend to form a "droplet"?

c. Increase the initial spacing between the particles. Use $Lx = Ly = 30$, and $rscale = 2$. What is the reduced density of the system? Estimate the initial density of the droplet. Is the total energy negative or positive? If we make $rscale$ sufficiently large, the droplet must eventually "evaporate" even though the total energy is negative. In a real system, the droplet would be in equilibrium with its vapor and the two phases would coexist. As the density of the initial droplet is decreased, more of the particles within the droplet would evaporate and the size of the droplet would shrink. Of course, any conclusions about the structure of the system based on simulations of only 16 particles must be viewed with caution.

d. Let $Lx = Ly = 30$ and $rscale = 0.8$ What is the reduced density of the system? Estimate the initial density of the droplet. Since the particles are initially closer together, it is necessary to choose a smaller value of Δt, e.g. $\Delta t = 0.01$. Why is the total energy positive? Consider at least 200 time steps and compute the average temperature and pressure over the last 100 time steps. Save the final configuration for use in Problem 6.5. What is the nature of your snapshots? Explain why the equilibrium state can be interpreted as a gas.

PROBLEM 6.5 Distribution of speeds

a. Use the final configuration from Problem 6.4d as the initial configuration for this problem. Our goal is to compute the equilibrium probability $P(v)\Delta v$ that a particle has a speed between v and $v + \Delta v$. Obtain an estimate of the maximum speed of the particles from the initial configuration. Choose bins of width Δv with the bin number k given by $v/\Delta v$ with v the speed of a particle. A reasonable choice for Δv is $0.1 * sqr(T)$, where T is the temperature. Use the array $prob(k)$ to record the number of times the speed of a particle corresponds to bin number k:

```
LET prob(k) = prob(k) + 1
```

Suppose that $\Delta v = 0.1$ and consider the speeds $v = 0.3, 0.49, 0.5, 0.51$ and 0.9. What are the corresponding values of k? Write a short program to determine the array $prob(k)$. Determine $prob(k)$ after each time step and average $prob(k)$ over at least 100 time steps. Normalize $prob(k)$ by dividing by the number of particles and by the number of time steps. Note that it is not necessary to observe the trajectories of the particles. Print a table of k, v, and $prob(k)$.

b. Plot the probability density $P(v)$ versus v. What is the qualitative form of $P(v)$? What is the most probable value for v? What is the approximate "width" of $P(v)$? This probability distribution is known as the Maxwell-Boltzmann distribution.

c. Determine the probability distribution for each component of the velocity. Make sure you distinquish between positive and negative values. What is the most probable values for the x- and y-components? What are the average values?

PROBLEM 6.6 Temperature dependence of the internal energy

a. One characteristic of the molecular dynamics method is that the total energy is determined by the initial conditions and the temperature is a derived quantity found only after the system has reached thermal equilibrium. Hence it is difficult to study the system at a particular temperature. The usual way to reach a desired temperature T_f is to choose the initial condition to be an equilibrium configuration at a temperature T_i, which is as close as possible to T_f. Define the "scale factor" f by the relation $T_f = f T_i$ and scale the velocities by $\vec{v} \rightarrow f^{1/d}\vec{v}$. More than one rescaling of the velocities might be necessary to reach T_f. Choose the initial configuration of the system to be an equilibrium configuration from Problem 6.5a with $Lx = Ly = 6, N = 16, rscale = 1$ and $\Delta t = 0.01$. Set $f = 1.2$ and find the total energy and the new equilibrium temperature. Allow at least 100 time steps for equilibration. After equilibrium has been established, average the kinetic energy per particle over 200 time steps to obtain a reasonable estimate of the mean temperature of the system. Also compute the time-dependence of the equilibrium temperature by averaging the kinetic energy per particle over intervals of five time steps. Repeat this rescaling four additional times and compute the total energy, the mean temperature, and the equilibrium fluctuations in the temperature for each case.

b. Compare the initial and final temperatures in part (a). Are they approximately related by $T_f = fT_i$?

c. Use your data for $T(E)$ found in part (a) to plot the total energy E as a function of T. Estimate the contribution to c_V, the specific heat per particle, from the potential energy and the kinetic energy. What percentage of the specific heat is due to the potential energy? Why are accurate determinations of c_V difficult to achieve?

d. Plot the equilibrium temperature averaged over intervals of five time steps as a function of time for each energy considered in part (a). Why does the equilibrium temperature fluctuate? Make a visual estimate of the magnitude of the temperature fluctuations for the temperatures considered in part (a). What is the qualitative dependence of the temperature fluctuations on T?

In Problem 6.7 we compute the pressure and hence the *equation of state* (the relation between pressure, temperature, and volume) of a gas.

PROBLEM 6.7 Equation of state of a non-ideal gas

a. Choose the initial configuration to be an equilibrium configuration from Problem 6.6a ($Lx = Ly = 6$, $N = 16$, $rscale = 1$, $\Delta t = 0.01$). Use **Program md** and **SUB output** to compute the mean pressure using the net momentum transfer method and the virial theorem. Allow at least 100 time steps for equilibration and 200 time steps to compute averages. Is the pressure constant or does it fluctuate? How does the pressure compare with the ideal gas result? Which method of computing the pressure is more accurate? Give an explanation for your answer.

b. An approximate equation of state for dense gases and liquids is the *van der Waals* equation:

$$P = k_B T \frac{\rho}{1 - b\rho} - a\rho^2 \quad . \tag{6.8}$$

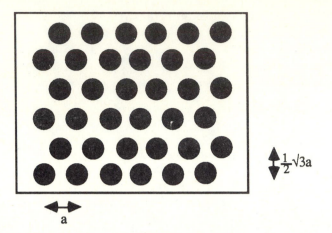

$\updownarrow \frac{1}{2}\sqrt{3}a$

$\leftrightarrow$
a

Fig. 6.6 The state of lowest energy of a two-dimensional Lennard-Jones system is a triangular rather than a square lattice (see Problem 6.8).

The phenomenological parameters b and a are related to the repulsive and attractive parts of the interaction respectively and are approximately independent of the temperature. Use the same configurations as in Problem 6.6a to find the dependence of P on T. Plot P versus T and use the form (6.8) to obtain an estimate for the parameters a and b.

*c. Change the density as in Problem 6.4a using *rscale* = 1.2. Compute the pressure for different values of T and estimate a and b. Do your values for a and b change significantly? Make a rough estimate of the uncertainties in your calculations.

Although the use of periodic boundary conditions minimizes surface effects, it is also important to choose the symmetry of the central "unit cell" to be consistent with the symmetry of the solid phase of the system. This choice of cell is essential if we wish to do simulations of the high density, low temperature behavior which are as realistic as possible. If the cell does not correspond to the correct crystal structure, the particles cannot form a perfect crystal and some of the particles will wander around in an endless search for their "correct" position. Consequently, a computer simulation of a small number of particles at high density and low temperature would lead to spurious results.

We know that the equilibrium structure of a crystalline solid at $T = 0$ is the configuration of lowest energy. In Problem 6.8 we verify that the state of lowest energy for a two-dimensional Lennard-Jones solid is a triangular lattice rather than a square lattice (see Fig. 6.6).

*PROBLEM 6.8 Ground state energy of two-dimensional lattices

a. The nature of the triangular lattice can be seen from Fig. 6.6. Each site has six nearest neighbors. Write a program to compare the energy per particle of a system of N particles interacting via the Lennard-Jones potential. Consider both the triangular and square lattices. Let L_x be the width of the triangular lattice, and n_c be the number of particles in a column or row. Each column of the triangular lattice is separated by a distance $a = L_x/n_c$, and each row is separated by a distance $\frac{\sqrt{3}}{2}a$. The sites in each row are displaced by $a/2$ from the preceding row. The height of the triangular lattice is $L_y = \frac{\sqrt{3}}{2}L_x$ and $N = n_c{}^2$. In order for both lattices to have the same density, choose the linear dimension of the square lattice to be $L = \sqrt{L_x L_y}$. Although it is possible to choose the unit cell of the triangular lattice to be a rhombus, it is more convenient to choose the unit cell to be rectangular. (There is no square unit cell for the triangular lattice.) Choose $n_c = 6$ and determine the energy for each lattice for $L_x = 5$ and 7. What is the density of the system for each case? Are your results for E/N independent of the size of the lattice? Which lattice has a lower energy? Explain your results in terms of the ability of the triangular lattice to pack the particles closer together.

b. Consider $n_c = 6$ and $L_x = 10, 20$, and $2^{1/6}n_c$. Which lattice structure has the lowest energy in each case? In all these cases the net force on a particle is zero. Why? The latter density corresponds to the case where the force between nearest neighbors is zero. Convince yourself that at this density the lattice is unstable, since the force on any particle which deviates from its lattice site is attractive. Consequently the system will collapse to a higher density, where the triangular lattice is always favored.

c. Repeat the previous calculations for $V(r) = 1/r^6$ and $1/r^4$. Is the triangular lattice still favored?

PROBLEM 6.9 The solid state and melting

a. Choose the parameters $N = 16$, $\Delta t = 0.01$, $L_x = 4$, and $L_y = 2\sqrt{3}$. Place the particles on a triangular lattice which fills the container and give each particle zero initial velocity. Measure the temperature and pressure as a function of time, and save several "snapshots" of the system. What is the total energy of the system? Does the system remain a solid?

b. Give the particles a random velocity in the interval $[-0.1, 0.1]$. What is the total energy? Equilibrate the system for approximately 50 timesteps and average the temperature and pressure over 100 time steps. Take snapshots of the system at intervals of 25 time steps. Save an equilibrium configuration for use in part (c).

c. Choose the initial configuration to be an equilibrium configuration from part (b) but increase the temperature by letting $v_i \to 2.0 v_i$. What is the new total energy? Take snapshots of the system at intervals of 25 time steps and describe the qualitative behavior of the motion of the particles in the system. What is the equilibrium temperature and pressure of the system? After equilibrium is reached, increase the temperature again by rescaling the velocities in the same way. Repeat this rescaling and measure $P(T)$ and $E(T)$ for six different temperatures.

d. Use your results from part (c) to plot $E(T) - E(0)$ and the pressure as a function of T. Is the difference $E(T) - E(0)$ proportional to T? What is the mean potential energy for a harmonic solid? Are your measured results for the temperature dependence of $E(T) - E(0)$ consistent with your expectations?

e. Decrease the density by multiplying L_x, L_y and the particle coordinates by a factor of 1.1. What are your results for the temperature and pressure? What is the nature of the snapshots? Continue rescaling the density and the positions until the system melts. What is your qualitative criterion for "melting" as observed from your snapshots?

6.7 SIMPLE TRANSPORT PROPERTIES

We now discuss several dynamical properties of a fluid at equilibrium. Suppose that we follow the trajectory of a single *tagged* particle (particle i) and that at some arbitrarily chosen time its position is $\vec{r}_i(t_1)$. At some later time t_2, we can determine its displacement $\vec{r}_i(t_2) - \vec{r}_i(t_1)$. We know that if particle i suffers zero net force, its displacement increases linearly with time. However, a particle in a fluid undergoes many collisions and on the average its net displacement would be zero. A more interesting quantity is the mean square displacement $R(t)^2$ defined by

$$R(t)^2 = <|\vec{r}_i(t_2) - \vec{r}_i(t_1)|^2> \tag{6.9}$$

where $t = t_2 - t_1$ and we have averaged over all particles. Since the system is at equilibrium, the zero of time is arbitrary and the average in (6.9) depends only on the time difference t. We will find in Problem 6.10 that the t-dependence of R(t) is consistent with the Einstein relation

$$R(t)^2 = 2dDt \qquad (t \to \infty) \tag{6.10}$$

where D is the *self-diffusion constant*. Note that $R(t)$ increases as $t^{1/2}$ for sufficiently long t.

Another single-particle property is the "velocity autocorrelation function" $Z(t)$ whose definition we now motivate. Suppose that particle i has velocity $\vec{v}_i(t_1)$ at time t_1. If particle i suffers zero net force, its velocity will remain constant and hence its velocity at a later time will remain "correlated" with its earlier velocity. However, the interactions with other particles in the fluid will change the particle's velocity, and we expect that after several collisions its velocity will not be strongly correlated with its earlier velocity. Hence we define $Z(t)$ as

$$Z(t) = <\vec{v}_i(t_2) \cdot \vec{v}_i(t_1)> \tag{6.11}$$

where $t = t_2 - t_1$. If we define the self-diffusion constant D by the relation (6.9), it can be shown that D is related to $Z(t)$ by

$$D = \frac{1}{d} \int_{-\infty}^{+\infty} Z(t)dt \quad . \tag{6.12}$$

The relation (6.12) which relates the self-diffusion constant to the time integral of an autocorrelation function is an example of a general relation between transport coefficients such as viscosity and thermal conductivity and autocorrelation functions.

The velocity autocorrelation function and the mean square displacement are computed in **SUB transport**. This subroutine should be called at the same time that the pressure and temperature are computed. Four arrays, *xs*, *ys*, *vxs*, and *vys*, are used to store the positions and velocities of the particles. The variable *ntrans* is the number of times **SUB transport** is called and is used to normalize the results in **SUB trans_output**. The latter subroutine is called at the end of the main program.

```
SUB transport(N,Lx,Ly,x(),y(),vx(),vy(),xs(,),ys(,),vxs(,),vys(,),ntrans,Z(),R2())
    ! compute velocity autocorrelation function and mean square displacement
    ! save 10 configurations before computing Z(t) and R2(t)
    IF ntrans > 10 then                  ! compute transport functions
        FOR itime = 1 to 10
            FOR i = 1 to N
                LET dx = x(i) - xs(i,itime)
                LET dy = y(i) - ys(i,itime)
                CALL separation(dx,dy,Lx,Ly)
                LET R2(itime) = R2(itime) + dx*dx + dy*dy
                LET Z(itime) = Z(itime) + vx(i)*vxs(i,itime) + vy(i)*vys(i,itime)
            NEXT i
        NEXT itime
        ! update arrays xs,ys,vxs,vys
        FOR itime = 10 to 2 step -1
            FOR i = 1 to N
                LET xs(i,itime) = xs(i,itime-1)
                LET ys(i,itime) = ys(i,itime-1)
                LET vxs(i,itime) = vxs(i,itime-1)
                LET vys(i,itime) = vys(i,itime-1)
            NEXT i
        NEXT itime
        FOR i = 1 to N                   ! store new configuration
            LET xs(i,1) = x(i)
            LET ys(i,1) = y(i)
            LET vxs(i,1) = vx(i)
            LET vys(i,1) = vy(i)
        NEXT i
    ELSE                                 ! store configurations if ntrans <=10
        FOR i = 1 to N
            LET xs(i,10 - ntrans) = x(i)
            LET ys(i,10 - ntrans) = y(i)
            LET vxs(i,10 - ntrans) = vx(i)
            LET vys(i,10 - ntrans) = vy(i)
    END IF
    LET ntrans = ntrans + 1              ! # of times transport properties measured
END SUB
```

```
SUB trans_output(N, ntrans,Z(),R2())
  ! normalize transport functions and print results
  LET ntrans = ntrans - 10
  LET norm = 1/(N* ntrans )
  FOR itime = 1 to 10
      PRINT itime, r2(itime)*norm,z(itime)*norm
  NEXT itime
END SUB
```

PROBLEM 6.10 Self-diffusion constant

a. Use an equilibrium configuration from Problem 6.5 and visually follow the motion of a particular particle (referred to as a *labeled* or *tagged* particle). Describe its motion qualitatively.

b. Modify **Program md** to compute the self diffusion constant. Use the following initial configuration.

```
LET N = 16
LET Lx = 6
LET Ly = 6
DATA 1.5,3.6,0.2,0.5,4.8,5.9,-0.8,-4.6,1.8,5.7,1.8,3.4,1.9
DATA 4.5,0.2,0.5,3.6,4.3,0.3,0.6,0.5,3.2,-3.2,-2.5,5.8,4.0
DATA 3.1,-2.8,3.1,5.8,2.5,-0.1,5.0,2.2,-0.1,0.4,6.0,1.7,2.1
DATA 1.2,4.2,5.2,-0.9,1.9,3.9,3.3,2.1,-0.1,4.3,1.0,-3.0,-1.4
DATA 3.0,0.9,-1.9,2.3,3.0,1.8,-0.0,-0.9,1.5,0.8,-2.3,1.8
FOR i = 1 to N
  READ x(i),y(i),vx(i),vy(i)
NEXT i
```

Choose $\Delta t = 0.01$ and compute $R(t)^2$ at intervals of five time steps. Also compute the mean temperature and pressure. Since $R(t)$ is much less than $L_x/2$ or $L_y/2$, finite size effects are minimized.

c. Plot $R(t)^2$ as a function of t. Does $R(t)^2$ increase as t^2 as for a free particle or more slowly? Use the relation (6.10) to estimate the magnitude of D from the plot of $R(t)^2$. Obtain D for several different temperatures. (A careful study of $R(t)^2$ for larger systems and longer times would find that $R(t)^2$ is not proportional to t in two dimensions. Instead $R(t)$ has a term proportional to $t\,log(t)$, which dominates the linear t term if t is sufficiently large. However, we will not be able to observe the effects of this logarithmic term, and we can interpret our results for $R(t)^2$ in terms of an "effective" diffusion constant. No such problem exists for three dimensions.)

d. Compute $R(t)^2$ for an equilibrium configuration corresponding to a harmonic solid. What is the qualitative behavior of $R(t)^2$? Is this behavior consistent with your snapshots?

e. Compute $R(t)^2$ for an equilibrium configuration corresponding to a dilute gas. Why is $R(t)^2$ not proportional to t for small times? Is it practical to use molecular dynamics to compute the self-diffusion constant of a dilute gas?

*PROBLEM 6.11 The velocity autocorrelation function

a. Compute $Z(t)$ for intervals of five time steps for the equilibrium configurations of Problem 6.10b. Plot $Z(t)$ versus t and describe its qualitative behavior. Estimate D by using the relation (6.12). (In order to estimate the integral of $Z(t)$, add your results for $Z(t)$ at the different values of t and multiply the sum by the time difference between successive values of t.)

b. Assume that $Z(t)$ satisfies the form $Z(t) \approx A\,exp(-t/\tau)$. What is the theoretical value of A? Substitute this assumed t-dependence of $Z(t)$ into (6.12) and determine the relationship between D and the *correlation time* τ. Plot the natural logarithm of $Z(t)$ versus t and estimate τ. Use this derived relationship between D and τ to deduce D. Compare your estimates for D found from the slope of $R(t)^2$, the relation (6.12) and the estimate of τ. Are these estimates consistent?

c. Choose an equilibrium configuration from part (a) and increase the density by changing L_x and L_y to 5.5 and rescaling all positions by the factor (5.5/6). After the system has equilibrated, compute $Z(t)$ at intervals of five time steps. What is the qualitative behavior of $Z(t)$? What is the implication of the fact that $Z(t)$ becomes negative after a relatively short time? Give a physical explanation of this effect.

d. Place $N = 16$ particles on a triangular lattice with $L_x = 4$, $L_y = 2\sqrt{3}$ and choose the velocities at random in the interval $[-1, 1]$. Take $\Delta t = 0.01$ and compute $Z(t)$ after equilibrium has been attained. Plot $Z(t)$ versus t and describe the qualitative behavior of $Z(t)$. Explain your results in terms of the oscillatory motion of the particles about their lattice sites.

6.8 EXTENSIONS

The primary goals of this chapter were to introduce some of the concepts of the kinetic theory of fluids and to introduce the method of molecular dynamics. Although we found that simulations of systems as small as sixteen particles do show some of the qualitative properties of macroscopic systems, we would need to simulate larger systems to make quantitative conclusions. In general the most time consuming parts of the computation are equilibration and the bookkeeping necessary for the force and energy calculations. If the force is sufficiently short range, there are a number of ways to reduce the equilibration time. For example, suppose we want to simulate a system of 864 particles in three dimensions. We can first simulate a smaller system of 108 particles and allow the small system to come to equilibrium at the desired temperature. After equilibrium has been reached, the small system can be replicated two times in each direction to generate the desired system of 864 particles. All of the velocities are reassigned using the Maxwell-Boltzmann distribution (see Problem 6.4), and equilibration is resumed. Equilibration of the complete system is usually established quickly.

The computer time required for our molecular dynamics program in its present form is roughly proportional to N^2 for each time step. The reason for this relation is that the energy and force calculations require sums over all pairs of N interacting particles. However if the interactions are short range, the time required at each time step for these sums can be reduced to order N. The idea is to take advantage of the fact that at any given time most pairs of particles are separated by a distance much greater than the effective range r_c of the interparticle potential ($r_c \approx 2.5\,\sigma$ for the Lennard-Jones potential). Hence the calculation of the force and the energy requires the summation of interactions only over those pairs whose separation is less than r_c. Of course, testing whether each pair satisfies this criterion is also an order N^2 calculation. Clearly we have to limit the number of pairs tested. One method is to divide the box into a number of small cells. At each time step, the molecules in each cell are listed in arrays. The arrays are then searched and the relative distances are calculated only for pairs of molecules in neighboring cells.

How do we know if the size of our system is large enough to yield quantitative results which are independent of N? The answer is simple—repeat the simulation for different N. Fortunately most simulations of equilibrium systems with simple potentials require only several hundred to several thousand particles for reliable results.

It is possible to do molecular dynamics simulations at constant temperature and/or pressure rather than at constant energy and volume. It is also possible to do simulations in which the shape of the cell is determined by the dynamics rather than imposed by the program. Such a simulation is essential for the study of solid-to-solid transitions where the major change is the shape of the crystal.

In addition to these technical advances, there is more to learn about the properties of the system from the trajectories. For example, how are the trajectories related to transport properties such as the viscosity and the thermal conductivity? What is the structure of a liquid, e.g. what is the probability that two particles are separated by a certain amount? The latter problem is addressed in Chapter 16 in the context of Monte Carlo methods.

Now that we are familiar with the molecular dynamics technique, we can briefly discuss the role of molecular dynamics and other simulation methods. In general molecular dynamics methods are used with two main purposes in mind. Suppose we want to develop a general theory of liquids. In order to make the theoretical analysis easier, it would be desirable to choose a simple model which preserves the essential features of liquids. Since such a model would not have a laboratory counterpart, molecular dynamics can provide essentially exact, quasi-experimental data. In addition, molecular dynamics can provide information on quantities which cannot be easily measured in the laboratory. On the other hand, the simulation might be compared with a real (physical) experiment in order to test the detailed predictions of the theory. As a result of this type of interplay between theory and computer and laboratory experiments, a well developed theory of the structure of simple liquids now exists.

The emphasis in current research in molecular dynamics is shifting from the studies of equilibrium fluids to studies of nonequilibrium systems. For example how does a solid form when the temperature of a liquid is lowered quickly? How does a crack propagate in a brittle solid? Computer simulation will play a crucial role in aiding our understanding of these and other problems.

REFERENCES AND SUGGESTIONS FOR ADDITIONAL READING

Farid F. Abraham, "Computational statistical mechanics: methodology, applications and supercomputing," *Adv. Phys.* **35**, 1 (1986). The author discusses both molecular dynamics and Monte Carlo (see Chapter 16) techniques. Of special interest is the author's views on the future role of supercomputers and new computer architectures on problems in science ranging from the structure of proteins to turbulent fluids.

B. J. Alder and T. E. Wainwright, "Studies in Molecular Dynamics. I. General Method," *J. Chem. Phys.* **31**, 459 (1960). Although we did not consider molecular dynamics methods for hard spheres, no discussion of molecular dynamics would be complete without mention of this pioneering work. R. P. Bonomo and F. Riggi, "The evolution of the speed distribution for a two-dimensional ideal gas: A computer simulation," Am. J. Phys. **52**, 54 (1984). The authors consider a system of hard disks and show that the system always evolves toward the Maxwell-Boltzmann distribution.

Jean-Pierre Hansen and Ian R. McDonald, *Theory of Simple Liquids*, Academic Press (1976). An excellent reference which derives most of the theoretical results used in this chapter.

J. Kushick and B. J. Berne, "Molecular dynamics methods: continuous potentials" in *Statistical Mechanics Part B: Time-Dependent Processes*, Bruce J. Berne, ed. Plenum Press (1977). Also see the article by Jerome J. Erpenbeck and William Wood on "Molecular dynamics techniques for hard-core systems" in the same volume.

A. Rahman, "Correlations in the Motion of Atoms in Liquid Argon," *Phys. Rev.* **136**, A405 (1964). The first application of molecular dynamics to systems with continuous potentials.

F. Reif, *Statistical Physics*, Vol. 5 of the Berkeley Physics Course, McGraw-Hill (1965). An introduction to the behavior of macroscopic systems with probably the first educational use of computer simulations to illustrate the approach of macroscopic systems to equilibrium.

F. Reif, *Fundamentals of Statistical and Thermal Physics*, McGraw-Hill (1965.) An intermediate level text on statistical mechanics with a more thorough discussion of kinetic theory than found in most undergraduate texts.

R. M. Sperandeo Mineo and R Madonia, "The equation of state of a hard-particle system: a model experiment on a microcomputer," *Eur. J. Phys.* **7**, 124 (1986).

Loup Verlet, "Computer 'Experiments' on Classical Fluids. I. Thermodynamical Properties of Lennard-Jones Molecules," *Phys. Rev.* **159**, 98 (1967). Another classic paper on molecular dynamics.

James H. Williams and Glenn Joyce, "Equilibrium properties of a one-dimensional kinetic system," *J. Chem. Phys.* **59**, 741 (1973). Simulations in one dimension are even simpler than in two dimensions.

APPENDIX 6A THE PRESSURE VIRIAL

The following derivation of the pressure of a fluid enclosed in a volume V is based on the derivation in Hansen and McDonald. Consider the quantity

$$G = \sum_i \vec{r}_i \cdot \vec{F}_i \tag{6.13}$$

where the sum is over all particles in the system and $\vec{F}_i$ is the total force acting on the ith particle. The time average of G can be written as

$$
\begin{aligned}
<G> &= \lim_{\tau \to \infty} \frac{1}{\tau} \int_0^\tau dt \sum_i \vec{r}_i(t) \cdot \vec{F}_i(t) \\
&= \lim_{\tau \to \infty} \frac{1}{\tau} \int_0^\tau dt \sum_i \vec{r}_i(t) \cdot m \frac{d^2 \vec{r}_i(t)}{dt^2} \\
&= -\lim_{\tau \to \infty} \frac{1}{\tau} \int_0^\tau dt \sum_i m |\frac{d\vec{r}_i(t)}{dt}|^2 = -3Nk_BT
\end{aligned} \tag{6.14}
$$

where we have done an integration by parts and used the equipartition theorem. G can be separated into a part arising from the interparticle forces and another part due to the external force of the walls. We can relate the latter to the pressure and write

$$d\vec{F}_i = -P\hat{n}dA \tag{6.15}$$

where $\hat{n}$ is a unit vector normal to the area $d\vec{A}$. We have

$$\sum_i \vec{r}_i \cdot \vec{F}_i = -P \int \vec{r} \cdot \hat{n} \, dA = P \int \vec{\nabla} \cdot \vec{r} \, dV = 3PV \tag{6.16}$$

where we have used Gauss' theorem. Hence we can write

$$-3PV + <G_{int}> = -3Nk_BT$$

or

$$PV = Nk_BT + \frac{1}{3} <\sum_{i=1} \vec{r}_i \cdot \vec{F}_i> \quad . \tag{6.17}$$

In two dimensions the fraction $1/3$ is replaced by $1/2$.

THE CHAOTIC MOTION OF DYNAMICAL SYSTEMS

7

We study simple deterministic non-linear models which exhibit complex patterns of behavior.

7.1 INTRODUCTION

The ideas to be discussed in this chapter are based on the use of the computer as a tool for making empirical observations. In fact computer-based investigations have led to major conceptual advances in our understanding of non-linear problems.

Most natural phenomena are intrinsically non-linear. Weather patterns and the turbulent motion of rapidly moving fluids are everyday examples. Although we might be aware that non-linear effects are important in these and other physical phenomena, it is easier to introduce some of the important concepts in the context of theoretical ecology. Our problem will be to analyze the one-dimensional difference equation

$$x_{n+1} = 4rx_n(1 - x_n) \tag{7.1}$$

where x_n is the ratio of the population in the nth generation to a reference population. We shall see that the dynamical properties of (7.1) are surprisingly intricate and have important implications in the development of a more general description of non-linear phenomena. The significance of recent results is indicated by the following quote by ecologist Robert May (see the references at the end of the chapter) on the study of the difference equation (7.1):

" ... Its study does not involve as much conceptual sophistication as does elementary calculus. Such study would greatly enrich the student's intuition about non-linear systems. Not only in research but also in the everyday world of politics and economics we would all be better off if more people realized that simple non-linear systems do not necessarily possess simple dynamical properties."

7.2 A SIMPLE ONE-DIMENSIONAL MAP

Many biological populations effectively consist of a single generation with no overlap between successive generations. For example we can imagine an island with an insect population which breeds in the summer and leaves eggs which hatch the following spring. Since the population growth occurs in discrete steps, it is appropriate to model the population growth using difference equations rather than differential equations. A simple model of density-independent growth which relates the population in generation $(n + 1)$ to the population in generation n is given by

$$P_{n+1} = aP_n \tag{7.2}$$

where a is a constant. Clearly if $a > 1$, then each generation will be a times larger than the previous one. This leads to geometric growth and an unbounded population. It is natural to formulate a more realistic model in which the population is bounded by the finite carrying capacity of its environment. A simple discrete model of density-dependent growth is

$$P_{n+1} = P_n(a - bP_n) \quad . \tag{7.3}$$

Note that (7.3), which is sometimes called the "logistic" difference equation, is non-linear due to the presence of the quadratic term in P_n. The first term represents the natural growth of the population; the quadratic term represents a reduction of this natural growth caused, for example, by overcrowding or the spread of disease.

It is convenient to "rescale" the population by letting $P_n = (a/b)x_n$ and rewriting (7.3) as

$$x_{n+1} = ax_n(1 - x_n) \quad . \tag{7.4}$$

This replacement of P_n by x_n changes the system of units used to define the various parameters. In order to write (7.4) in the standard form (7.1), we introduce the "growth" parameter $r = a/4$ and obtain

$$x_{n+1} = f(x_n) \tag{7.5}$$

where the function $f(x)$ can be written as

$$f(x) = 4rx(1 - x) \quad . \tag{7.6}$$

The rescaled form (7.6) has the desirable feature that its dynamics are determined by a single control parameter r (also called λ in the literature). Note that if $x_n > 1$, x_{n+1} will be negative. In order to avoid this unphysical feature, we impose the conditions that x is restricted to the interval $0 \leq x \leq 1$ and that $0 \leq r \leq 1$. Since the function $f(x)$ transforms any point on this one-dimensional interval into some other point in the same interval, the function f is called a one-dimensional *map*. In the following discussion, we will refer to the form (7.6) of $f(x)$ as the "standard" map.

Many of the interesting properties of the standard map were discovered by Feigenbaum (cf. Feigenbaum 1978) using a programmable calculator. In Table 7.1 we list the first sixteen iterations of (7.5) to indicate the diversity of behavior for different values of r but the same initial value $x_0 = 0.75$. These values are also plotted in Fig. 7.1. Notice that the behavior for the first few iterations is irregular but, except for the case $r = 0.9$, a pattern emerges. The initial part of the sequence is called the transient behavior and the latter part is the steady state behavior. The sequence of x_n values is called the *orbit* of the map.

TABLE 7.1 The first 16 iterations of the map $x_{n+1} = 4rx_n(1 - x_n)$ for four values of r. Note the different steady state behavior in each case.

n	$r = 0.1$	0.6	0.8	0.9
0	0.750000	0.750000	0.750000	0.750000
1	0.075000	0.450000	0.600000	0.675000
2	0.027750	0.594000	0.768000	0.789750
3	0.010792	0.578794	0.570163	0.597762
4	0.004270	0.585100	0.784247	0.865593
5	0.001701	0.582619	0.541452	0.418829
6	0.000679	0.583618	0.794502	0.876281
7	0.000271	0.583219	0.522460	0.390286
8	0.000109	0.583379	0.798386	0.856667
9	0.000043	0.583315	0.515091	0.442040
10	0.000017	0.583341	0.799271	0.887906
11	0.000007	0.583330	0.513398	0.358303
12	0.000003	0.583334	0.799426	0.827719
13	0.000001	0.583333	0.513102	0.513360
14	0.000000	0.583334	0.799451	0.899357
15	0.000000	0.583333	0.513054	0.325849
16	0.000000	0.583333	0.799455	0.790817

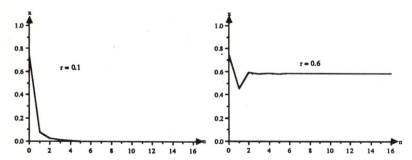

Fig. 7.1a Plot of the iterated values of x for $r = 0.1$ and $r = 0.6$

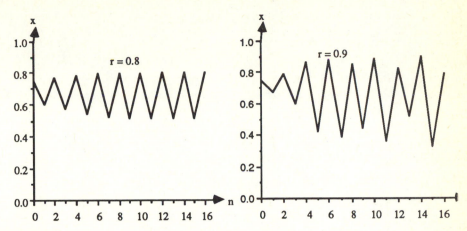

Fig. 7.1b Plot of the iterated values of x for $r = 0.8$ and $r = 0.9$

The following programs calculate the orbit of x for the one-dimensional map $f(x)$. In **Program map_table**, the results for x_n are listed eight iterations per line. The value of r can be changed by typing any key. In **Program map_plot**, x is plotted versus the iteration number n. The value of r can be changed by an amount Δr during the plotting by typing 'i' (increase) or 'd' (decrease).

```
PROGRAM map_table                          ! iterate one-dimensional map f(x)
DO
   CALL initial(x,r)
   CALL map(x,r)
   INPUT  prompt "continue y/n ? ": choice$
LOOP until choice$ = "n"
END


SUB initial(x,r)
   INPUT prompt "growth parameter (0 < r < 1) = ": r
   INPUT prompt "initial value of x (0 < x < 1) = ": x
END SUB
```

```
SUB map(x,r)
  LET iterations = 0
  DO
    LET x = 4*r*x*(1 - x)
    LET iterations = iterations + 1              ! number of iterations
    PRINT USING "#.######": x;
    IF mod(iterations,8) = 0 then PRINT          ! new line
  LOOP until key input
  PRINT
  PRINT "number of iterations = "; iterations
END SUB

PROGRAM map_plot
CALL initial(x,r,nmax)
CALL plot_output(x,r,nmax)
END

SUB initial(x,r,nmax)
  INPUT prompt "initial value of growth parameter r = ": r
  INPUT prompt "initial value of x = ": x
  INPUT prompt "maximum number of iterations = ": nmax
  SET WINDOW -0.1*nmax,nmax,-0.1,1.1
  PLOT LINES: 0,1; 0,0; nmax,0                  ! draw x and y axis
END SUB

SUB plot_output(x,r,nmax)
  DECLARE DEF f
  LET dr = 0.01                      ! change in r
  FOR i = 1 to nmax
    IF key input then                ! type i to increase r by dr, d to decrease r
      GET KEY k
      IF k = ord("i") then LET  r = r + dr
      IF k = ord("d") then LET  r = r - dr
      SET cursor 4,1
      PRINT using "r = ##.#####": r
    END IF
    LET x = f(x,r)
    PLOT POINTS: i,x
  NEXT i
END SUB
```

DEF f(x,r) = 4*r*x*(1 - x)

In Problems 7.1 and 7.2 we use **Program map table** and **Program map plot** to explore the dynamical properties of the standard map (7.6).

PROBLEM 7.1 Exploration of period doubling

a. Explore the dynamical behavior of (7.6) for $r = 0.2$ and $r = 0.24$ for different values of the *seed* x_0. Show that $x = 0$ is a *stable fixed point*. That is, for sufficiently small r, the iterated values of x converge to $x = 0$ independent of the initial value x_0. If x represents the population of insects, describe the qualitative behavior of the population.

b. Explore the dynamical behavior of (7.6) for $r = 0.26, 0.5, 0.7, 0.72, 0.74$, and 0.748. (For $r = 0.748$ approximately 1000 iterations are necessary to obtain convergent results.) Do the iterated values of x converge to $x = 0$? A fixed point is *unstable* if, for almost all x_0, the iterates diverge from it. Do your results indicate that $x = 0$ is an unstable fixed point? Does x iterate to a non-zero fixed point? Show that after many generations the iterated values of x do not change, i.e. the dynamical behavior is static or *period* 1. What are the stable fixed points for the different values of r? The sequence of values $x_0, x_1, x_2, \ldots$ is called the *orbit* or *trajectory* of x. Show that for any one of the suggested values of r the orbits of x become independent of the seed after an initial transient behavior.

c. Explore the dynamical properties of (7.6) for $r = 0.752, 0.76, 0.8$, and 0.862. (For $r = 0.752$ and 0.862 approximately 1000 iterations are necessary to obtain convergent results.) Show that if r is increased slightly beyond 0.75, x is found after an initial transient behavior to oscillate between two values. That is, instead of a stable cycle of period 1 corresponding to one fixed point, the system has a stable cycle of period 2. The value of r at which the single fixed point x^* splits or *bifurcates* into two oscillating values x_1^* and x_2^* is $r_1 = 3/4$. The pair of x values (x_1^* and x_2^*) form a *stable attractor* of period 2.

d. Describe an ecological scenario of an insect or human population which exhibits dynamical behavior similar to that observed in part (c).

e. What are the stable attractors of (7.6) for $r = 0.863$ and 0.88? What is the corresponding period?

f. What are the stable attractors and corresponding periods for $r = 0.89$, 0.891, and 0.8922?

PROBLEM 7.2 The chaotic regime

a. The region $r > r_c = 0.892486417967\ldots$ is called the *chaotic* regime where neighboring seeds can give rise to very different trajectories after a small number of iterations. As an example choose $r = 0.91$ and consider the seeds $x_0 = 0.500$ and 0.501. How many iterations are necessary in order that the iterated values of x differ by more than ten percent?

b. We know that the accuracy of floating point numbers retained on a digital computer is finite. In order to test the effect of the finite accuracy of your computer, first choose $r = 0.91$ and $x_0 = 0.5$ and obtain the numerical value of x after approximately 200 iterations. Then modify your program so that after each iteration, the operations $x = x/10$ followed by $x = 10*x$ are performed. This combination of operations truncates the last digit that your computer retains. (A similar effect can be obtained by using the **truncate** function in True BASIC.) Obtain the iterated value of x under the same conditions and compare your results. Do you find the same discrepancy for $r < r_c$?

c. What are the dynamical properties for $r = 0.958$. Can you find other "windows" in the chaotic region?

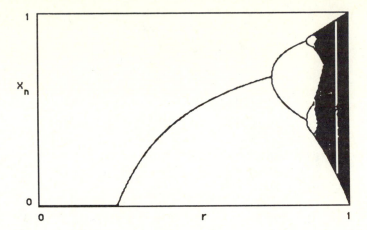

Fig. 7.2 Plot of the iterated values of x_n as a function of the growth parameter r. Note the transition from periodic to chaotic behavior. Also, note the narrow window of periodic behavior within the region of chaos.

Program **map_table** and Program **map_plot** print or plot the values of the population x as a function of the number of iterations. Another way to understand the behavior of (7.6) is to plot the values of x as a function of the control parameter r (see Fig. 7.2). The iterated values of x in Fig. 7.2 are plotted only after the transient behavior is completed. Such a plot can be obtained by modifying **Program map_plot** so that for a given value of r the first *ntransient* values of x are calculated but not plotted, and the next *nplot* values of x are calculated and plotted. This process is repeated for a new value of r until the desired range of r values is reached. A typical value of *ntransient* should be in the range 100—1000 iterations. A typical value of *nplot* should be at least as large as the longest period you wish to observe.

PROBLEM 7.3 Qualitative features of the quadratic map

a. Modify **Program map_plot** so that the iterates x_n are plotted as a function of r. Make the range of r and the range of x input parameters and change the **SET window** statement so that you can "zoom in" on any portion of the plot shown in Fig. 7.2. Do not plot the first *ntransient* iterations. Begin in the range $0.8 \leq r \leq 0.9$. How many period doublings can you discern?

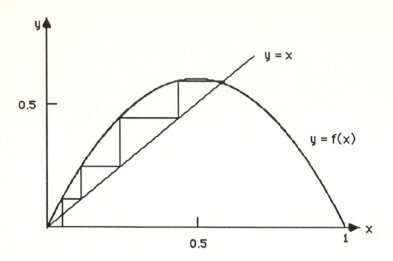

Fig. 7.3 Iterations of the map $x_{n+1} = 4rx_n(1 - x_n)$ with $r = 0.6$ and the seed $x_0 = 0.05$. The trivial fixed point at $x = 0$ is unstable and the fixed point at $x = 0.58333$ is stable.

b. Change the scale so that you can follow the iterations of x from the period 4 to the period 32 behavior. How does the plot look on this scale compared to that of the period 4 map on the original scale?

c. Give a brief qualitative description of the shape of the curve near the bifurcations.

7.3 PERIOD DOUBLING

The above "computer experiments" on the behavior of the standard map led us to develop a new vocabulary to describe our observations and probably convinced you that the dynamical properties of simple deterministic systems can be quite complicated!

In order to understand how the dynamical behavior depends on r, we present a simple and elegant graphical method for iterating $f(x)$. In Fig. 7.3, we show a graph of $f(x)$ for $r = 0.6$. A diagonal line corresponding to $y = x$ intersects the curve $y = f(x)$ at the two fixed points $x^* = 0$ and $x^* = 0.58333$. That is, repeated iterations of $f(x)$ for $x_0 = 0$ and $x_0 = 0.58333$ yield an unchanging sequence. If x_0 is not one of the fixed points, we can find the orbit in the following manner. First draw a vertical line from $\{x = x_0, y = 0\}$ to the intersection with the curve $y = f(x)$ at $\{x_0, y_0 = f(x_0)\}$. Next draw a horizontal line from $\{x_0, y_0\}$ to the intersection with the diagonal line at $\{y_0, y_0\}$. Since along this diagonal line y equals x, the value of x at this intersection is the first iteration $x_1 = y_0$. The second iteration x_2 can be found in the same way. From the point $\{x_1, y_0\}$, draw a vertical line to the intersection with the curve $y = f(x)$. Keep y fixed at $y = y_1 = f(x_0)$ and draw a horizontal line until it intersects the diagonal line; the value of x at this intersection is x_2. Further iterations can be found by repeating this process:

1. move vertically until the line intersects the curve $y = f(x)$;
2. move horizontally until the line intersects the diagonal line $y = x$;
3. repeat the steps 1 and 2 indefinitely.

This graphical process is illustrated in Fig. 7.3 for $x_0 = 0.05$ and $r = 0.6$. Note that if we begin with any x_0 ($x \neq 0$ and $x \neq 1$), continued iterations will converge to the fixed point $x^* = 7/12 \approx 0.58333$. (Use a pencil and try it yourself on Fig. 7.3.) Such a fixed point is stable (an attractor of period 1). In contrast, no matter how close x_0 is to the fixed point at $x = 0$, the iterates diverge away from it. Such a fixed point is unstable.

How can we explain the qualitative difference between the fixed points $x^* = 0$ and $x^* = 0.58333$ for $r = 0.6$? The local curvature of the curve $y = f(x)$ determines the distance moved horizontally each time f is iterated. A steep slope (greater than 45 degrees) leads to a value of x further away from its initial value. Hence the criterion for the stability of a fixed point is that the magnitude of the slope at the fixed point must be less than 45 degrees. That is, if $|df(x)/dx|_{x=x^*} < 1$, then x^* is stable; conversely if $|df(x)/dx|_{x=x^*} > 1$, then x^* is unstable. Inspection of $f(x)$ in Fig. 7.3 shows that $x = 0$ is unstable because the slope of $f(x)$ at $x = 0$ is greater than unity. In contrast the magnitude of the slope of $f(x)$ at $x = 0.58333$ is less than unity. In Appendix 7A, we use similar analytical arguments to show that

$$x^* = 0 \ is \ stable \ for \ 0 < r < 1/4 \qquad (7.7a)$$

and

$$x^* = 1 - \frac{1}{4r} \ is \ stable \ for \ 1/4 < r < 3/4 \ . \qquad (7.7b)$$

Thus for $0 < r < 3/4$, the eventual behavior after many iterations is known.

What happens if r is in the range $3/4 < r < 1$? We know from our observations that as r is increased, the fixed point of f becomes unstable and gives birth (bifurcates) to a cycle of period 2. Now x returns to the same value only after every second iteration, i.e.

$$x_i = f(f(x_i)) \qquad i = 1, 2 \tag{7.8}$$

and the attractors of $f(x)$ are the fixed points of $g(x) = f(f(x))$. What happens as we increase r still further? Eventually the magnitude of the slope of the fixed points of $g(x)$ exceeds unity and the fixed points of g bifurcate. Now the cycle of f is period 4 and we can study the stability of the fixed points of the fourth iterate $h(x) = g(g(x)) = f(f(f(f(x))))$. These fixed points will also eventually bifurcate, and we are led to the phenomena of *period-doubling*, i.e. period 1 → period 2 → period 4 → period 8 → period 16 → period 32 → ... as we observed in Problem 7.4.

Program map_graph implements the graphical analysis of $f(x)$. Note that in the definition of $f(x, r, iterate)$, the second iterate $g(x) = f(f(x))$ and the fourth iterate $h(x) = g(g(x)) = f(f(f(f(x))))$ are defined using recursion, that is, the function calls itself. (The quantity *iterate* is 1, 2, and 4 for the functions $f(x)$, $g(x)$ and $h(x)$ respectively.)

```
PROGRAM map_graph
CALL parameter(x,r,iterate)
CALL graph(r,iterate)
CALL map(x,r,iterate)
END

SUB parameter(x,r,iterate)
  INPUT prompt " r = ": r
  INPUT prompt "initial x = ": x
  INPUT prompt "iterate of f(x) = ": iterate
END SUB
```

```
SUB graph(r,iterate)
  DECLARE DEF f
  LET n = 200                        ! number of points at which function computed
  LET delta = 1/n
  LET margin = 0.1
  SET window -margin,1 + margin,-margin,1 + margin
  PLOT LINES: 0,0;1,1               ! draw line y = x
  PLOT LINES: 0,1;0,0;1,0           ! draw axes
  PLOT
  FOR i = 1 to n
     LET x = x + delta
     LET y = f(x,r,iterate)
     PLOT x,y
  NEXT i
END SUB

SUB map(x,r,iterate)
  DECLARE DEF f
  LET n = 100                        ! number of iterations of map
  LET y0 = 0
  LET x0 = x
  FOR i = 1 to n
     LET y = f(x,r,iterate)
     PLOT LINES: x0,y0; x0,y; y,y
     LET x0 = y
     LET y0 = y
     LET x = y
  NEXT i
END SUB

DEF f(x,r,iterate)                   ! f defined by recursive procedure
  IF iterate > 1 then
     LET y = f(x,r,iterate - 1)
     LET f = 4*r*y*(1 - y)
  ELSE
     LET f = 4*r*x*(1 - x)
  END IF
END DEF
```

In Problem 7.4, we use **Program map_graph** to explore the dynamical properties of the standard map and its higher order iterates.

PROBLEM 7.4 Qualitative properties of the fixed points

a. Use **Program map_graph** to show graphically that there is a single stable fixed point of $f(x)$ for $r < 3/4$. The function $f(x)$ is symmetrical about $x = 1/2$, at which $f(x)$ is a maximum. What are the qualitative features of the second iterate $g(x) = f(f(x))$? Is $g(x)$ symmetrical about $x = 1/2$? Is x^* also a fixed point of $g(x)$? For what value of x does $g(x)$ have a minimum? Let r_1 denote the value of r at which the fixed point of $f(x)$ becomes unstable and verify that $r_1 = 0.75$.

b. Describe the orbit of $f(x)$ for $r = 0.785$. What is the period of $f(x)$? What are the numerical values of the unstable attractors? Iterate $g(x)$ and find its two fixed points x_1^* and x_2^*. (Try the seeds $x_0 = 0.1$ and $x_0 = 0.3$.) Are the fixed points of g stable or unstable? How do the values of x_1^* and x_2^* compare with the values of the unstable attractors of $f(x)$? Verify that the slopes of $g(x)$ at x_1^* and x_2^* are equal.

c. Verify the following properties of the fixed points of $g(x)$. As r is increased the fixed points of $g(x)$ move apart and the slope of $g(x)$ at the fixed points decreases. What is the value of $r = r^{(1)}$ when one of the fixed points of g equals $1/2$? What is the value of the other fixed point? At this value of r both slopes at the fixed points equal zero. As r is further increased, the slopes at the fixed points become negative. Finally at $r = r_2 \approx 0.8623$, the slopes at the two fixed points of $g(x)$ equal -1 and the two fixed points of g become unstable.

d. Show that for r slightly greater than r_2, e.g. $r \approx 0.87$, there are four stable fixed points of the function $h(x) = g(g(x))$. What is the value of $r = r^{(2)}$ when one of the fixed points equals $1/2$? What are the values of the three other fixed points at $r = r^{(2)}$? At what value of $r = r_3$ do the four fixed points of h become unstable?

7.4 UNIVERSAL PROPERTIES OF NON-LINEAR MAPS

So far our observations have been applied to the simple map (7.6). In order to determine the generality of period doubling, we consider two other one-dimensional maps in Problem 7.5.

PROBLEM 7.5 Additional one-dimensional maps

Perform numerical experiments to determine the qualitative properties of the maps

$$f(x) = xe^{r(1-x)} \tag{7.9}$$

$$f(x) = r[1 - (2x - 1)^4] \quad . \tag{7.10}$$

What is the behavior of (7.9) for $r \sim 2$ and $r \sim 2.7$? Note that r and the initial value of x must be between 0 and 1 for the map (7.10). Do these maps exhibit similar qualitative properties, for example period doubling and a chaotic region? The map (7.9) has been used by ecologists (cf May) to study a population limited at high densities by the effect of epidemic disease. Although it is more complicated than (7.6), this map has the compensatory advantage that the population remains positive no matter what positive value is taken for the initial population. There are no restrictions on the maximum value of r, but if r becomes large enough, x will eventually become effectively zero, thus rendering the population extinct.

We will find in the following discussion that it is convenient to define the "order" of a map. Let x_{max} be the value of x where $f(x)$ is a maximum, i.e. $df/dx = 0$ at $x = x_{max}$. If $d^m f/dx^m = 0$ for $m < n$ and $d^n f/dx^n < 0$ at $x = x_{max}$, then $f(x)$ is a nth order map. Show that this criterion implies that the maps (7.6) and (7.9) are second-order or quadratic. In contrast, show that the map (7.10) is a fourth-order map, i.e. $d^2 f/dx^2 = d^3 f/dx^3 = 0$, but $d^4 f/dx^4 < 0$ at $x = 1/2$.

We now give qualitative arguments to indicate that some of the quantitative properties of the standard quadratic map (7.6) in the period doubling regime apply equally well to all quadratic maps. Consider $f(x, r)$ at a value of r such that $f(x, r)$ has period 4 (see Fig. 7.4).

Next let us consider the second iterate $g(x, r) = f(f(x, r))$ for the same value of r (see Fig. 7.5). Clearly $g(x, r)$ has period 2 and for the seed $x_0 = 0.5$, $g(x, r)$ oscillates between the two fixed points $x_1^* = 0.373$ and $x_2^* = 0.512$. We can see that $g(x, r)$ is qualitatively similar to $f(x, r')$, where r' is a smaller value of r such that $f(x, r')$ has period 2. In Fig. 7.6, we show $f(x, r')$ for the arbitrarily chosen value $r' = 0.8$. Note that $f(x, r = 0.8)$ oscillates between 0.513 and 0.799. Now compare the shape of $g(x, r = 0.88)$ within its circulation square in Fig. 7.5 and the shape of $f(x, r' = 0.8)$ within its circulation square shown

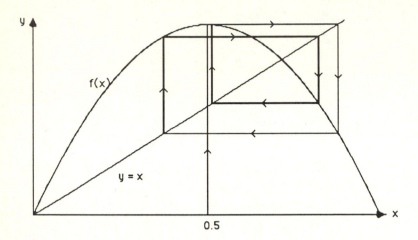

Fig. 7.4 Iterations of $f(x)$ for $r = 0.88$. Note that for this value of r, $f(x)$ has period 4.

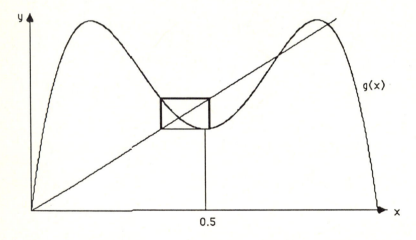

Fig. 7.5 Iterations of $g(x)$ for $r = 0.88$ starting from $x_0 = 0.5$. Note the shape of $g(x)$ in the "circulation square" bounded by $x_1{}^* = 0.373$ and $x_2{}^* = 0.512$.

in Fig. 7.6. We see that if we flip g about the horizontal axis passing through the center of the square and then *magnify* g so that the circulation squares of f and g are of the same size, the two functions within the square are qualitatively similar. We can determine the magnification factor α by noting that the range of $g(x, r = 0.88)$ is $0.512 - 0.373 = 0.139$ and the range of $f(x, r = 0.8)$ is $0.799 - 0.513 = 0.286$. Hence if we choose $\alpha = 0.286/0.139 = 2.06$, the two functions should exhibit similar shape. This procedure is illustrated in Fig. 7.7, where we have superimposed the circulation squares of $f(x, r = 0.8)$ and $g(x, r = 0.88)$

The above argument is an example of a *scaling* argument; we scaled g and changed *(renormalized)* the value of r in order to compare g to f. (See Chapter 12 for a discussion of scaling and the renormalization in another context.) Our arguments were only meant to be suggestive. For example, we did not give a reason for choosing $r' = 0.8$. It turns out that it is sufficient to compare circulation squares for r-values corresponding to the fixed point $x = 1/2$ and the fixed point closest to $x = 1/2$. A precise approach shows that if we continue the comparison of the higher order iterates, e.g. $h(x)$ to $g(x)$, etc., the superposition of functions will converge to a universal function which is independent of the form of the original function $f(x)$ for all maps of the same order.

We can determine the number α by a related argument. Look at the "pitchfork" bifurcations in Fig. 7.3 and Fig. 7.8. Note that each pitchfork gives birth to "twins" with the new generation more densely packed than the previous generation. In order to quantify this increased density of fixed points, consider the

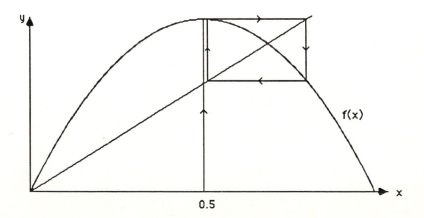

Fig. 7.6 The two-cycle behavior of $f(x)$ for $r = 0.8$. Compare the form of $f(x)$ in the circulation square bounded by $x_1^* = 0.513$ and $x_2^* = 0.799$ to the form of $g(x)$ in the circulation square shown in Fig. 7.5.

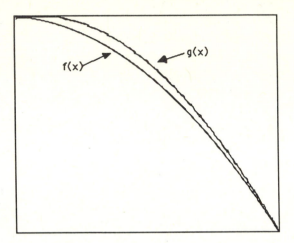

Fig. 7.7 The superposition of the suitably magnified circulation squares of $f(x, r = 0.8)$ and $g(x, r = 0.88)$.

behavior of $f(x)$ at $r = r^{(n)}$ for which one of the fixed points is $1/2$. For example in Problem 7.4, we found $r^{(1)} \approx 0.809$ and $r^{(2)} \approx 0.875$. One measure of the density is the quantity $d_n = x_n{}^* - 1/2$, where $x_n{}^*$ is the value of the fixed point nearest to the fixed point $x^* = 1/2$. The first two values of d_n are shown in Fig. 7.8, where $d_1 \approx 0.309$ and $d_2 \approx -0.117$. Note that the fixed point nearest to $x = 1/2$ alternates from one side of $x = 1/2$ to the other. We define the quantity α by the ratio

$$\alpha = \lim_{n \to \infty} -\frac{d_n}{d_{n+1}} \quad . \tag{7.11}$$

The estimate $\alpha = 0.309/0.117 = 2.64$ is consistent with our earlier estimate and the asymptotic limit $\alpha = 2.50290787509589284855 \ldots$. (The number of decimal places is shown to indicate that this number is known rather precisely!)

We can quantify the period doubling behavior and the transition to chaos still further. Recall that r_n is the value of r at which a 2^n cycle first appears. In Problem 7.4, we found $r_1 = 0.75$, $r_2 \approx 0.862$, and $r_3 \approx 0.880$. As n becomes very large, Feigenbaum showed (using a calculator) that r_n approaches the limiting value r_c in a simple manner:

$$r_n - r_c = A\delta^{-n} \quad . \tag{7.12}$$

The remarkable result of Feigenbaum's work is that the constant δ like α is *universal*. That is, δ is independent of the detailed properties of $f(x)$ and depends only on the order of the map. In contrast, the constant A depends on the detailed structure of $f(x)$. It is straightforward to show that (7.12) implies that δ can also be determined by the relation

$$\delta = \lim_{n \to \infty} \frac{r_{n+1} - r_n}{r_{n+2} - r_{n+1}} \,. \tag{7.13}$$

If we use the above values of r_1, r_2, and r_3, we find $\delta \approx 6.22$; the asymptotic result is $\delta = 4.66920160910299097\ldots$.

PROBLEM 7.6 Further estimates of the universal exponents α and δ

a. Use arguments similar to those discussed in the text and compare the behavior of $g(x)$ in its circulation square about $x = 1/2$ for $r = r^{(2)} \approx 0.875$ to the behavior of $f(x)$ about its corresponding circulation square for $r^{(1)} \approx 0.809$. Find the appropriate scaling factor α and superimpose f and the rescaled form of g.

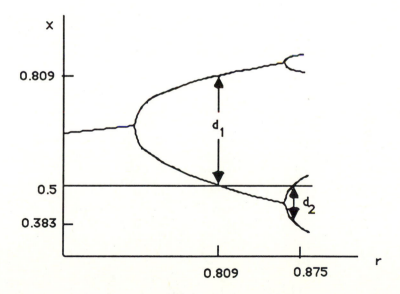

Fig. 7.8 Values of x as a function of the growth parameter r. The quantity d_n is the distance from $x^* = 1/2$ to the nearest element of the attractor of period 2^n.

b. Do an analysis similar to part (a) and compare $h(x)$ at $r = r^{(3)} \approx 0.880$ to $g(x)$ at $r = r^{(2)}$. Determine the scaling factor α and superimpose the two functions.

c. Compute the values of r_n for the $8 \to 16$ and $16 \to 32$ period doublings. Use these values of r_n to improve your estimate for δ.

d. Obtain additional values for $r^{(n)}$, the values of r at which the 2^n iterates of $f(x)$ have a fixed point at $x^* = 1/2$. Obtain additional estimates of δ by using (7.13) with r_n replaced by $r^{(n)}$.

*e. Calculate α and δ for the maps (7.9) and (7.10).

From the above considerations we can conclude that there are *universal* quantities α and δ which are independent of the detailed form of $f(x)$. Why is the universality of the bifurcation process and the existence of the universal numbers δ and α more than a curiosity? One reason is that it is unlikely that a population will evolve exactly according to the map (7.6) or any other simple map of the type we have discussed. However, if the behavior is independent of the details, then there might exist realistic systems whose underlying dynamics would yield the same behavior as the simple maps we have discussed. If the underlying dynamics were similar, we would then know that the dynamics of a system with many degrees of freedom could be simplified under certain circumstances.

Of course physical systems are usually described by differential rather than difference equations. Can these systems exhibit period doubling behavior? Several workers (cf Testa et al.) have constructed non-linear RLC circuits driven by an oscillatory source voltage. The output voltage shows bifurcations and the measured values of α and δ are consistent with the predictions of the simple quadratic map.

Since electrical circuits can be described by a few variables, it might not seem surprising that they show similar behavior. Of more interest is the nature of turbulence in fluid systems, one of the major areas of research by scientists of many disciplines. Consider for example a stream of water flowing past several obstacles. From our experience we know that at low flow speeds, the water flows past obstacles in a regular and time-independent fashion, called *laminar* flow. As the flow speed is increased (as measured by a dimensionless parameter called the Reynolds number), some swirls develop but the motion is still time-independent. As the flow speed is increased still further, the swirls break away and start moving downstream. The flow pattern as viewed from the bank becomes time-dependent. For still larger flow speeds, the flow pattern becomes very complex and looks chaotic. We say that the flow pattern has made a transition from laminar flow to *turbulent* flow.

This qualitative description of the transition to chaos in fluid systems is superficially similar to the description of the simple quadratic map. Can fluid systems be analyzed in terms of the simple models of the type we have discussed here? In a few specialized instances such as turbulent convection in a heated saucepan, period-doubling and other types of transitions to turbulence have been observed. In general, the type of theory and analysis we have discussed has been suggestive of new concepts and approaches. However, genuine understanding of turbulent flows remains a subject of much current investigation.

*7.5   CHAOTIC BEHAVIOR IN CLASSICAL MECHANICS

Since at least some of the qualitative features of the quadratic map appear in laboratory systems, it is interesting to consider the dynamical properties of a mechanical system described by a differential equation rather than a difference equation. The general problem in classical mechanics is the determination of the positions and velocities of a system of particles subjected to certain forces. For example, we considered in Chapter 4 the celestial two-body problem and were able to predict the motion at any time. It is remarkable that we are not able to make long-time predictions for most orbits. Most mechanical systems must be solved approximately using a combination of analytical and numerical methods. Under certain conditions these systems exhibit chaos, i.e. their orbits are very sensitive to the initial conditions and to any approximations made in calculating the orbit. (Remember our results in Problem 7.2b for the orbit of the standard map in the chaotic regime.) Classical mechanics is not as simple as described in traditional textbooks!

The specific example of a non-linear system we consider is the familiar simple pendulum (see Chapter 5). In order to make its dynamics more interesting, we assume that there is a linear damping term present and that the pivot is forced to move vertically. Newton's second law for this system is (McLaughlin, also see Percival and Richards)

$$\frac{d^2\theta}{dt^2} = -\gamma\frac{d\theta}{dt} - [\omega_0{}^2 + 2A\cos\omega t]\sin\theta \tag{7.14}$$

where θ is the angle the pendulum makes with the vertical axis, γ is the damping coefficient, $\omega_0{}^2 = g/L$ is the natural frequency of the oscillator, and ω and A are the frequency and amplitude of the external force. Note that the effect of the vertical acceleration of the pivot is equivalent to a time-dependent gravitational field.

Of course we can in principle (and in Problem 7.7) solve for the dynamics of such a system. But how do we analyze our results? In Chapter 5 we analyzed the motion of the harmonic oscillator by constructing a phase space plot, i.e. a plot of the velocity versus the position. (It would be a good idea to complete Problems 5.2g, 5.3d, and 5.5g if you have not done them already.) If the velocity is constant, then the trajectory in phase space is simply a horizontal line. Is it possible to have a vertical line in phase space? For simple harmonic motion, the trajectory in phase space is an ellipse. If there is damping present, the trajectory will spiral toward the origin. What would be the trajectory in phase space for a ball thrown vertically in the air? A phase space plot can take on many forms. If there are no time-dependent forces, it can be shown (cf Marion) that a phase space plot cannot cross itself. Phase space curves which are closed are said to be periodic.

Now how do we expect the driven, damped simple pendulum to behave? Since there is damping present, we expect that if there is no external force, the motion will come to rest. That is $\{x = 0, v = 0\}$ is a stable attractor. For larger A, we can expect steady state periodic motion, i.e. a limit cycle, with the period $T = 2\pi/\omega$ of the external force. Does the system exhibit similar behavior for larger A? Since we are mainly interested in the fixed points (stable and unstable) of the motion, an easy way to analyze the motion is to plot a point in phase space after every cycle of the external force. Thus, we will plot $d\theta/dt$ versus θ for values of t equal to nT. Such a phase space plot is called a *Poincare map*. If the system has a period T, then the Poincare map will consist of a single point. If the period of the system is nT, there will be n points.

Program nonlinear plots a Poincare map for the pendulum described by (7.14). The values of θ and $d\theta/dt$ are printed at $t = nT$ and a box is drawn at $\{\theta, d\theta/dt\}$. If the system has period 1, i.e. if the same values of $\{\theta, d\theta/dt\}$ are drawn at $t = nT$, the box will flicker, indicating that there is already a box at that position. The keys 'i' and 'd' can be pressed to increase or decrease A by an amount dA. Since the first few values of $\{\theta, d\theta/dt\}$ show the transient behavior, it might be desirable to clear the screen and to begin a new Poincare map without changing A, θ or $d\theta/dt$. This clearing can be done by pressing any key other than 'i', 'd' or 's'. The latter key stops the execution of the program.

```
PROGRAM nonlinear                        ! plot Poincare map
CALL initial(theta,ang_vel,gamma,A,n,t,dt,dA,r)
DO
   CALL Euler(theta,ang_vel,gamma,A,n,t,dt)
   CALL Poincare(theta,ang_vel,A,k,dA,r)
LOOP UNTIL k = ord("s")
END

SUB initial(theta,ang_vel,gamma,A,n,t,dt,dA,r)
   INPUT prompt "initial angle = ": theta
   INPUT prompt "initial angular velocity = ": ang_vel
   INPUT prompt "damping constant = ": gamma
   INPUT prompt "amplitude of external force = ": A
   LET n = 500                ! number of iterations between plots
   LET dt = 2*pi/n            ! time step
   LET t = 0                  ! initial time
   LET dA = .01          ! incremental increase in amplitude of external force
   SET WINDOW -4,4,-4,4
   PRINT using "A = #.#####": A
   PLOT LINES: -4,0; 4,0      ! draw axes
   PLOT LINES: 0,-4; 0,4
   LET r = 0.05               ! dimension of box
END SUB

SUB Euler(theta,ang_vel,gamma,A,n,t,dt)          ! use Euler-Cromer algorithm
   FOR i = 1 to n
      LET accel = -gamma*ang_vel
      LET accel = accel - (1 + 2*A*cos(2*t))*sin(theta)
      LET ang_vel = ang_vel + accel*dt
      LET theta = theta + ang_vel*dt
      IF theta > pi then LET theta = theta - 2*pi
      IF theta < -pi then LET theta = theta + 2*pi
      LET t = t + dt
   NEXT i
END SUB
```

```
SUB Poincare(theta,ang_vel,A,k,da,r)
    ! plot points and allow for change in amplitude of external force
    BOX CLEAR theta-r,theta+r,ang_vel-r,ang_vel+r
    BOX AREA theta-r,theta+r,ang_vel-r,ang_vel+r
    SET CURSOR 1,20
    PRINT using "theta = ##.#####": theta
    SET CURSOR 1,40
    PRINT using "ang_vel = ##.#####": ang_vel
    IF key input then
        GET KEY k
        IF k = ord("i") then LET A = A + da
        IF k = ord("d") then LET A = A - da
        CLEAR
        PLOT LINES: -4,0; 4,0             ! redraw axes
        PLOT LINES: 0,-4; 0,4
        PRINT using "A = ##.#####": A
    END IF
END SUB
```

*PROBLEM 7.7 Dynamics of a driven, damped simple pendulum

a. Program nonlinear plots a Poincare map for the driven damped simple pendulum. We choose $\omega_0 = 1$ and $\omega = 2$ so that the period T of the external force equals π. For these parameters, a convenient choice of Δt is $\Delta t = 0.03$. Use $\gamma = 0.2$ and $A = 0.85$ and compute the period of the pendulum. Vary the initial values of θ and $d\theta/dt$. Is the attractor independent of the initial conditions? Remember to ignore the initial transient behavior.

b. The amplitude A plays the role of the control parameter for the dynamics of the system. Find the period and the attractors for $A = 0.1, 0.25, 0.5, 0.7,$ 0.75, 0.85, 0.95, 1.00, 1.02, 1.031, 1.033, 1.036, and 1.05. Note that unlike the quadratic map, the period is 2π for $A < 0.71$, π for $0.72 < A < 0.79$, and then 2π again.

c. In order to see the relation between the results of the Poincare plot and the usual plots of the time-dependence of θ, change **Program nonlinear** so that θ and $d\theta/dt$ are plotted at each time step rather than only when $t = n\pi$. Describe the behavior of the oscillator in each of the cases considered in part (b).

d. The first period doubling occurs for $A \approx 0.79$. Find the values of A for further period doublings and use these values of A to compute the exponent δ defined by (7.13). Compare your result for δ with the result found for the one-dimensional quadratic map. Are your results consistent with those found for the quadratic map?

e. Repeat the the calculations of parts (b)–(d) for $\gamma = 0.05$. What can you conclude about the effect of damping? (The analysis of this system can be found in the article by McLaughlin (1981)).

7.6   A TWO-DIMENSIONAL MAP

At this time you probably have either become very interested in non-linear systems and have already read some of the references, or you are ready to go on to Chapter 8 and consider linear systems again. However, we cannot resist describing in Problem 7.8 a two-dimensional system which exhibits "strange" behavior.

*PROBLEM 7.8 A two-dimensional map

Consider the sequence of points $\{x_n, y_n\}$ generated by the two-dimensional map

$$x_{n+1} = y_n + 1 - a{x_n}^2 \qquad (7.15a)$$
$$y_{n+1} = bx_n \quad . \qquad (7.15b)$$

The map (7.15) was proposed by Henon (see references) who found that the form (7.15) exhibits behavior similar to that found from a set of differential equations proposed in the study of long-range weather patterns.

a. Iterate (7.15) for $a = 1.4$ and $b = 0.3$ and plot the first $10,000$ points starting from the seed $\{x_0 = 0, y_0 = 0\}$. Make sure you compute the new value of y using the old value of x and not the new value of x. Choose the **SET window** statement such that all values of the orbit within the box drawn by the statement **BOX LINES** $-1.5, 1.5, -0.45, 0.45$ are plotted. Make a similar plot beginning from the second seed $\{x_0 = 0.63135448, y_0 = 0.18940634\}$. Compare the shape of the two plots. Is the shape of the two curves independent of the initial conditions?

b. Increase the scale of your plot so that all points with the box drawn by the statement **BOX LINES** $0.50, 0.75, 0.15, 0.21$ are shown. Make a new plot beginning from the second seed and increase the number of computed points to 10^5. Then make another plot showing all points within the box drawn by **BOX LINES** 0.62, 0.64, 0.185, 0.191. If patience permits, make an additional enlargement and plot all points within the box drawn by **BOX LINES** 0.6305, 0.6325, 0.1889, 0.1895. What is the structure of the curves within each box? Do the curves appear to have an underlying structure? (You will have to increase the number of computed points to order 10^6). Do your results suggest that the process of multiplication of "curves" will continue indefinitely and that each "curve" is made of an indefinite number of quasi-parallel curves? Is there a region in the plane from which the points cannot escape? This region is known as the *Henon attractor,* which is an example of a *strange attractor.*

REFERENCES AND SUGGESTIONS FOR ADDITIONAL READING

Ralph H. Abraham and Christopher D. Shaw, *Dynamics—The Geometry of Behavior,* Vols. 1–4, Aerial Press, Santa Cruz, CA (1984). In these four volumes and the Shaw monograph (see below), the authors explain the dynamics of complex dynamical systems using an abundance of visual representations.

Hao Bai-Lin, *Chaos,* World Scientific (1984). A collection of reprints including articles by Feigenbaum, Henon, May, Testa et al. which were cited in this chapter. Also of interest are papers on experimental studies of chaotic phenomena.

James P. Crutchfield, J. Doyne Farmer, Norman H. Packhard and Robert S. Shaw, "Chaos," *Sci. Amer.* **255**, No. 6, 46–57, (December, 1986).

J. P. Crutchfield, J. D. Farmer, and B. A. Huberman, "Fluctuations and Simple Chaotic Dynamic," *Phys. Repts.* **92**, 45 (1982).

Predrag Cvitanovic, *Universality in Chaos,* Adam Hilger (1984). Another reprint collection which includes several of the articles cited in the Bai-Lin collection. Also of interest are reprints on applications to chemical, optical, and biological systems.

Robert Devaney, *Introduction to Chaotic Dynamical Systems,* Benjamin/ Cummings (1986).

J. P. Eckmann, "Roads to turbulence in dissipative dynamical system," *Rev. Mod. Phys.* **53**, 643 (1981).

M. Henon, "A two-dimensional mapping with a strange attractor," *Commun. Math. Phys.* **50**, 50 (1976). Reprinted in the Bai-Lin and Cvitanovic collections.

T. A. Heppenheimer, "Routes to chaos," *Mosaic* **17**, No. 2, pg. 2, (Summer, (1986).

Douglas R. Hofstadter, "Metamagical Themas," *Sci. Amer.* **245**, 22-43, (November, 1981). An expanded version of this article is in Douglas R. Hofstadter, *Metamagical Themas,* Basic Books (1985).

Leo P. Kadanoff, "Roads to chaos," *Physics Today* **36**, 46 (December, 1983).

Jerry B. Marion, *Classical Dynamics of Particles and Systems,* second ed., Academic Press (1970). Chapter 5 discusses phase space plots and non-linear equations in a variety of contexts.

Robert M. May, "Simple Mathematical Models with Very Complicated Dynamics," *Nature* **261**, 459 (1976). Reprinted in the Bai-Lin and Cvitanovic collections.

J. B. McLaughlin, "Period-doubling bifurcations and chaotic motion for a parametrically forced pendulum," *J. Stat. Phys.* **24**, 375 (1981).

E. Ott, "Strange attractors and chaotic motions of dynamical systems," *Rev. Mod. Phys.* **53**, 655 (1981).

Ian Percivel and Derek Richards, *Introduction to Dynamics,* Cambridge University Press (1982). An advanced undergraduate text which introduces many of the ideas of phase curves and the theory of stability. A derivation of the Hamiltonian for the driven damped pendulum considered in Sec. 7.4 is given in Chapter 5, example 5.7.

Robert Shaw, *The Dripping Faucet as a Model Chaotic System,* Aerial Press, Santa Cruz, CA (1984).

James Testa, Jose Perez and Carson Jeffries, "Evidence for universal chaotic behavior of a driven nonlinear oscillator," *Phys. Rev. Lett.* **48**, 714 (1982). (Reprinted in Bao-Lin and Cvitanovic.)

N. B. Tufillaro and A. M. Albano, "Chaotic dynamics of a bouncing ball," *Amer. J. Phys.* **54**, 939 (1986). The authors describe an undergraduate level experiment of a bouncing ball subject to repeated impacts with a vibrating table.

APPENDIX 7A STABILITY OF FIXED POINTS

We derive analytical expressions for the fixed points of the standard quadratic map given by (7.6). The fixed-point condition for $f(x)$ is

$$x^* = f(x^*) \tag{7.16}$$

which using (7.6) yields the two fixed points

$$x^* = 0 \quad and \quad x^* = 1 - \frac{1}{4r} \quad . \tag{7.17}$$

Since x is restricted to be positive, the only fixed point for $r < 1/4$ is $x = 0$. To determine the stability of x^*, we let

$$x_n = x^* + \Delta_n \tag{7.18a}$$

and

$$x_{n+1} = x^* + \Delta_{n+1} \quad . \tag{7.18b}$$

Then since $|\Delta_n| \ll 1$, we have

$$x_{n+1} = f(x^* + \Delta_n) \approx f(x^*) + \Delta_n f'(x^*)$$
$$= x^* + \Delta_n f'(x^*) \quad . \tag{7.19}$$

Hence using (7.18b) and (7.19), we obtain

$$\Delta_{n+1}/\Delta_n = f'(x^*) \quad . \tag{7.20}$$

If $|f'(x^*)| > 1$, then the trajectory will iterate away from x^* since $|\Delta_{n+1}| > |\Delta_n|$. The opposite is true for $|f'(x^*)| < 1$. Thus, the local stability criteria for a fixed point x^* are

1. $|f'(x^*)| < 1$, x^* is stable;
2. $|f'(x^*)| = 1$, x^* is marginally stable;
3. $|f'(x^*)| > 1$, x^* is unstable.

If x^* is marginally stable, the second derivative $f''(x)$ must be considered and the iterates approach x^* with deviations from x^* inversely proportional to the square root of the number of iterations. For $f(x)$ given by (7.6), the derivatives at the fixed points are respectively

$$f'(0) = \frac{d}{dx}[4rx(1-x)]|_{x=0} = 4r \tag{7.21}$$

and

$$f'(x^*) = \frac{d}{dx}[4rx(1-x)]|_{x=1-\frac{1}{4r}} = 2 - 4r \quad . \tag{7.22}$$

It is straightforward to use (7.22) to find the range of r for which $x^* = 0$ and $x^* = 1 - \frac{1}{4r}$ are stable.

WAVE PHENOMENA

8

We simulate a linear chain of coupled oscillators, emphasize the properties of the chain which are applicable to wave phenomena, and obtain the linear wave equation as the limit of a continuous chain. Wave phenomena such as interference, diffraction, refraction and polarization are demonstrated. Fourier series and Fermat's principle are also discussed.

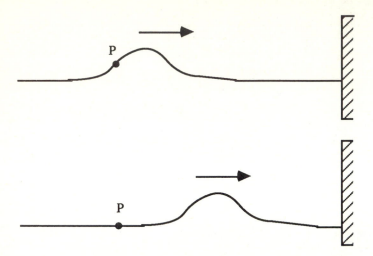

Fig. 8.1 A wave pulse traveling down a stretched rope. The motion of the segment P is localized and is perpendicular to the wave motion.

8.1 INTRODUCTION

We use concepts such as period, amplitude, and frequency to describe both waves and oscillatory motion. In order to understand the relation between the two phenomena, consider a uniform flexible rope which is under tension with one end fixed (see Fig. 8.1). If we flip the other end, a wave pulse will *propagate* along the rope with a speed which depends on the tension and on the inertial properties of the rope. As the wave pulse travels along the rope, each segment of the rope moves up and down perpendicular to the direction of the pulse. We know that at the *macroscopic* level, we observe a transverse wave which moves along the length of the rope and the motion of the individual segments of the rope is not relevant. In contrast, at the *microscopic* level we see discrete particles undergoing oscillatory motion in a direction perpendicular to the motion of the wave.

We begin from a microscopic point of view and consider in Sec. 8.2 the oscillatory motion of a linear chain of particles coupled by springs. For a sufficiently large number of particles in the chain, we can simulate the motion of a longitudinal wave by obtaining numerical solutions to Newton's equations of motion for the individual particles. We find for example that energy is transported along the chain although each oscillator remains near its equilibrium position. We also find that the most general motion of the N particle system can be represented as a superposition of N independent simple harmonic motions. This representation applies more generally, and we introduce in Sec. 8.3 the Fourier series representation of an arbitrary periodic function. In Sec. 8.4 we make the transition from the microscopic to the macroscopic description of a linear chain by obtaining the wave equation for mechanical waves. The properties of solutions to the wave equation are also studied.

The remainder of the chapter is devoted to the analysis of wave motion. In Sec. 8.5 we consider interference and diffraction phenomena, and in Sec. 8.6 we illustrate the different types of polarized waves. In Sec. 8.7 we apply Fermat's principle of least time to problems in geometrical optics.

8.2 COUPLED OSCILLATORS

In Chapter 6 we simulated the dynamics of an N particle system of interacting particles but did not discuss their collective motion, for example the propagation of sound waves. We now discuss a much simpler N particle system for which the propagation of waves can be examined. Our main purpose will be to introduce the concepts of normal modes, beats, and energy propagation.

Consider a one-dimensional chain of N particles each of mass m with equal equilibrium separation a. The particles are coupled by massless springs with force constant k_c, except for the two end springs which have spring constant k (see Fig. 8.2). We let u_i be the displacement from equilibrium of the ith mass along the axis of the system. The ends of the left- and right-hand springs are assumed fixed. We incorporate the condition of fixed endpoints by the condition

$$u_0 = u_{N+1} = 0 \quad . \tag{8.1}$$

Since the force on an individual mass is determined solely by the compression or extension of the adjacent springs, the equation of motion for particle i is given by

$$m\frac{d^2 u_i}{dt^2} = -k_c(u_i - u_{i+1}) - k_c(u_i - u_{i-1}) \cdot$$
$$= -k_c(2u_i - u_{i+1} - u_{i-1}) \qquad i = 2, \ldots, N-1 \quad . \tag{8.2}$$

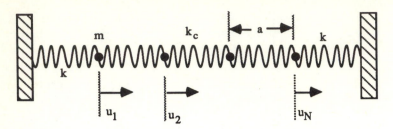

Fig. 8.2 Longitudinal oscillations of mass points connected by massless springs.

The equations for particles $i = 1$ and N next to the walls are given by

$$m\frac{d^2u_1}{dt^2} = -k_c(u_1 - u_2) - ku_1 \tag{8.3a}$$

$$m\frac{d^2u_N}{dt^2} = -k_c(u_N - u_{N-1}) - ku_N \quad . \tag{8.3b}$$

Note that for $k_c = 0$, the above equations for u_i decouple and the motion of mass point is independent of its neighbors. The above equations of motion describe *longitudinal* oscillations, i.e. motion along the length of the system. It is straightforward to show that equations of the same form hold for the *transverse* oscillations of N identical mass points equally spaced on a stretched massless string (cf French).

In order to simulate the dynamical behavior of N coupled masses, we use the Euler-Cromer algorithm to compute the displacements and velocities of the particles. **Program oscillators** graphs the displacement as a function of time for a maximum of four particles. We consider the case where each particle has the same mass, which we set equal to unity.

```
PROGRAM oscillators            ! calculate displacement of N coupled oscillators
DIM u(0 to 21),vel(20)
CALL initial(N,u,vel,kc,k,dt,tmax)
CALL screen(N,nplot,tmax,dy)
CALL move(N,u,vel,kc,k,dt,nplot,tmax,dy)
END
```

```
SUB initial(N,u(),vel(),kc,k,dt,tmax)
   INPUT prompt "number of particles = ": N
   INPUT prompt "time step = ": dt
   INPUT prompt "duration = ": tmax
   INPUT prompt "spring constant kc = ": kc      ! intraspring coupling constant
   LET k = 1                                      ! coupling to walls
   DATA 0.5,0,0                                   ! data for N = 2
   FOR i = 1 to N                                 ! initial conditions
      LET vel(i) = 0
      READ u(i)
   NEXT i
END SUB

SUB screen(N,nplot,tmax,dy)
   LET dy = 2                    ! distance between plots on screen
   SET window -1,tmax + 1,-dy,3*dy
   LET ntick = 100
   LET dx = tmax/ntick           ! distance between ticks
   LET Ly = 0.1*dx               ! "height" of tick marks
   LET nplot = min(4,N)          ! number of oscillators to be graphed
      LET row = -1
      FOR iplot = 1 to nplot
         PLOT LINES: 0,row; tmax,row       ! draw equilibrium displacement
         FOR itick = 1 to ntick            ! draw tick marks
            LET col = itick*dx
            PLOT LINES: col,row; col,row + Ly      ! draw tick marks
         NEXT itick
         LET row = row + dy
      NEXT iplot
END SUB
```

```
SUB move(N,u(),vel(),kc,k,dt,nplot,tmax,dy)
   DIM a(20)
   DO
      LET t = t + dt                      ! time
      FOR i = 2 to (N - 1)                ! accel of particles not connected to wall
         LET a(i) = kc*(u(i+1) + u(i-1) - 2*u(i))
      NEXT i
      LET a(1) = kc*(u(2) - u(1)) - k*u(1)       ! accel of end masses
      LET a(N) = kc*(u(N-1) - u(N)) - k*u(N)
      FOR i = 1 to N           ! Euler-Cromer algorithm
         LET vel(i) = vel(i) + a(i)*dt
         LET u(i) = u(i) + vel(i)*dt
      NEXT i
      LET row = -1
      FOR iplot = 1 to nplot
         PLOT POINTS: t,u(iplot) + row
         LET row = row + dy
      NEXT iplot
   LOOP until t > tmax
END SUB
```

In the following three problems, we explore the effects of the superposition of sinusoidal motions of different frequencies. We will see that, in general, complicated patterns can arise and that these patterns can be described as a superposition of *normal modes* of oscillation.

PROBLEM 8.1 Motion of two coupled oscillators

a. Use **Program oscillators** with N, the number of particles, equal to 2. The arrays $u(i)$, $vel(i)$, and $a(i)$ represent the displacement, velocity, and acceleration of particle i. Set the initial velocities of both particles equal to zero for all runs in this problem. Choose the initial conditions $u_0(1) = 0.5$, $u_0(2) = 0$ and compute the time-dependence of $u(1)$ and $u(2)$ for $\{k = 1, k_c = 0.8\}$ and $\{k = 1, k_c = 1\}$. Determine reasonable values for the time step dt and the time of the run, $tmax$. (Remember that the mass of the particles has been set equal to unity.) Describe the qualitative behavior of $u(1)$ and $u(2)$ in each case. Is it possible to define a period of motion in the first case? What is the period of motion for the second pair of k-values?

b. Set $k = 1$ and $k_c = 0.2$. Since $k_c < k$, we can describe the springs as being *weakly coupled*. Observe the time-dependence of the displacement of particle one. Can you identify two kinds of oscillations superimposed upon each other? What is the time between the oscillations of the amplitude? What is the time between the zeros of the displacement? Compute the corresponding angular frequency of each oscillation. How does the displacement of particle two correspond to that of particle one? Determine the qualitative changes in the frequencies of each oscillation for $k_c = 0.1$.

c. Choose the initial conditions $u_0(1) = u_0(2) = 0.5$ so that both particles have equal initial displacements. Set $k_c = 0.1$ and $k = 1$ and describe the observed motion. Compute the energy (kinetic plus potential) of each particle as a function of time and describe its qualitative behavior. Does the period of motion depend on k_c? What is the dependence of the period on k?

d. Consider the initial conditions $u_0(1) = -u_0(2) = 0.5$ so that both particles have equal but opposite initial displacements. Is there a simple sinusoidal oscillation in this case? Compute the period T_1 for $\{k = 1, k_c = 1\}$, $\{k = 2, k_c = 1\}$ and $\{k = 1, k_c = 2\}$. Analyze your results for ω_1^2 ($\omega_1 = 2\pi/T_1$) and determine the dependence of ω_1^2 on k and k_c. What is the behavior of the energy of each particle as a function of time?

PROBLEM 8.2 Response to an external force

Add an external driving force $F(t)$ to particle 1, such that $F(t) = F_0 \cos \omega t$. Plot $u_1(t)$ and determine its maximum steady-state amplitude $A(\omega)$ for each value of ω. Confirm that near a resonance $A(\omega)$ exhibits a rapid increase with ω, and $u_1(t)$ increases without bound at the resonant frequency. (Remember that the system is not damped.) Determine the resonant frequencies for the pairs of k-values already considered in parts (b)–(d) of Problem 8.1. How do these values of ω compare with those found in Problem 8.1?

PROBLEM 8.3 Superposition of motion

The results in Problems 8.1 and 8.2 make plausible the assumption that an arbitrary motion of the system can be written as

$$u(1) = A_1 \cos(\omega_1 t + \delta_1) + A_2 \cos(\omega_2 t + \delta_2) \tag{8.4a}$$
$$u(2) = A_1 \cos(\omega_1 t + \delta_1) - A_2 \cos(\omega_2 t + \delta_2) \quad . \tag{8.4b}$$

The constants A_1, A_2, δ_1, and δ_2 can be expressed in terms of the initial values of the displacement and velocity of each particle. Determine these constants for $u_0(1) = 0.5$, $u_0(2) = 0$, and $v_0(1) = v_0(2) = 0$. Verify that the motion predicted by (8.4) is consistent with your measured values for $u(1)$ and $u(2)$ for $k = 1$ and $k_c = 0.8$ found in part (a). What is the periodicity of $u(1)$ and $u(2)$?

Let us review the results we found in Problem 8.1 for the two coupled particles. The effect of the spring k_c is to couple the motions of the two particles so that they no longer move independently. For special initial conditions, only one frequency of oscillation appears. The resulting motion is called a *normal mode* and the corresponding frequencies are called the *normal mode frequencies*. The higher frequency is given by $\omega_1 = [(k + 2k_c)/m]^{1/2}$. In this mode, the two particles oscillate exactly out of phase; that is, their displacements are in opposite directions. The motion at the lower frequency $\omega_2 = (k/m)^{1/2}$ corresponds to the two particles oscillating exactly in phase. Why is ω_2 independent of k_c?

The general motion of this two particle system is a superposition of the two normal modes. Unless there is a simple relation between ω_1 and ω_2, the resultant displacement is a complicated function of time. However if the coupling is small, ω_1 and ω_2 are nearly equal and $u(1)$ and $u(2)$ exhibit *beats*. In this case the displacements oscillate rapidly at the angular frequency $\frac{1}{2}(\omega_1 + \omega_2)$ with an amplitude which varies sinusoidally at the beat frequency $\frac{1}{2}(\omega_1 - \omega_2)$. The phenomena of beats is common in nature. You probably have heard two sources of sound with slightly different frequencies, for example two out-of-tune violins playing the same note. The result is perceived as a single sound with a varying loudness.

We also found that if we drive the system by an external force applied to either particle (or both), the system is in resonance if the frequency of the applied force corresponds to either of the normal modes. We use this method for determining the normal mode frequencies in Problems 8.4 and 8.5.

PROBLEM 8.4 Three coupled oscillators

a. Run **Program oscillators** with $N = 3$, $k_c = 0.2$, $k = 1$ and arbitrary but nonzero initial displacements. Describe the time-dependence of the displacement of the particles.

b. Consider the following initial conditions shown in Table 8.1. (The initial velocities are all zero.) If these initial conditions correspond to normal modes, determine the normal mode frequencies.

TABLE 8.1 Initial conditions considered in Problem 8.4b.

	$u_0(1)$	$u_0(2)$	$u_0(3)$
case 1	0.5	0.5	0.5
case 2	0.5	-0.5	0.5
case 3	0.5	0	-0.5

c. Add an external driving force to particle 1 and determine the normal mode frequencies. Compare your results with the frequencies you obtained in part (b). How many normal modes are there?

*PROBLEM 8.5 N coupled oscillators

a. Choose $k_c = k = 1$, and $N = 10$. (The optimum choice of N depends on the speed of your computer and your patience.) Find the normal modes by applying an external force to one of the particles and determine the resonant frequencies. Drive the system for at least several periods of the external force and compute the steady-state amplitude of the displacement of each particle for each value of w. Try values of w in the range $0.2(k/m)^{1/2}$ to $3(k/m)^{1/2}$. If you think that you are close to a resonance, use several other values of w to obtain a better estimate. How many normal modes are there? A more systematic method for determining the normal modes has been given by Williams and Maris (see references) who applied their method to disordered systems with random masses.

b. Compare your results in part (a) with the analytical result

$$\omega_n{}^2 = \frac{4k}{m} sin^2 \frac{n\pi}{2(N+1)} \qquad (8.5)$$

where N is the number of particles and the mode number $n = 1, 2, \ldots, N$.

Another interesting property of a system of coupled oscillators is the propagation of energy. In Problem 8.6, we disturb the chain at one end and determine the time it takes for the disturbance to travel a given distance.

PROBLEM 8.6 Propagation speed in a linear chain

a. Consider a linear chain of coupled oscillators at rest with $k_c = k$. Create a disturbance by giving particle 1 an initial displacement, $u_0(1) = 1$. Determine the time it takes for particles $N/2$ and N to first satisfy the conditions, $|u(N/2)| \geq d$ and $|u(N)| \geq d$. Choose $N = 10$, $k = 1$, and $d = 0.3$ for your initial runs. Use your results to estimate v, the speed of propagation of the disturbance. Consider larger values of N to ensure that your estimate of v is independent of N. (Qualitative results for v are sufficient.)

b. Do you expect the speed of propagation to be an increasing or decreasing function of the spring constant k? Do a simulation and estimate v for different values of k.

c. Create a disturbance by applying an external force $F(t) = \cos \omega t$ to particle 1. Estimate the speed of propagation of the disturbance as in part (a). Set $k = 1$ and consider the values $\omega = 0.1$ and 1. Explain why the propagation speed depends on ω. Can a disturbance propagate for $\omega = 4$? In what way does the system act as a mechanical filter? Explain the "filtering" property of the system in terms of the frequency of the normal modes.

*d. Consider a "disordered" system with different masses assigned to the particles. How does the disorder effect the speed of propagation? (See the article by Williams and Maris for a discussion of related research problems.)

8.3 FOURIER ANALYSIS

In Problem 8.3, we found that the displacement of a particle could be written as a linear combination of normal modes, i.e. a linear superposition of sinusoidal terms. This decomposition of the motion into its various frequencies is more general. It can be shown that, in general, an arbitrary periodic function $f(t)$ of period T can be written as a Fourier series of sines and cosines:

$$f(t) = \frac{1}{2}a_0 + \sum_{n=1}^{\infty}(a_n \cos n\omega_0 t + b_n \sin n\omega_0 t) \tag{8.6}$$

where ω_0 is the fundamental angular frequency given by

$$\omega_0 = \frac{2\pi}{T} . \tag{8.7}$$

The sine and cosine terms in (8.6) for $n = 2, 3, \ldots$ represent the second, third, $\ldots$ harmonics. The *Fourier coefficients* a_n and b_n are given by

$$a_n = \frac{2}{T} \int_{-T/2}^{T/2} f(t)\, cos\, n\omega_0 t\, dt \qquad\qquad (8.8a)$$

$$b_n = \frac{2}{T} \int_{-T/2}^{T/2} f(t)\, sin\, n\omega_0 t\, dt \quad . \qquad\qquad (8.8b)$$

The constant term $\frac{1}{2}a_0$ is the average value of $f(t)$.

In general an infinite number of terms is needed to represent an arbitrary function $f(t)$ exactly. In practice, a good approximation to $f(t)$ can usually be obtained by including a relatively small number of terms. **Program Fourier**, listed in the following, plots the sum (8.6) for various n and helps us visualize the accuracy of our finite sum of harmonic terms.

```
PROGRAM Fourier
DIM a(0 to 100),b(100)
CALL initial(N)
CALL screen(xmin,xmax,ymin,ymax,title$)
CALL coefficients(N,a,b)
CALL plot(N,a,b)
END

SUB initial(N)
    SET CURSOR 1,10
    INPUT prompt "enter number of modes = ": N
END SUB

SUB screen(xmin,xmax,ymin,ymax,title$)
    LET xmin = 0
    LET xmax = 2*pi
    LET ymin = -2
    LET ymax = 2
    LET title$ = "Fourier transform"
    CALL plot_axis(xmin,xmax,ymin,ymax,title$)        ! see Chapter 2 listing
END SUB
```

```
SUB coefficients(N,a(),b())    ! generate Fourier coefficients for special case
    LET a(0) = 0
    FOR imode = 1 to N
        LET a(imode) = 0
        IF mod(imode,2) <> 0 then
            LET b(imode) = 2/(pi*imode)
        ELSE
            LET b(imode) = 0
        END IF
    NEXT imode
END SUB

SUB plot(N,a(),b())                    ! compute Fourier series and plot function
    LET npoint = 100
    LET dx = 2*pi/npoint
    FOR ipoint = 1 to npoint
        LET x = dx*ipoint
        LET f = a(0)/2
        FOR imode = 1 to N
            IF a(imode) <> 0 then LET f = f + a(imode)*cos(imode*x)
            IF b(imode) <> 0 then LET f = f + b(imode)*sin(imode*x)
        NEXT imode
        PLOT LINES: x,f;
    NEXT ipoint
END SUB
```

PROBLEM 8.7 Fourier analysis

a. Use **Program Fourier** to see how a sum of harmonic functions can represent an anharmonic (but periodic) function. Consider the following sum represented by **SUB coefficients**

$$f(t) = \frac{2}{\pi}(sin\, t + \frac{1}{3} sin\, 3t + \frac{1}{5} sin\, 5t + \ldots) \quad . \tag{8.9}$$

What is the form of $f(t)$ if only the first three terms in (8.9) are retained? Increase the number of terms until you are satisfied that (8.9) represents the desired function sufficiently accurately. What function is represented by the infinite sum?

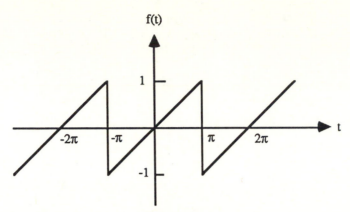

Fig. 8.3 The "sawtooth" function studied in Problem 8.7b.

b. Use (8.8) to show that the Fourier coefficients of the "sawtooth" function shown in Fig. 8.3 are given by $a_n = 0$, $b_n = (2/n\pi)(-1)^{n-1}$ for $n = 1, 2, 3, \ldots$. Modify **Program Fourier** to plot the sum and confirm your results.

c. What function is represented by the sum (8.6) with the coefficients $a_0 = 0$ and $a_n = b_n = 1/n^2$ for $n \neq 0$?

8.4 WAVE MOTION

So far we have stressed the similarities between oscillatory phenomena and wave motion. In particular we found that for a system of N coupled oscillators, the individual oscillations of the particles leads to a propagation of energy over arbitrary distances. The difference between waves and the oscillatory motion of coupled systems is one of scale. In order to understand the transition between oscillatory and wave phenomena, we consider again the longitudinal oscillations of a linear chain of N particles with identical spring constants k and equal equilibrium separation a. The equations of motion can be written as (see (8.1))

$$\frac{d^2 u_i}{dt^2} = -\frac{k}{m}(2u_i - u_{i+1} - u_{i-1}) \quad i = 1, \ldots N \quad . \tag{8.10}$$

We consider the limits

$$N \to \infty, \quad a \to 0 \tag{8.11}$$

with the length of the chain equal to a constant. The main result is that in the limit (8.11), the discrete equations of motion (8.10) can be replaced by the continuous *wave equation*

$$\frac{\partial^2 u(x,t)}{\partial t^2} = \frac{1}{v^2} \frac{\partial^2 u(x,t)}{\partial x^2} \tag{8.12}$$

where v has the dimension of velocity.

The wave equation (8.12) can be obtained as follows. We replace $u_i(t)$, where i is a discrete variable, by the function $u(x,t)$, where x is a *continuous* variable. We then rewrite (8.10) in the form

$$\frac{\partial^2 u(x,t)}{\partial t^2} = \frac{ka^2}{m} \frac{1}{a^2}[u(x+a,t) - 2u(x,t) + u(x-a,t)] \quad . \tag{8.13}$$

We have written the time derivative as a partial derivative since the function u depends on two variables. Since the particles are distributed continuously, we can introduce the quantities $\mu = m/a$ and $T = k/a$. If we use the Taylor series expansion

$$u(x \pm a) = u(x) \pm a\frac{\partial u}{\partial x} + (a^2/2)\frac{\partial^2 u}{\partial x^2} + \dots \tag{8.14}$$

it is easy to show that as $a \to 0$,

$$\frac{1}{a^2}[u(x+a,t) - 2u(x,t) + u(x-a,t)] \to \frac{\partial^2 u(x,t)}{\partial x^2} \quad . \tag{8.15}$$

The substitution of (8.15) into (8.13) leads to the wave equation (8.12) with $v^2 = T/\mu$. (T is the tension and μ is the linear mass density.)

There are many solutions to the wave equation. Examples of solutions are

$$u(x,t) = A\cos\frac{2\pi}{\lambda}(x \pm vt) \tag{8.16a}$$

$$u(x,t) = A\sin\frac{2\pi}{\lambda}(x \pm vt) \quad . \tag{8.16b}$$

In fact it is straightforward to check that any function of the form $f(x - vt)$ or $f(x + vt)$ is a solution to (8.12). Since the wave equation is a linear equation and hence satisfies a superposition principle, we can understand the behavior of a wave of arbitrary shape by using Fourier's theorem to represent its shape as a sum of sinusoidal waves. Hence in the following we need only consider harmonic (sinusoidal) solutions of the wave equation.

We will use **Program waves** to make the nature of the solutions of (8.12) more explicit.

```
PROGRAM waves
CALL initial(A,v,lambda,dt)
CALL screen(A,lambda,dt,xmax,ntime,space)
CALL wavemotion(A,v,xmax,ntime,dt,space)
END

SUB initial(A,v,lambda,dt)
    INPUT prompt "v = ": v              ! cm/sec
    LET A = 1                          ! amplitude of wave
    LET lambda = 2*pi                  ! (cm)
    INPUT prompt "time (sec) between plots = ": dt
END SUB

SUB screen(A,lambda,dt,xmax,ntime,space)
    LET xmax = 6*lambda
    LET ntime = 5                      ! number of times wave is plotted
    LET space = 0.5*A                  ! spacing between plots
    LET ymax = ntime*(space + 2*A) + 1
    SET window -xmax,1.4*xmax,0,ymax
    LET dx = lambda/4
    PRINT "distance between tick marks = "; dx
    LET dy = A/10                      ! height of tick mark
    LET row = A
    LET t = 0
    LET ntick = xmax/dx
    FOR itime = 1 to ntime             ! draw x axis ntime times
        PLOT LINES: -xmax,row; xmax,row
        PLOT TEXT, at xmax,row: using$(" t =##.##",t)
        FOR itick = -ntick to ntick
            PLOT LINES: itick*dx,row; itick*dx,row + dy          ! draw tick marks
        NEXT itick
        LET row = row + space + 2*A
        LET t = t + dt
    NEXT itime
END SUB
```

```
SUB wavemotion(A,v,xmax,ntime,dt,space)      ! plot displacement 5 times
    DECLARE DEF u
    LET npoint = 200
    LET dx = xmax/npoint
    LET row = A                    ! y coordinate on screen for  u = 0
    FOR itime = 1 to ntime
        LET t = t + dt             ! time
        FOR ipoint = -npoint to npoint
            LET x = ipoint*dx
            PLOT x,u(A,v,x,t) + row;
        NEXT ipoint
        PLOT
        LET row = row + space + 2*A
    NEXT itime
END SUB


DEF u(A,v,x,t)
    LET u = A*cos(x - v*t)
END DEF
```

PROBLEM 8.8 Velocity of waves

a. Program waves plots the shape of $u = A\cos(x - vt)$ for a range of values of x and at $ntime = 5$ different times. Set the parameter $v = 1$ and determine the velocity of the wave by measuring the distance a peak moves in the time interval t between plots. Which direction does the wave move for $v > 0$? Set $v = -1$ and determine the direction of the wave.

b. Replace $cos(x - vt)$ by $exp[-(x - vt)^2]$ and answer the same questions as in part (a).

How do we characterize a harmonic wave? Consider the form $u(x, t) = A\cos(kx - \omega t)$, where ω and k are parameters. (The parameter k should not be confused with the spring constant.) This form satisfies the wave equation if $\omega/k = v$. In order to interpret k and ω, we first set $t = 0$ so that $u(x) = A\cos kx$. Since the cosine is a periodic function of its argument, the distance λ between two maxima of u is given by $k\lambda = 2\pi$, or $\lambda = 2\pi/k$. This distance is the *wavelength* and the quantity $k = 2\pi/\lambda$ is the *wave number*. The same argument at a fixed position yields the relation $T\omega = 2\pi$, where T is the *period*. Since the frequency $f = 1/T$, we find that $f = \omega/2\pi$ and hence $v = f\lambda$. In the following, we will often use the parameters k and ω rather than f and λ to characterize a harmonic wave.

PROBLEM 8.9 Superposition of waves

a. Use **Program waves** to observe the propagation of the wave described by the function

$$u(x, t) = \frac{4}{\pi}[1 + sin(x - vt) + \frac{1}{3} sin\, 3(x - vt) + \frac{1}{5} sin\, 5(x - vt)] \quad . \quad (8.17)$$

(It is only necessary to change the definition of the external function in **Program waves**.) What are the values of the wavenumber k represented in (8.17)? Describe the motion of u.

b. Use **Program waves** to observe the propagation of the wave described by the function

$$u(x, t) = sin(x - vt) + sin(x + vt) \quad\quad (8.18)$$

with $v = 1$ cm/s and $2\pi/\lambda = 1$. Describe the resultant wave.

c. Consider the result of two sinusoidal waves of equal amplitude both propagating in the positive x direction but with different frequencies ω_1 and ω_2. Assume that for both waves, $\omega = vk$, where the speed $v = 1$cm/s. The sum of the waves becomes $u(x, t) = A[sin(k_1 x - \omega_1 t) + sin(k_2 x - \omega_2 t)]$. Choose $k_1 = 1.0, k_2 = 1.05$ and modify **Program waves** to follow $u(x, t)$ for different times. Describe the qualitative form of $u(x, t)$ for fixed t. What is the distance between modulations of the amplitude? Estimate the *phase velocity*, the velocity of the fine ripples of the amplitude. The envelope or clump formed by several groups of waves moves with the *group velocity*. Estimate the group velocity for this case. Compare the magnitudes of the phase and group velocities.

In Problem 8.9, the waves of various shapes retained their form as time increased. Such a wave is said to be *nondispersive* and is a consequence of the linear relationship between ω and k, that is, each harmonic of the wave moves with the same speed. If the speed of propagation depends on the wavelength (or wavenumber), the wave is said to be *dispersive* and the form of the wave changes with time. We illustrate this effect in the following problem.

PROBLEM 8.10 Dispersive waves

a. Modify **Program waves** to consider the propagation of the wave form
(8.17) through a dispersive medium in which the speed depends on k according to the relation $v(k) = v_0(1.1 + 0.1k)$ and $\omega(k) = v(k)k$. Modify the
form of $u(x, t)$ to include dispersion. Set $v_0 = 1$ for simplicity. Does the wave
retain its shape? Compute the phase velocity by finding the distance traveled by a given "ripple" of the amplitude. Also compute the group velocity
by measuring the distance traveled by the envelope of the wave. Compare
the magnitude of the phase and group velocities. Note that solutions to the
wave equation (8.12) all have constant propagation velocities independent of
k.

b. Repeat the same computation for the wave form considered in Problem
8.9b.

8.5 INTERFERENCE AND DIFFRACTION

Interference is one of the most fundamental characteristics of all wave phenomena. Conventionally the term *interference* is used when relatively few sources of
waves separately derived from the same source are brought together. However,
the term *diffraction* has a similar meaning and is commonly used if there are
many sources. Since it is relatively easy to observe interference and diffraction
phenomena with light, we will discuss these phenomena in this context.

The classic example of interference involving light is Young's double slit
experiment (see Fig. 8.4). Imagine two narrow parallel slits separated by a distance a and illuminated by a light source which emits light of only one frequency
(monochromatic light). If the light source is placed on the line bisecting the two
slits and the slit opening is very narrow, the two slits become coherent light
sources with equal phase. We will ignore for now the fact that the slits act as
line light sources and assume that they are point sources, e.g. pinholes. A screen
which displays the intensity of the light from the two sources is placed a distance
L away. What do we see on the screen?

The light emitted from a monochromatic point source is a spherical wave of
the form

$$E(r, t) = \frac{A}{r} \cos(kr - \omega t + \phi) \quad . \tag{8.19}$$

The factor of $1/r$ in (8.19) is consistent with the fact that the intensity of the light

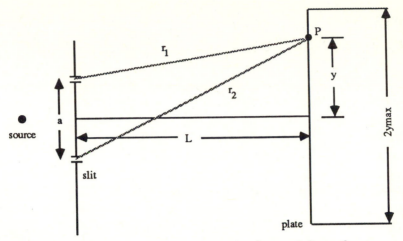

Fig. 8.4 Young's double slit experiment. The figure defines the parameters a, L, y, and $ymax$ which are used in **Program interfere**.

decreases with the distance from the source. We know from the superposition principle that the total electric field at point P (see Fig. 8.4) is

$$E = E_1 + E_2 = \frac{A}{r_1} cos(kr_1 - \omega t) + \frac{A}{r_2} cos(kr_2 - \omega t) \quad . \qquad (8.20)$$

The observed intensity is proportional to the time-averaged value of $|E|^2$.

Program interfere displays the interference pattern due to light emanating from N pinholes. It is assumed that each slit has an equal amplitude harmonic wave propagating from it in all directions. The notation of the program and its main features are summarized in the following:

1. The program plots the time-averaged intensity as a function of the distance y, the distance along the screen (see Fig. 8.4). The most complicated part of the program is defining the parameters to draw the graph. The input parameter $ymax$ is the maximum distance along the screen for which the intensity is to be plotted.
2. The observed intensity of a harmonic wave of the form $E(x,t) = A\, cos[\omega t + \phi]$ is $(1/2)A^2$, where the factor of $1/2$ arises from the time-average. In lieu of averaging over a continuous range of values of t, we instead average the intensity over the set of values $\omega t = 0$, $2\pi/3$ and $4\pi/3$. It is easy to confirm that the cross-terms cancel and that the sum $[cos^2(0+\phi) + cos^2(2\pi/3+\phi) + cos^2(4\pi/3 + \phi)]/3 = 1/2$, independent of ϕ. This average is done in **SUB pattern**.

```
PROGRAM interfere
CALL initial(nslit,a,L,lambda,ymax,nbar)
CALL pattern(nslit,a,L,lambda,ymax,nbar)
END

SUB initial(nslit,a,L,lambda,ymax,nbar)
    INPUT prompt "number of slits = " : nslit
    INPUT prompt "distance between slits (mm) = ": a
    INPUT prompt "distance to the screen (mm) = ": L
    INPUT prompt "wavelength (angstroms)= ": lambda
    INPUT prompt "max. position on photographic plate (mm) = ": ymax
    INPUT prompt "# times to average intensity = ": nbar
    LET lambda = lambda*1e-7          ! convert angstroms to millimeters
    LET Imax = (nslit/L)^2            ! maximum value of intensity
    SET window -1.1*ymax,1.1*ymax,-0.1*Imax,1.1*Imax
    PLOT LINES: -ymax,0;ymax,0        ! draw horizontal axis
    PLOT LINES: 0,Imax;0,0            ! draw intensity axis
    PRINT "intensity versus vertical distance on screen"
    LET dy = lambda*L/a               ! distance between maxima if L >> a
    LET ntick = int(ymax/dy)
    LET Lt = 0.01*Imax                ! height of vertical tick
    FOR itick = -ntick to ntick
        PLOT LINES: i*dy,0; i*dy,Lt
    NEXT itick
END SUB
```

```
SUB pattern(nslit,a,L,lambda,ymax,nbar)
    LET k = 2*pi/lambda              ! wavenumber
    LET npoint = 200                 ! # points in positive y-direction
    LET dy = ymax/npoint             ! distance between points to be plotted
    LET delta = a/(nslit - 1)        ! distance between slits
    LET phase = 2*pi/nbar
    LET L2 = L*L
    FOR ipoint = -npoint to npoint
        LET y = ipoint*dy            ! position on screen
        LET intensity = 0            ! intensity of light
        FOR t = 1 to nbar            ! average over intensity not amplitude
            LET amplitude = 0
            FOR islit = 1 to nslit
                LET yslit =  -0.5*a + (islit - 1)*delta       ! position of slit
                LET yslit = yslit - y  ! vertical distance between slit and point on screen
                LET r2 = L2 + yslit*yslit
                LET r = sqr(r2)          ! distance of slit from screen
                LET amplitude = (1/r)*cos(k*r - phase*t) + amplitude
            NEXT islit
            LET intensity = intensity + amplitude*amplitude
        NEXT t
        LET intensity = intensity/nbar
        PLOT y,intensity;
    NEXT ipoint
END SUB
```

PROBLEM 8.11 Double slit interference

a. Use **Program interfere** to find the intensity of light on a screen a distance L from a double slit. Let a be the distance between the slits and y be the position along the screen. Set $L = 200$ mm, $a = 0.1$ mm, $ymax = 5.0$mm, and the wavelength of light $\lambda = 5000\,\mathring{A}$. The program converts angstroms to millimeters ($1\,\mathring{A} = 10^{-7}$ mm). The quantity $nbar$ is the number of times the intensity is averaged. Observe the interference pattern for $nbar = 1$ and 2. Why is the pattern very jagged for these values of $nbar$? Now let $nbar = 3$ and observe the pattern. Does the pattern change much if $nbar$ is greater than 3? The simple averaging procedure used in **Program interfere** has the same effect as the actual time average that occurs in a real experiment.

b. Vary λ from 4000 to 6000 Å in equal increments. How do the positions of the minima change as a function of λ? What happens if $\lambda = 1$Å?

c. For fixed λ, vary L from 1 to 100 mm. How do the positions of the maxima of the intensity depend on L if $L \gg a$?

One of the original purposes of the double-slit apparatus was to measure the wavelength of light. However, a much better method employs a *diffraction grating*, a large number of evenly spaced parallel slits. In its simplest form, the grating consists of a plane glass sheet with carefully arranged scratches on it. We investigate the intensity pattern from such a grating in Problem 8.12.

PROBLEM 8.12 Multiple slit diffraction

Use **Program interfere** with $\lambda = 5000$ Å, $a = 0.01$mm, $L = 200$ mm, $ymax = 15$ mm, and $nbar = 3$. Consider N, the number of slits, equal to 3, 4, 5 and 10. How does the intensity of the peaks vary with N? Does the separation between the peaks change?

In our analysis of Young's double-slit experiment and the diffraction grating, we assumed that each slit was a pinhole which emitted only one spherical wave. In practice, real slits are much wider than a wavelength of visible light. In Problem 8.13 we consider the pattern of light produced when a plane wave is incident on an aperture such as a single slit. We use *Huygens' principle* and replace the slit by N coherent sources of spherical waves. This equivalence is not exact but is applicable when the aperture width is large compared with the wavelength.

PROBLEM 8.13 Single slit diffraction

a. Compute the intensity of light of $\lambda = 5000$Å from a single slit of width 0.02mm by replacing it by $N = 20$ point sources 0.001 mm apart. Set $L = 200$ mm, $nbar = 3$, and $ymax = 30$ mm and determine the width of the central peak of the intensity. How does the width of the central peak compare to the width of the slit? Do your results change if N is increased?

b. Determine the position of the first minimum of the diffraction pattern as a function of wavelength, slit width, and distance to the screen.

c. Observe the intensity pattern for $L = 1$ mm and 50mm. How do the patterns differ?

PROBLEM 8.14 A more realistic double slit simulation

We now reconsider the intensity distribution for double-slit inteference using slits of finite width. Modify **Program interfere** to simulate two "thick" slits by replacing each slit by 20 point sources spaced 0.001 mm apart. Set the centers of the thick slits 0.1 mm apart. How does the intensity pattern compare with the single and double slit patterns? How does the pattern change with wavelength?

*PROBLEM 8.15 The diffraction pattern due to a rectangular aperture

We can use a similar approach to determine the diffraction pattern due to an aperture of finite width and height. The simplest approach is to divide the aperture into little squares and to consider each square as a source of spherical waves. Similarly we can divide the screen or photographic plate into small regions or cells and calculate the time-averaged intensity at the center of each cell. The necessary calculations are straightforward but time-consuming because of the necessity of evaluating the cosine function many times. The less straightforward part of the problem is deciding how to plot the different values of the calculated intensity on the computer screen. One way to proceed is to plot "points" at random locations in each cell with the number of points proportional to the calculated intensity at the center of the cell. Suggested parameters are $\lambda = 5000\,\text{Å}$, $L = 200$ mm, for an aperture of dimensions 1 mm ×3 mm.

8.6 POLARIZATION

So far we have not been concerned with the direction of oscillation of the wave. For example our description in Sec. 8.1 of the longitudinal oscillations of a linear chain applied equally well to the transverse oscillations of a string. We now consider several phenomena which depend on the *polarization* of the wave.

The specification of the direction of travel of a longitudinal wave automatically specifies the direction of vibration of the medium. For a transverse wave, the only restriction on the direction of oscillation is that it must be in a plane perpendicular to the direction of travel. Let us consider the transverse oscillations of the electric field of an electromagnetic wave propagating in the z-direction. The electric field can be represented by a two-dimensional vector function $\vec{E}(z,t)$

with components $E_x(z,t)$ and $E_y(z,t)$. For ideal monochromatic light, the electric field oscillates at a definite frequency. However, the x and y-components of E oscillate independently and can be represented by

$$E_x(z,t) = E_{x0}\cos(kz - \omega t - \phi) \tag{8.21}$$

$$E_y(z,t) = E_{y0}\cos(kz - \omega t) \tag{8.22}$$

where E_{x0} and E_{y0} are the respective amplitudes and ϕ is the relative phase of the two components. In order to find the electric field produced by (8.21) and (8.22), we add E_x and E_y vectorially to find the resultant $\vec{E}$.

In the following, we use **Program polarize** to help us visualize the nature of $\vec{E}$. The main part of the program shows the time-dependence of the quantities E_x, E_y, and $\vec{E}$ for an "incoming" wave at $z = 0$. The fourth plot represents an "outgoing" wave $\vec{E}(z,t)$ at $z > 0$. This latter plot will be used in Problem 8.17 to represent the effect of passing light through a birefringent material.

Since **Program polarize** is a demonstration program, its output is more hardware and software dependent. For example, we used the animation features of True BASIC to represent the value of E_x and E_y. Since our "tip" is represented by a rectangular box, rather than an arrow or triangle, you might wish to rewrite the program. On the other hand, remember that our purpose is to learn physics rather than to make the ideal visual display. The main features of the program include the following:

1. A horizontal and vertical line is drawn to represent the range of possible values of E_x and E_y. The values of E_x and E_y are calculated according to (8.21) and (8.22), and their "tip" is drawn at the current value of E_x and E_y.
2. The vector sum of E_x and E_y is represented by a rotating straight line whose angle θ with respect to the horizontal is given by $\tan\theta = E_y/E_x$. The previous position of the rotating line is not erased before a new line is drawn a time Δt later. You might wish to modify the program so that most of the line is erased, leaving only the tip of the line to sketch the motion of the tip of the electric field vector.

It is suggested that you run the program first to see the nature of the display before you try to make any changes in it.

```
PROGRAM polarize
CALL initial(Ex,Ey,phase,width,nx,ny,lambda,ymax,tip$,erase$)
CALL polar(Ex,Ey,phase,width,nx,ny,lambda,ymax,tip$,erase$)
END
```

```
SUB initial(Ex0,Ey0,phase,width,nx,ny,lambda,ymax,tip$,erase$)
    INPUT prompt "ratio (>=1) of Ex to Ey = ": ratio
    INPUT prompt "phase difference (rads) = ": phase
    ! following three statements needed for Problem 8.17
    ! INPUT prompt "width of crystal (mm) = ": width
    ! INPUT prompt "index of refraction of crystal in x-direction = ": nx
    ! INPUT prompt "index of refraction of crystal in y-direction = ": ny
    LET lambda = 5.4e-4              ! wavelength (millimeters)
    LET Ex0 = ratio
    LET Ey0 = 1
    LET aspect_ratio = 1.5          ! monitor-dependent
    LET Lmax = 10*ratio             ! horizontal distance
    LET ymax = Lmax/aspect_ratio
    SET window -1,Lmax,-0.5*ymax,0.5*ymax
    PLOT TEXT, at 0.1*Lmax,0.45*ymax: "incoming wave"
    ! PLOT TEXT, at 0.8*Lmax, 0.45*ymax: "outgoing wave"        ! Problem 8.17
    LET r = 0.1                     ! linear dimension of "tip" representing Ex and Ey
    BOX AREA 1,1 + r,1,1 + r
    BOX KEEP 1,1 + r,1,1 + r in tip$
    BOX CLEAR 1,1 + r,1,1 + r
    BOX KEEP 1,1 + r,1,1 + r in erase$
END SUB

SUB polar(Ex0,Ey0,phase,width,nx,ny,lambda,ymax,tip$,erase$)
    LET spacing = 2.5*Ex0           ! horizontal distance between plots
    LET Lx = 0.9*Ex0                ! horizontal position of plot of Ex
    PLOT TEXT, at Lx, 0.25*ymax: "Ex"
    LET Ly = Lx + spacing
    PLOT TEXT, at Ly, 0.25*ymax: "Ey"
    LET Lin = Ly + spacing
    PLOT TEXT, at Lin, 0.25*ymax: "Ein"
    LET Lout = Lin + spacing
    ! PLOT TEXT, at Lout, 0.25*ymax: "Eout"               ! Problem 8.17
    LET t = 0                       ! time
    LET k = 2*pi/lambda             ! wavevector
    LET c = 3e11                    ! speed of light (mm/sec)
    LET w = k*c                     ! angular frequency
    LET dt = 0.1/w
```

```
    DO
      BOX SHOW erase$ at Lx + Ex,0
      PLOT LINES: Lx - Ex0,0;Lx + Ex0,0         ! draw line from -Ex0 to +Ex0
      BOX SHOW erase$ at Ly,Ey
      PLOT LINES: Ly,-Ey0;Ly,Ey0                ! draw line from -Ey0 to +Ey0
      LET t = t + dt
      LET Ex = Ex0*cos(w*t - phase)
      LET Ey = Ey0*cos(w*t)
      ! LET Exout = Ex0*cos(w*t - k*width/nx - phase)     ! Problem 8.17
      ! LET Eyout = Ey0*cos(w*t - k*width/ny)             ! Problem 8.17
      BOX SHOW tip$ at Lx + Ex,0
      BOX SHOW tip$ at Ly,Ey
      PLOT LINES: Lin,0; Lin + Ex,Ey
      ! PLOT LINES: Lout,0; Lout + Exout,Eyout            ! Problem 8.17
    LOOP UNTIL key input
  END SUB
```

In Problem 8.16, we use **Program polarize** to explore the various types of olarized waves.

ROBLEM 8.16 Polarization

a. In **Program polarize**, E_{y0} is set equal to unity and the relative value of E_{x0} is determined by the quantity $ratio = E_{x0}/E_{y0}$. Choose $E_{x0} = E_{y0}$ and $\phi = 0$ and determine the nature of the resultant electric field vector. Why is the resultant oscillation said to be *linearly polarized*? What is the polarization of the wave if $E_{x0} = 2, E_{y0} = 1$, and $\phi = 0$?

b. If the end of the electric field vector travels around a circle, the light is said to be *circularly polarized*. Produce such an oscillation by choosing $E_{x0} = E_{y0} = 1$ and $\phi = \pi/2$. If the end of the electric field vector moves counterclockwise (as viewed from the positive z direction), the light is right-circularly polarized. What is the direction of the polarization for $\phi = \pi/2$? What value of ϕ produces a left-circularly polarized wave?

c. What is the shape of the resultant for $E_{x0} = 2, E_{y0} = 1$, and $\phi = \pi/2$? What is the shape for arbitrary relative values of E_{x0} and E_{y0} and ϕ?

d. The wavelength in **Program polarize** was chosen to be $5400\,\text{Å}$. Vary the wavelength and determine if the wavelength affects the shape of the resultant $\vec{E}$.

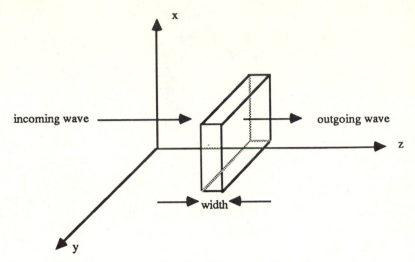

Fig. 8.5 A birefringent material with different indices of refraction in the x- and y-direction.

In some materials such as quartz and calcite, the speed of a wave depends on the direction in which the electric field vector is oscillating. Such materials are called *birefringent* or *doubly refracting*. As demonstrated in Problem 8.17, these materials can be used to change the state of polarization of a ray traversing it (see Fig. 8.5).

PROBLEM 8.17 Quarter-wave plates

Modify **Program polarize** by removing the exclamation points (!) at the beginning of statements which determine the change of state of polarization of a light ray passing through a birefringent material. Let the index of refraction in the x-direction be 1.2 and the index of refraction of light in the y-direction be 1.1. Assume that the light entering the crystal is circularly polarized. Find the width of the crystal *width* (in millimeters) which converts circularly polarized light to linearly polarized light when it emerges from the crystal. What happens when linearly polarized light passes through a crystal of the same width? A birefringent material with this thickness is called a "quarter wave" plate.

8.7 GEOMETRICAL OPTICS AND THE PRINCIPLE OF LEAST TIME

Our everyday experience of light leads naturally to the concept of rays of light, propagating in straight lines and reflected or refracted according to geometrical laws. This description of light propagation, called *geometrical* or *ray optics*, is applicable when the wavelength of light is small compared to the linear dimensions of any obstacles or detectors we might use. Geometrical optics treats the phenomena of reflection, refraction, and the design of lens systems such as telescopes and microscopes.

The propagation of light rays is governed by a simple principle due to Fermat: *A ray of light follows the path between two points (consistent with any constraints) which requires the least amount of time.* Fermat's principle of least time can be adopted as the basis of geometrical optics. Fermat's principle is not the only extremal principle in physics. An analogous principle known as the *principle of least action* can be used instead of Newton's laws of motion as the foundation for all of classical mechanics.

A simple application of the principle of least time is to the path of light from point A to point B in the same medium. Since the velocity is constant along any path within the medium, the path of shortest time is the path of shortest distance, i.e. a straight line from A to B. Hence we reach the rather obvious conclusion that light travels in a straight line in a homogeneous medium. Show what happens if we impose the constraint that the light must strike a mirror before reaching B.

More interesting applications of the principle of least time are to problems of refraction where the light is incident on a surface between two materials where the speed of light is different. It is conventional to give the speed of light in a medium v in terms of the speed of light in a vacuum c and the *index of refraction* n of the medium:

$$n = \frac{c}{v} \quad . \tag{8.23}$$

The indices of refraction of some common substances are given in Table 8.2.

TABLE 8.2 Indices of refraction for visible light for several common substances.

Substance	Index of Refraction
air	1.0003
water	1.33
glass	1.5
diamond	2.4

We consider some of the consequences of the principle of least time in Problems 8.18 to 8.19. Our strategy is to develop a computer program which allows us to draw various paths and to find by trial and error the path of least time. Some of the features of **Program Fermat** are as follows:

1. We consider the propagation of light from left to right through N media (see Fig. 8.6).
2. The coordinates of the light "source" and the "detector" are at $\{0, y(0)\}$ and $\{N, y(N)\}$ respectively where $y(0) = -y(N)$.
3. The width of each region equals unity and the index of refraction is uniform in each region. There are $N - 1$ boundaries separating the N media with the index of refraction $n(i)$ in region i given by $n(i) = n(i) + (i - 1) * dn$. (The index i increases from left to right.) The speed of light in a vacuum is set equal to unity.
4. Since the light propagates in a straight line in each medium, the path of the light is given by the coordinates $y(i)$ at each boundary.
5. The initial path is taken to be a straight line between the two fixed endpoints. The path of light is altered by changing the value of $y(i)$ at the intersection of the path with the boundary between two media. The value of $y(i)$ is changed by moving the cursor to the left or the right until the desired boundary is reached and then moving the cursor up or down.
6. The four possible moves of the cursor are considered with the **SELECT CASE** decision structure which is equivalent to a sequence of else-if statements. The variable to be evaluated is the ASCII code corresponding to a key pressed on the keyboard. If a 'u' or a 'd' key is pressed, the point on the path is moved up or down by an amount *delta*. Similarly, pressing the 'l' or 'r' moves the cursor to the left or right respectively. Typing 's' stops the program.
7. As the path is changed, the new path is drawn while the current "best" path is redrawn. The current minimum path time and the time of the trial path are shown on the screen.

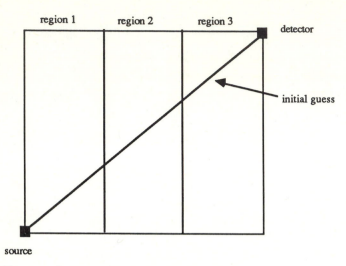

Fig. 8.6 Nature of screen for **Program Fermat**.

```
PROGRAM Fermat
DIM y(0 to 30),ybest(0 to 30)
CALL initial(y,ybest,N,tpath,tbest,dn,delta,cursor$,rx,ry)
CALL path(y,ybest,N,tpath,tbest,dn,delta,cursor$,rx,ry)
END

SUB initial(y(),ybest(),N,tpath,tbest,dn,delta,cursor$,rx,ry)
    INPUT prompt "number of regions = ": N
    INPUT prompt "change in index of refraction = ": dn
    INPUT prompt "y coordinate of detector = ": y(N)
    LET y(0) = -y(N)                  ! position of source
    LET ybest(0) = y(0)              ! end coordinates fixed
    LET ybest(N) = y(N)
    LET slope = (y(N) - y(0))/(N)      ! slope of initial path
    FOR i = 1 to N
        LET y(i) = y(0) + slope*i
        LET ybest(i) = y(i) ! initial guess straight line between source and detector
    NEXT i
    ! each region has width 1
    SET window -1,N + 1,y(0),y(N)
    BOX LINES 0,N,y(0),y(N)              ! draw box around region
```

```
   FOR i = 1 to (N - 1)
      PLOT LINES: i,y(0); i,y(N)        ! draw vertical lines separating regions
   NEXT i
   LET ry = 0.1
   LET rx = 0.02
   BOX AREA - rx,rx,y(0) - ry,y(0) + ry        ! draw box at detector and source
   BOX AREA N - rx,N + rx,y(N) - ry, y(N) + ry
   LET ry = 0.025
   LET rx = 0.01
   BOX KEEP N - rx,N + rx, y(N) - ry,y(N) + ry in cursor$
   FOR i = 1 to N
      PLOT LINES: i,y(i); i-1,y(i-1)
      PLOT LINES: i,ybest(i); i-1,ybest(i-1)
      LET dy2 = (y(i) - y(i-1))*(y(i) - y(i-1))
      LET length = sqr(1 + dy2)                ! length of path
      LET tpath = tpath + length*(1 + (i-1)*dn)
   NEXT i
   LET tbest = tpath
   LET delta = 0.01*abs(y(N) - y(0))        ! change in path for one key input
   PRINT using "time of trial path =##.###": tpath
   PRINT using "best time among trials =##.###": tbest
END SUB

SUB path(y(),ybest(),N,tpath,tbest,dn,delta,cursor$,rx,ry)
   LET i = 1                        ! start at boundary between region 1 and 2
   BOX SHOW cursor$ at i-rx,y(i)-ry
   DO
      LET choice = 0
      IF key INPUT then                ! input u,d,l,r or s
         GET KEY choice
         SELECT CASE choice

         CASE 108                    ! move cursor to left
            IF i > 1 then
               LET deltax = -1
               CALL boundary(y,i,deltax,cursor$,rx,ry)
            END IF
```

```
          CASE 114                    ! move cursor to right
             IF i < N - 1 then
                LET deltax = 1
                CALL boundary(y,i,deltax,cursor$,rx,ry)
             END IF
          CASE 117                    ! move cursor up
             CALL newpath(y,ybest,i,N,tpath,tbest,dn,delta,cursor$,rx,ry)
          CASE 100                    ! move cursor down
             CALL newpath(y,ybest,i,N,tpath,tbest,dn,-delta,cursor$,rx,ry)
          CASE ELSE      ! needed if key other than u, d, l, r or s is pressed
          END SELECT
       END IF
    LOOP until choice = ord("s")
END SUB

SUB boundary(y(),i,deltax,cursor$,rx,ry)
    BOX CLEAR i - rx,i + rx, y(i) - ry,y(i) + ry              ! erase cursor
    PLOT LINES: i,y(i) - ry; i,y(i) + ry       ! redraw line which was partially erased
    LET i = i + deltax
    BOX SHOW cursor$ at i - rx,y(i) - ry
END SUB

SUB newpath(y(),ybest(),i,N,tpath,tbest,dn,delta,cursor$,rx,ry)
    CALL erase(i,y,rx,ry)
    LET y(i) = y(i) + delta
    CALL draw(i,y,ybest)
    BOX SHOW cursor$ at i - rx,y(i) - ry
    CALL pathtime(N,i,dn,delta,y,ybest,tpath,tbest)
END SUB

SUB erase(i,y(),rx,ry)
    BOX CLEAR i - rx,i + rx,y(i) - ry,y(i) + ry
    SET color "background"
    PLOT LINES: i,y(i); i - 1,y(i-1)
    PLOT LINES: i,y(i); i + 1,y(i+1)
END SUB
```

```
SUB draw(i,y(),ybest())
   SET color "black"
   PLOT LINES: i,y(i); i - 1,y(i-1)
   PLOT LINES: i,y(i); i + 1,y(i+1)
   PLOT LINES: i,ybest(i); i - 1,ybest(i-1)
   PLOT LINES: i,ybest(i); i + 1,ybest(i+1)
END SUB


SUB pathtime(N,i,dn,delta,y(),ybest(),tpath,tbest)
   LET v1 = 1/(1 + (i-1)*dn)          ! velocity of light in region i - 1
   LET v2 = 1/(1 + i*dn)              ! velocity of light in region i
   LET dy2 = (y(i) - y(i-1))*(y(i) - y(i - 1))
   LET t1 = sqr(1 + dy2)/v1           ! time of path in region i - 1
   LET dy2 = (y(i) - y(i+1))*(y(i) - y(i+1))
   LET t2 = sqr(1 + dy2)/v2           ! time of path in region i
   LET dy2 = (y(i) - delta - y(i-1))*(y(i) - delta - y(i-1))
   LET t1old = sqr(1 + dy2)/v1
   LET dy2 = (y(i) - delta - y(i+1))*(y(i) - delta - y(i+1))
   LET t2old = sqr(1 + dy2)/v2
   LET tpath = tpath + t1 + t2 - t1old - t2old
   IF tpath <= tbest then
      LET tbest = tpath
      FOR j = 1 to N
         SET color "background"
         PLOT LINES: j,ybest(j); j - 1,ybest(j-1)          ! erase old "best" path
         SET color "black"
         PLOT LINES: j,y(j); j - 1,y(j-1)                  ! draw new best path
      NEXT j
      FOR j = 1 TO N
         LET ybest(j) = y(j)
      NEXT j
   END IF
```

```
     IF delta > 0 then
        PLOT LINES: i,y(i) - 2*delta; i,y(i) + delta
     ELSE
        PLOT LINES: i,y(i) + delta; i,y(i) - 2*delta
     END IF
     SET cursor 4,1
     PRINT using "time of trial path =##.###": tpath
     PRINT using "best time among trials =##.###": tbest
  END SUB
```

PROBLEM 8.18 The law of refraction

a. Use **Program Fermat** to determine the angle of incidence θ_1 and the angle of refraction θ_2 between two media of different indices of refraction. The angles θ_1 and θ_2 are measured from the normal to the boundary. Set $N = 2$ and let the first medium be air ($n \approx 1$) and the second medium be glass ($n \approx 1.5$). A reasonable value of $y(N)$, the coordinate of the detector, is $y(N) = 3$. (The "default" value of the coordinate of the source $y(0)$ is $-y(N)$ and the default value of *delta*, the incremental vertical change of the path, is 1% of $[y(N) - y(0)]$.) After you have found the path of least time, "copy" the screen and measure the angle of incidence θ_1 and the angle of refraction θ_2.

b. Modify the program so that the first medium represents glass and the second medium represents water ($n \approx 1.33$). Verify that your results in (a) and (b) are consistent with Snell's law: $n_2 \sin\theta_2 = n_1 \sin\theta_1$.

c. What is the fractional change in the time of the path for paths near the initial "guess"? What is the fractional change in the time of the path for paths near the optimum path? Which fractional change is smaller? As discussed by Feynman et al. (see references), a better way to state Fermat's principle is that light takes a path such that there are many other paths nearby which take almost the *same* time.

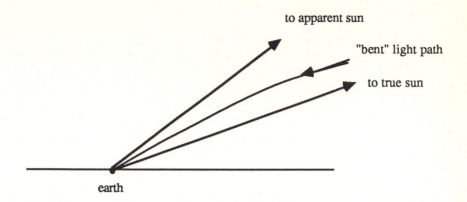

Fig. 8.7 Near the horizon, the apparent (exaggerated) position of the sun is higher than the true position of the sun.

PROBLEM 8.19 Spatially varying index of refraction

a. In order to obtain practice in finding the least path for many boundaries, run **Program Fermat** with $N = 3$ and 4, $y(N) = 3$, and $dn = 0.2$. How quickly can you make your trial paths converge to the least time?

b. Suppose we have a medium in which the index of refraction is spatially dependent. An example is the earth's atmosphere which is thin at the top and dense near the earth's surface. We can model such an inhomogeneous medium by dividing the system into equal width segments each of which is assumed to be homogeneous. The index of refraction of region i is $n(i) = 1 + (i - 1)*dn$. Run **Program Fermat** for $N = 10$ and $dn = 0.01$ and find the path of least time. Use your results to explain the fact that when we see the sun set it is already below the horizon (see Fig. 8.7). An example of a similar phenomenon is the mirage that can be seen while driving on hot roads. The road ahead might appear "wet" although in reality it is dry. Since the air near the road surface is very hot, it is less dense than the air up higher. Use your results to explain the origin of such a mirage.

REFERENCES AND SUGGESTIONS FOR FURTHER READING

Frank S. Crawford, *Waves,* Berkeley Physics Course, Vol. 3, McGraw-Hill (1968). A delightful book on waves of all types. The home experiments are highly recommended. One observation of wave phenomena equals many computer demonstrations.

N. A. Dodd, "Computer simulation of diffraction patterns", Phys. Educ. **18**, 294 (1983).

Robert M. Eisberg and Lawrence S. Lerner, *Physics,* Vol. II, McGraw-Hill (1981). The authors of this introductory text discuss Fermat's principle as well as traditional topics in optics and waves.

David Falk, Dieter Brill and David Stork, *Seeing the Light,* Harper and Row (1986). A beautifully illustrated book on optical phenomena written for the non-science major. In spite of its lower level, the authors discuss Babinet's principle, a subject many intermediate level optics books ignore.

Richard P. Feynman, Robert B. Leighton and Matthew Sands, *The Feynman Lectures on Physics*, Vol. 1, Addison-Wesley (1963). An excellent discussion of the principle of least time is given in Chapter 26. Other chapters relevant to wave phenomena include Chapters 28–30 and Chapter 33.

A. P. French, *Vibrations and Waves,* W. W. Norton & Co. (1971). An introductory level text which emphasizes mechanical systems.

Akira Hirose and Karl E. Lonngren, *Introduction to Wave Phenomena,* John Wiley & Sons (1985). An intermediate level text which treats the general properties of waves in various contexts.

F. Graham Smith and J. H. Thomson, *Optics,* John Wiley & Sons (1971). An intermediate level optics text which is based on wave concepts.

Garrison Sposito, *An Introduction to Classical Dynamics,* John Wiley & Sons (1976). A discusssion of the coupled harmonic oscillator problem is given in Chapter 6.

Michael L. Williams and Humphrey J. Maris, "Numerical study of phonon localization in disordered systems," *Phys. Rev.* **B31**, 4508 (1985). The authors rediscover what we have termed the Euler-Cromer algorithm and apply it to obtain the normal modes of a two-dimensional system of coupled oscillators with random masses.

THE STATIC FIELDS
OF CHARGES
AND CURRENTS

9

We calculate the electric and magnetic fields from fixed charge or current distributions. The relaxation method for obtaining numerical solutions of Laplace's and Poisson's equation is also discussed.

9.1   INTRODUCTION

We know that the force on a charge q moving with velocity $\vec{v}$ is given by the Lorentz force

$$\vec{F} = q(\vec{E} + \vec{v} \times \vec{B}) \qquad (9.1)$$

where $\vec{E}$ is the *electric field* and $\vec{B}$ is the *magnetic field* at the location of the charge. Hence if we know $\vec{E}$ and $\vec{B}$, we can find the motion of a charged particle. In this chapter we use several methods for calculating $\vec{E}$ and $\vec{B}$ from fixed charge or current distributions. We also apply the relaxation method to find numerical solutions of Laplace's and Poisson's equation.

9.2   ELECTRIC FIELDS AND POTENTIAL

Suppose we want to find the electric field $\vec{E}(\vec{r})$ at the point $\vec{r}$ due to the point charges $q_1, q_2, \ldots, q_N$. We know that $\vec{E}(\vec{r})$ satisfies a superposition principle and is given by

$$\vec{E}(\vec{r}) = K \sum_{i}^{N} \frac{q_i}{|\vec{r} - \vec{r}_i|^3}(\vec{r} - \vec{r}_i) \qquad (9.2)$$

where $\vec{r}_i$ is the fixed location of the ith charge and K is a constant which depends on the choice of units. In SI units, C is given by

$$K = 1/4\pi\epsilon_0 \approx 9.0 \times 10^9 \ N\text{--}M^2/C^2 \qquad (9.3)$$

where the coulomb (C) is the SI unit of charge and the constant ϵ_0 is the electrical permittivity of free space. From a microscopic point of view, the coulomb is a very large unit of charge. For example the charge e of the electron is $e \approx 1.6 \times 10^{-19} \ C$. Hence we expect that in many of our simulations, we will have to choose different units.

Note that $\vec{E}$ is a *vector* field. At each point in space the field is character-ized by a magnitude and a direction. How can we represent such a vector field visually? One possible way is to divide space into a discrete grid, find $\vec{E}$ at the various points, and draw arrows in the direction of $\vec{E}$ at these points. However, this way would not display any information about the magnitude of the electric field. A better way to visualize a vector field is to draw *electric field lines*. The properties of these lines are as follows:

1. An electric field line is a directed line whose tangent at every position is parallel to the electric field at that position.
2. The lines are smooth and continuous except at singularities such as point charges. (It makes no sense to talk about the electric field *at* a point charge.)
3. The total number of electric field lines emanating from a point charge is proportional to the magnitude of that charge. The value of the proportionality constant is chosen to provide the clearest pictorial representation of the field. The drawing of field lines is art plus science.

Program fieldline which follows draws electric field lines in two dimensions using the following algorithm:

1. Choose a point (x, y) and compute the components E_x and E_y of the electric field vector $\vec{E}$ using the relation (9.2).
2. Draw a small line segment of fixed length Δs in the direction of $\vec{E}$ at that point. The components of the line segment are given by

$$\Delta x = \Delta s \frac{E_x}{|\vec{E}|} \qquad and \qquad \Delta y = \Delta s \frac{E_y}{|\vec{E}|} \ .$$

3. Repeat the process beginning at the new point $(x + \Delta x, y + \Delta y)$. Continue until the field line moves off toward infinity or until it approaches a negative charge.

Program fieldline does not automatically draw the correct density of lines. Instead the strategy is for you to choose a point in space at which the computer begins to draw the field line. In order to obtain the correct density of lines, it is necessary for you to begin at a point where the field-line distribution is obvious. For example we know that field lines always start radially outward from a positive point charge. Hence you should begin drawing the field lines near a positive charge such that the number of field lines beginning at each positive charge is proportional to the magnitude of the charge on the particle. For example, if we have a $2\mu C$ and $4\mu C$ charge, the number of lines beginning near the $4\mu C$ charge would be twice that originating from the $2\mu C$ charge. The cursor can be moved to the desired point on the screen by pressing 'u', 'd', 'l', and 'r' representing up, down, left, and right. To draw the field line beginning at the current position of the cursor, press 'p'. To stop drawing a line, press any key.

The main features of **Program fieldline** are associated with its graphics statements. The symbol for the cursor is saved as a string variable using **BOX AREA** and **BOX KEEP** statements. The **save$** variable is used to save the part of the screen at which the cursor is to be drawn. Since the placement of the cursor might erase lines already present, the **save\$** variable is used to redraw the lines after the cursor has been moved to a new position.

```
PROGRAM fieldline
DIM x(20),y(20),q(20)
CALL charges(N,x,y,q,ymax)        ! input locations of charges
CALL screen(N,x,y,q,xmax,ymax,dx,dy,r,cursor$,save$)
CALL move(N,x,y,q,xmax,ymax,dx,dy,r,cursor$,save$,xcursor,ycursor)
END

SUB charges(N,x(),y(),q(),ymax)   ! input charge values and location
    INPUT prompt"number of charges = ": N
    FOR i = 1 to N
        PRINT "charge (microcoulombs) on particle ";i;
        INPUT q(i)
        PRINT "x and y coordinates (meters) of particle ";i;
        INPUT x(i),y(i)
        IF xmax < abs(x(i)) then LET xmax = abs(x(i))
        IF ymax < abs(y(i)) then LET ymax = abs(y(i))
    NEXT i
    LET ymax = max(xmax,ymax)
    LET ymax = 1.5*ymax
    IF ymax = 0 then LET ymax = 2
END SUB

SUB screen(N,x(),y(),q(),xmax,ymax,dx,dy,r,cursor$,save$)
    LET aspect_ratio = 1.5       ! depends on shape of monitor
    LET xmax = aspect_ratio*ymax
    SET WINDOW -xmax,xmax,-ymax,ymax
    LET r = 0.01*xmax
    FOR i = 1 to N
        BOX CIRCLE x(i)-r,x(i)+r,y(i)-r,y(i)+r  ! draw charges as circles of radius r
        IF q(i) < 0 then FLOOD x(i),y(i)    ! negative charges are filled circles
    NEXT i
```

```
        LET dx = 0.025*xmax          ! dx and dy minimum step sizes of cursor
        LET dy = 0.025*ymax
        BOX KEEP -r,r,-r,r in save$
        LET xtemp = 0.9*xmax
        LET ytemp = 0.9*ymax
        ! define shape of cursor
        BOX AREA xtemp-r,xtemp+r,ytemp-r,ytemp+r
        BOX KEEP xtemp-r,xtemp+r,ytemp-r,ytemp+r in cursor$
        BOX CLEAR xtemp-r,xtemp+r,ytemp-r,ytemp+r
        BOX SHOW cursor$ at -r,-r
END SUB

SUB move(N,x(),y(),q(),xmax,ymax,dx,dy,r,cursor$,save$,xcursor,ycursor)
        LET xcursor = 0              ! initial x-coordinate of cursor
        LET ycursor = 0              ! initial y-coordinate of cursor
        DO
          LET choice = 0
          IF KEY input then
            GET KEY choice
            LET xold = xcursor
            LET yold = ycursor
            SELECT CASE choice
            CASE 108                 ! move cursor to left
               IF xcursor > -xmax then LET xcursor = xcursor - 2*dx
            CASE 114                 ! move cursor to right
               IF xcursor < xmax then LET xcursor = xcursor + 2*dx
            CASE 117                 ! move cursor up
              IF ycursor > -ymax then LET ycursor = ycursor + 2*dy
            CASE 100                 ! move cursor down
               IF ycursor < ymax then LET ycursor = ycursor - 2*dy
```

```
      CASE 112              ! print field lines
          ! redraw field lines under cursor
          BOX SHOW save$ at xcursor-r,ycursor-r
          CALL draw(N,x,y,q,xcursor,ycursor)
          BOX KEEP xcursor-r,xcursor+r,ycursor-r,ycursor+r in save$
      CASE ELSE
      END SELECT
      BOX SHOW save$ at xold-r,yold-r
      BOX KEEP xcursor-r,xcursor+r,ycursor-r,ycursor+r in save$
      BOX SHOW cursor$ at xcursor-r,ycursor-r
    END IF
  LOOP until choice = 115      ! stop
END SUB

SUB draw(N,x(),y(),q(),xcursor,ycursor)
  LET xline = xcursor
  LET yline = ycursor
  LET delta = 0.01
  LET stop_plot = 0
  DO
    LET Ex = 0.0
    LET Ey = 0.0
    FOR i = 1 to N
       LET dx = xline - x(i)  ! x-distance from point to charge i
       LET dy = yline - y(i)  ! y-distance from point to charge i
       LET r = sqr(dx*dx + dy*dy)
       IF r > 0.001 then
          LET E0 = q(i)/(r*r*r)
          LET Ex = Ex + E0*dx
          LET Ey = Ey + E0*dy
       ELSE
          LET stop_plot = 1
       END IF
    NEXT i
    LET E = sqr(Ex*Ex + Ey*Ey)
    IF E > 0.001 then
       LET xline = xline + delta*Ex/E    ! new position on field line
       LET yline = yline + delta*Ey/E
```

```
     ELSE
        LET stop_plot = 1
     END IF
     IF stop_plot = 0 then PLOT xline,yline;
   LOOP until key input or stop_plot = 1
     PLOT    ! turn beam off
  END SUB
```

PROBLEM 9.1 Electric field lines from point charges

a. In **Program fieldline**, Coulomb's constant does not appear. Why not? Are the units of charge and distance relevant?

b. Use **Program fieldline** to draw the field lines for $q(1) = 1$, $x(1) = 1$, $y(1) = 0$. Note the use of arbitrary units. Next add a charge $q(2) = -4$ at $x(2) = -1$, $y(2) = 0$. Finally add a third charge $q(3) = 3$ at $x(3) = 0$, $y(3) = 1$. Remember to choose the number of field lines emanating from a positive charge to be proportional to its charge. Verify that the field lines never end at positive charges and always go towards negative charges. Why do field lines never cross?

c. Draw the field lines for the electric dipole $q(1) = 1$, $x(1) = 1$, $y(1) = 0$, and $q(2) = -1$, $x(2) = -1$, $y(2) = 0$.

d. Draw the field lines for the electric quadrupole $q(1) = 1$, $x(1) = 1$, $y(1) = 1$, $q(2) = -1$, $x(2) = -1$, $y(2) = 0$, $q(3) = 1$, $x(3) = -1$, $y(3) = -1$, and $q(4) = -1$, $x(4) = 1$, $y(4) = -1$.

PROBLEM 9.2 Electric field lines from semi-continuous charge distributions

a. A continuous charge distribution can be represented by a large number of closely spaced point charges. Plot the electric field lines due to a row of ten equally spaced unit charges between -5 and 5 on the x axis. How does the electric field distribution compare to the distribution due to a point charge?

b. Repeat part (a) with two rows of equally spaced positive charges on the $y = 0$ and $y = 1$ axes respectively.

c. Repeat part (b) with one row of positive charges and one of negative charges.

PROBLEM 9.3 Motion of a charged particle in an electric field

a. Add a subroutine to **Program fieldline** to compute the motion of a particle of charge q in the presence of the electric field created by a distribution of fixed point charges. Use the velocity form of Verlet's algorithm (see Appendix 5A or Chapter 6) to determine the position and velocity of the particle. The charge has mass m so that the acceleration of the charge is given by $(q/m)\vec{E}$, where $\vec{E}$ is the electric field due to the fixed point charges. We measure charge in μC (10^{-6} coulombs) and distance in centimeters. In these units the constant K in (9.3) becomes $K = 90$ newton-cm$^2/\mu C^2$.

b. Assume that E is due to a charge $q(1) = 1$ fixed at the origin. Simulate the motion of a charged particle of mass $m = 1$ gm and charge $q = 0.1$ initially at $x = 1, y = 0$. Consider the following initial conditions for its velocity: (i) $v_x = 0$, $v_y = 0$; (ii) $v_x = 1$, $v_y = 0$; (iii) $v_x = 0$, $v_y = 1$; and (iv) $v_x = -1$, $v_y = 0$. (Remember the units of charge and distance.) Draw electric field lines beginning at the initial values of x, y and draw lines showing the particle's trajectory. Why does the trajectory of the particle not follow a field line?

c. Assume the electric field arises from a point charge $q(1) = 1$ at the origin and determine the trajectory of the particle for $x_0 = 1$, $y_0 = 0$, $v_{x0} = 0$, and $v_{y0} = 9.5$. What is the nature of the trajectory in this case?

d. Assume that there are two fixed point charges with $q(1) = 1$, $x(1) = 2$, $y(1) = 0$, and $q(2) = -1$, $x(1) = -2$, and $y(2) = 0$. Place a charge $q = 1$ at $x_0 = 0.05$ and $y_0 = 0$. What do you expect the motion of this charge to be? Do the simulation and determine the qualitative nature of the motion.

*e. Consider the motion of a particle in the vicinity of an electric dipole. Can you find any bound orbits?

In Chapter 4 we made many simulations of bodies moving in the influence of the gravitational force. Since the gravitational interaction is attractive, we emphasized the study of bound orbits. In Problem 9.4, we consider the *scattering* of a positively charged particle by a positively charged nucleus.

PROBLEM 9.4 Alpha-particle scattering

a. Write a program using the velocity form of the Verlet algorithm (see Appendix 5A or Chapter 6) to compute the trajectory of an alpha particle in the vicinity of a gold nucleus (the target nucleus in the original Rutherford scattering experiment). The relevant parameters are $m_\alpha = 6.65 \times 10^{-27}$ kg, $m_{Au} = 3.27 \times 10^{-25}$ kg, $q_\alpha = +2e$ and $q_{Au} = +79e$, where $e = 1.60 \times 10^{-19} C$. We will assume that the gold nucleus is stationary. A more precise calculation would write the equations of motion in relative coordinates and would use the reduced mass. It is assumed that the α particle does not actually penetrate the nucleus so that the interaction between the particle and the nucleus is given by Coulomb's law. Then the magnitude of the acceleration of the alpha particle is proportional to the quantity κ which is given by

$$\kappa = K(2e)(79e)/m_\alpha \approx 5.60 \, m^3/s^2 \quad . \tag{9.4}$$

Since a typical interaction distance is the order of 10^{-13} cm, the resultant force in Newtons would be a very large number to use on a computer. We choose to measure lengths in fermis, $1\,F = 10^{-15}\,m$, and velocity in terms of the speed of light, $c = 3 \times 10^8$ m/s. In these units the force constant κ becomes

$$\kappa \approx 5.60 \times (3 \times 10^8)^2 (1 \times 10^{-15}) = 5.04 \times 10^2 F c^2 \quad . \tag{9.5}$$

In the usual scattering experiment, the scatterer is initially far away from the target nucleus where the Coulomb force is negligible, and the particle approaches the nucleus along a straight line at constant speed. After the scattering, the particle will move in a straight line with constant speed $v' = v$. The quantities of interest are the *impact parameter b*, the *scattering angle* θ (see Fig. 9.1), and the scattering cross section which is related to the probability of scattering between θ and $\theta + \Delta\theta$. The cross section is the effective area for the scattering event.

b. Choose the initial coordinates for the α particle to be $x_0 = -300\,F$, $y_0 = 30\,F$, $v_{x0} = 0.1\,c$, and $v_{y0} = 0$. The nucleus is at the origin. Compare the initial distance of the α particle from the nucleus to the radius of the Au nucleus which is about $10\,F$. What is the impact parameter? Compute the trajectory of the α particle and determine the scattering angle.

c. Determine the scattering angle for the initial condition $y_0 = 60\,F$ and $y_0 = 120\,F$. Explain why the scattering angle is an increasing or decreasing function of the impact parameter.

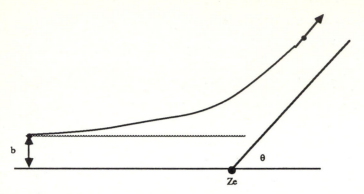

Fig. 9.1 The scattering of an alpha particle in terms of the impact parameter b and the scattering angle θ.

*d. Choose at random 100 values of the impact parameter between $b = 0$ and $b = 500$ and compute the number of times $N(\theta)\Delta\theta$ a particle is scattered between the angle θ and $\theta + \Delta\theta$. Choose a reasonable value of $\Delta\theta$ and plot $N(\theta)$ as a function of θ. A random value of the impact parameter can be found using the **rnd** statement, e.g. LET b = 500*rnd. Explain the qualitative dependence of $N(\theta)$.

We know that it is often easier to analyze the behavior of a system using energy rather than force concepts. Hence it is useful to define the electric potential $V(r)$ by the relation

$$V(\vec{r}_2) - V(\vec{r}_1) = -\int_{\vec{r}_1}^{\vec{r}_2} \vec{E} \cdot d\vec{r} \qquad (9.6a)$$

or

$$\vec{E}(\vec{r}) = -\nabla V(\vec{r}) \quad . \qquad (9.6b)$$

Note that $V(r)$ is a scalar quantity and that only differences in the potential between two points have physical significance. The gradient operator ∇ is given in Cartesian coordinates by

$$\nabla V(\vec{r}) = \frac{\partial V(\vec{r})}{\partial x}\hat{\imath} + \frac{\partial V(\vec{r})}{\partial y}\hat{\jmath} + \frac{\partial V(\vec{r})}{\partial z}\hat{k} \quad . \qquad (9.7)$$

The vectors $\hat{\imath}$, $\hat{\jmath}$, and $\hat{k}$ are unit vectors along the x, y, and z axes. In one dimension (9.6b) reduces to $E - -dV/dx$. If V depends only on the magnitude of $\vec{r}$, then (9.6b) becomes $E = -dV/dr$. In both cases the direction of $\vec{E}$ is in the direction in which the electric potential decreases most rapidly, a general property of $\vec{E}$. We note that V for a point charge q relative to a zero potential at infinity is given by

$$V(r) = \frac{q}{4\pi\epsilon_0 r} \quad . \tag{9.8}$$

The surface on which the electric potential has an equal value everywhere is called an *equipotential surface* (curve in two dimensions). It is easy to show that the electric field lines are orthogonal to the equipotential surfaces at any point. We can use this property of the electric field lines and the equipotential lines to use **Program fieldline** to draw the latter. Since the vector components of the line segment Δs of the electric field line are given by $\Delta x = \Delta s(E_x/E)$ and $\Delta y = \Delta s(E_y/E)$, the components of the line segment perpendicular to $\vec{E}$ and hence parallel to the equipotential line are given by $\Delta x = -\Delta s(E_y/E)$ and $\Delta y = \Delta s(E_x/E)$. It is unimportant whether the minus sign is assigned to the x or y component since the only difference will be the direction of the plot.

PROBLEM 9.5 Equipotential lines

a. Modify **Program fieldline** to find the equipotential lines for the charge distributions considered in Problem 9.1.

b. What would a higher density of equipotential lines mean if we produced lines such that each adjacent line differed from a neighboring one by a fixed potential difference?

c. Explain why equipotential surfaces never cross.

*PROBLEM 9.6 The electric potential due to a uniformly charged plate

Consider a uniformly charged square plate of total charge Q and linear dimension L in the x-z plane (see Fig. 9.2). In the limit $L \to \infty$ with the charge density $\sigma = Q/L^2$ a constant, we know that the electric field is normal to the sheet and is given by $E_n = \sigma/2\epsilon_0$. Our goal is to find the electric field for a finite sheet of charge. One way to proceed is to divide the plate into a grid of N cells on a side such that each cell is small enough to be considered a point charge of magnitude $dq = Q/N^2$. Since the potential is a scalar quantity, it is easier to compute the total potential rather than the total electric field from the N^2 point charges. The electric field can be determined using the relation (9.6b). Use the relation (9.8) for the potential from a point charge and write a program to calculate $V(y)$ and hence E_y for points along the y-axis and perpendicular to the sheet. Take $L = 1$ cm, $Q = 1$ C, and

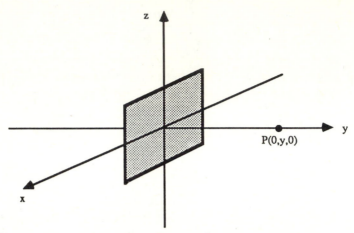

Fig. 9.2 A plate of total charge and area L^2 in the x-z plane.

$N = 10$ for your initial calculations. Increase N until your results for $V(y)$ are not affected significantly. Plot $V(y)$ and E_y as a function of y and compare the y-dependence of $V(y)$ and E_y to their infinite sheet counterparts for intermediate distances and to a point charge for large distances.

9.3 MAGNETISM AND MAGNETIC FIELD LINES

Our study of electrostatics in Sec. 9.1 was based on Coulomb's law for the electric field of a point charge. There is an analogous relation for the magnetic field due to a current. This relation is known as the *Biot-Savart law* and is given by:

$$\Delta \vec{B}(\vec{r}) = \frac{\mu_0 I}{4\pi} \left(\frac{\Delta \vec{L} \times \vec{r}}{r^3} \right) \tag{9.9}$$

where the current I is measured in amperes, B in tesla, and the magnetic permeability constant μ_0 is given by

$$\mu_0 = 4\pi \times 10^{-7} \, tesla-meter/ampere \quad . \tag{9.10}$$

$\Delta \vec{B}(\vec{r})$ is the magnetic field at point $\vec{r}$ due to a segment of wire $\Delta \vec{L}$ which carries a steady electric current I and is located at the origin. The Biot-Savart law is

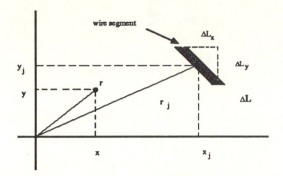

Fig. 9.3 A segment of wire in two dimensions of length ΔL at x_j, y_j. The components of $\Delta \vec{L}$ are ΔL_x and ΔL_y. The point $\vec{r}$ is the location at which the magnetic field is being computed and $\vec{r}_j$ is the location of the current segment.

completely general and in principle can be used to find the total magnetic field at any point. Of course there are no isolated current segments and a wire must be either a closed loop or sufficiently long that the contributions from the end points are negligible. However, we can approximate a continuous wire by a series of discrete segments. For each segment of length $\Delta \vec{L}$ at $\vec{r}_j$, the contribution to the magnetic field at $\vec{r}$ is given by (see Fig. 9.3)

$$\Delta B_x(\vec{r}) = (\mu_0 I/4\pi)[\Delta L_y(z - z_j) - \Delta L_z(y - y_j)]/|\vec{r} - \vec{r}_j|^3$$
$$\Delta B_y(\vec{r}) = (\mu_0 I/4\pi)[\Delta L_z(x - x_j) - \Delta L_x(z - z_j)]/|\vec{r} - \vec{r}_j|^3 \qquad (9.11)$$
$$\Delta B_z(\vec{r}) = (\mu_0 I/4\pi)[\Delta L_x(y - y_j) - \Delta L_y(x - x_j)]/|\vec{r} - \vec{r}_j|^3$$

where
$$|\vec{r} - \vec{r}_j|^3 = [(x - x_j)^2 + (y - y_j)^2 + (z - z_j)^2)]^{3/2} \qquad . \qquad (9.12)$$

Since it is not possible to perform analytical calculations using (9.11) unless the magnetic field has a high degree of symmetry, we are motivated to use the computer to calculate the magnetic field due to arbitrary configurations of current-carrying wires. The most important geometrical configurations of wires for which we wish to know the magnetic field distribution are a straight wire, a circular loop, and a coil (solenoid). We discuss the circular loop here. The magnetic field along the axis through the center of the circular loop can be calculated analytically using the Biot-Savart law without much difficulty. However, the calculation off the axis is very difficult. **Program magnetism** considers a circular wire loop in the x-z plane and draws the magnetic field lines in the x-y plane

(see Fig. 9.4). The structure of the program is similar to **Program fieldline**.
Note that the components of the N wire segments are stored in arrays.

```
PROGRAM magnetism
DIM x(50),y(50),z(50),dLx(50),dLy(50),dLz(50)
CALL wire(N,a,delta,x,y,z,dLx,dLy,dLz)
CALL screen(a,xmax,ymax,dx,dy,r,cursor$,save$)
CALL move(N,delta,x,y,z,dLx,dLy,dLz,xmax,ymax,dx,dy,r,cursor$,save$)
END

SUB wire(N,a,delta,x(),y(),z(),dLx(),dLy(),dLz())
    ! read in current segments
    ! assume current equal to one amp
    INPUT prompt "radius of loop = ": a
    INPUT prompt "number of segments = ": N
    INPUT prompt "delta = ": delta   ! magnitude of magnetic field line segment
    LET delta_angle = 2*pi/N
    LET angle = 0
    LET dL = 2*pi*a/N
    FOR i = 1 to N
        LET x(i) = a*cos(angle)
        LET y(i) = 0
        LET z(i) = a*sin(angle)
        LET dLx(i) = -dL*sin(angle) ! direction of current segment at (x,y,z)
        LET dLy(i) = 0
        LET dLz(i) = dL*cos(angle)
        LET angle = angle + delta_angle
    NEXT i
END SUB
```

```
SUB screen(a,xmax,ymax,dx,dy,r,cursor$,save$)
    ! draw projection of current loop onto x-y axis
    LET ymax = 3*a
    LET aspect_ratio = 1.5
    LET xmax = aspect_ratio*ymax
    SET window -xmax,xmax,-ymax,ymax
    ! dx and dy are minimum step sizes
    LET dx = 0.025*xmax
    LET dy = 0.025*ymax
    LET r = 0.01*xmax
    LET xtemp = 0.9*xmax
    LET ytemp = 0.9*ymax
    BOX KEEP xtemp - r,xtemp + r,ytemp - r,ytemp + r in save$
    BOX AREA xtemp - r,xtemp + r,ytemp - r,ytemp + r
    BOX KEEP xtemp - r,xtemp + r,ytemp - r,ytemp + r in cursor$
    BOX CLEAR xtemp - r,xtemp + r,ytemp - r,ytemp + r
    BOX SHOW cursor$ at -r,-r
    BOX CIRCLE -a,a,-0.4,0.4
END SUB
```

```
SUB move(N,delta,x(),y(),z(),dLx(),dLy(),dLz(),xmax,ymax,dx,dy,r,cursor$,save$)
   LET xcursor = 0
   LET ycursor = 0
   DO
      LET choice = 0
      IF KEY input then
         GET KEY choice
         LET xold = xcursor
         LET yold = ycursor
         SELECT CASE choice
         CASE 108              ! ascii code for "l"
            IF xcursor > -xmax then LET xcursor = xcursor - 2*dx
         CASE 114              ! ascii code for "r"
            IF xcursor < xmax then LET xcursor = xcursor + 2*dx
         CASE 117              ! ascii code for "u"
            IF ycursor > -ymax then LET ycursor = ycursor + 2*dy
         CASE 100              ! ascii code for "d"
            IF ycursor < ymax then LET ycursor = ycursor - 2*dy
         CASE 112              ! ascii code for "p"
            BOX SHOW save$ at xcursor-r,ycursor-r
            CALL draw(N,delta,x,y,z,dLx,dLy,dLz,xcursor,ycursor)
            BOX KEEP xcursor - r,xcursor + r,ycursor - r,ycursor + r in save$
         CASE ELSE
         END SELECT
         BOX SHOW save$ at xold - r,yold - r
         BOX KEEP xcursor - r,xcursor + r,ycursor - r,ycursor + r in save$
         BOX SHOW cursor$ at xcursor - r,ycursor - r
      END IF
   LOOP until choice = 115        ! ascii code for "s"
END SUB
```

```
SUB draw(N,delta,x(),y(),z(),dLx(),dLy(),dLz(),xcursor,ycursor)
    LET rx = xcursor
    LET ry = ycursor
    DO
        LET Bx = 0.0
        LET By = 0.0
        LET Bz = 0.0
        FOR i = 1 to N
            ! compute displacement from position to current segment
            LET dx = rx - x(i)
            LET dy = ry - y(i)
            LET dz = zcursor - z(i)
            LET r = sqr(dx*dx + dy*dy + dz*dz)
            LET B0 = 1/(r*r*r)     ! assume current equals 1 Amp
            ! B proportional to dL x r
            LET Bx = Bx + B0*(dLy(i)*dz - dLz(i)*dy)
            LET By = By + B0*(dLz(i)*dx - dLx(i)*dz)
            LET Bz = Bz + B0*(dLx(i)*dy - dLy(i)*dx)
        NEXT i
        LET B = sqr(Bx*Bx + By*By + Bz*Bz)
        LET rx = rx + delta*Bx/B  ! new position on flux line
        LET ry = ry + delta*By/B
        LET rz = rz + delta*Bz/B
        PLOT rx,ry;
    LOOP until key input
    PLOT
END SUB
```

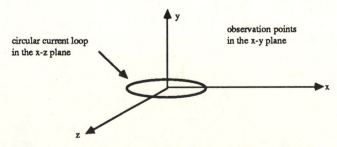

Fig. 9.4 The geometry of the circular loop for Problem 9.7.

PROBLEM 9.7 Magnetic field from a current loop

a. Use **Program magnetism** to determine the magnetic field lines of a circular loop located in the x-z plane and centered at the origin (see Fig. 9.4). We place the loop in the x-z plane since we wish to consider the screen as the x-y plane. The interesting field lines are in a plane perpendicular to the plane of the loop. Let the radius a of the circle equal 5 cm, and let *delta*, the length of a line segment of the magnetic field lines, equal 0.1cm. Is the magnitude of the current relevant? Describe the nature of the field lines. The field far away from the loop is called a dipole magnetic field and the loop is referred to as a dipole.

b. When you start a flux line near the current loop, you might find that the flux line bends sharply and does not form a closed loop. What should be the exact result? How can you improve the results for the magnetic field lines?

*PROBLEM 9.8 The motion of charged particles in a magnetic lens

a. Consider the motion of a charged particle which traverses the magnetic field due to a short solenoid, which is a cylindrical coil of wire (see Fig. 9.5). Assume the wire is closely and evenly spaced with n turns per unit length. Although the current path is actually helical, we can regard the solenoid as equivalent to a stack of current rings. (The field inside the solenoid is not effected by the helicity of the coil.) Write a subroutine to compute the magnetic field inside and near the coil. Assume $I = 1.0$amp, the radius $a = 0.5$cm, the length of the coil $L = 1.0$cm, and the number of loops $n = 10$.

b. Assume that an electron enters the solenoid from the left with the initial conditions $z = 0$, $v_z = 0.1$cm, $y = 0.125$ cm, and $v_y = 0.5$cm/s. Write a program to compute the trajectory of the electron in the magnetic field of the solenoid. Note that you need not find the magnetic field everywhere first. Instead find the magnetic field at the locations of the charge as it moves. Describe the motion of electrons approaching the solenoid in a direction roughly parallel to the axis. Consider small changes in the initial values y and explain how the solenoid acts as a lens.

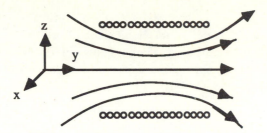

Fig. 9.5 The geometry of the short solenoid considered in Problem 9.8.

9.4   NUMERICAL SOLUTIONS OF LAPLACE'S EQUATION

In Sec. 9.1 we found the net electric field and electric potential due to a fixed distribution of source charges. In many cases we do not know the location of the source charges and instead know only the electric potential along the boundaries of a region. For example, suppose we have a fixed distribution of conductors in otherwise empty space and that each conductor is connected to a battery. We can easily perform a measurement to determine the potential V of each conductor. (Remember that V has the same value everywhere in a conducting body.) However, it is not easy to measure the locations of the charges on each conductor since their locations are given by a complicated nonuniform distribution which depends on the shape of the body.

Suppose we are given the potential on a set of boundaries and wish to find the potential $V(r)$ at any point within a charge-free region. Once we know V within a region, we can use the relation $\vec{E} = -\vec{\nabla}V(\vec{r})$ to determine $\vec{E}$. This problem is called a *boundary value* problem. The direct method of solving for $V(x, y, z)$ is based on Laplace's equation which is given in Cartesian coordinates by

$$\nabla^2 V(x, y, z) \equiv \frac{\partial^2 V}{\partial x^2} + \frac{\partial^2 V}{\partial y^2} + \frac{\partial^2 V}{\partial z^2} = 0 \quad . \tag{9.13}$$

In this direct approach the problem is to find a function $V(x, y, z)$ which satisfies (9.13) and also satisfies the specified boundary conditions. Since there are no analytical methods for conductors of arbitrary shape, the only general approach is to use approximate numerical methods.

Laplace's equation is not a new law of physics but can be derived from Gauss' law. Since a derivation of Laplace's equation is given in many introductory level textbooks (cf. Eisberg and Lerner or Purcell), we use **Program fieldline** to verify a difference equation version of Laplace's equation which is useful for numerical analysis. We divide all of space into a grid or lattice of small square cells (cubic cells in three dimensions). Then we show in the following that in the absence of a charge at (x, y), the potential $V(x, y)$ is given in two dimensions by

$$V(x, y) \approx \frac{1}{4}[V(x+\Delta x, y)+V(x-\Delta x, y)+V(x, y+\Delta y)+V(x, y-\Delta y)] \quad . \ (9.14)$$

That is, $V(x, y)$ is the average of the neighboring cells to the right, left, up, and down. (There are six neighboring cells in three dimensions.) This remarkable property of $V(x, y)$ is simply a discrete version of Laplace's equation. The approximate form (9.14) can also be verified by approximating the partial derivatives in (9.13) by finite differences.

In order to verify (9.14), we use the form (9.8) for the potential $V(r)$ due to a point charge q. Equation (9.8) is a consequence of Gauss' law and satisfies Laplace's equation for $r \neq 0$. Our strategy is to modify **Program fieldline** so that the value of the potential is printed at the position of the cursor. In Problem 9.9, we choose a cell, calculate the potential there, and then move the cursor to the four adjacent cells. As (9.14) indicates, the average of the potential in the neighboring cells should equal the potential of the center cell.

The following subroutine will be used in Problem 9.9. **SUB potential** prints the value of the potential at the position of the cursor.

```
SUB potential(N,x(),y(),q(),xcursor,ycursor)
    FOR i = 1 to N
        LET dx = xcursor - x(i)
        LET dy = ycursor - y(i)
        LET r = sqr(dx*dx + dy*dy)
        LET V = V + q(i)/r
    NEXT i
    PRINT "x,y,V = ",xcursor;ycursor,V
END SUB
```

PROBLEM 9.9 Verification of the two-dimensional difference equation for the potential

a. In order to compute the potential at any desired location, replace **SUB draw** in **Program fieldline** by **SUB potential**. Assume that the source of the potential is a point charge of $1\,\mu C$ at the origin. Choose reasonable

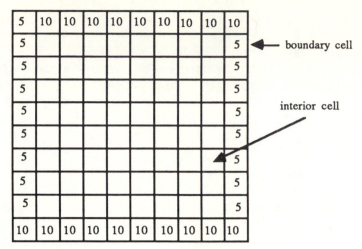

Fig. 9.6 Potential distribution for Problem 9.10c. Note that the potential at two of the four corners is ambigious.

values for Δx and Δy and consider an arbitrary location on the screen not too close to the origin. Print the value of the potential at the location of the cursor by typing 'p'. Move the cursor to each of the four neighboring cells and print the value of V for each one. Compute the average of V for the four neighboring cells and compare it with the value of V for the center cell. Do similar measurements for other positions. Does the relative agreement with (9.14) depend on the distance of the cell to the origin?

b. Repeat part (a) with smaller values of Δx and Δy. Does it matter whether Δx and Δy have the same value? Explain your answer. Are your results in better agreement with (9.14)?

c. Repeat part (a) with two point charges of $1\,\mu C$ each, fixed at $x(1) = 10\,cm$ and $x(2) = -10\,cm$ with $y(1) = y(2) = 0$.

Now that we have seen that (9.14) is consistent with Coulomb's law, we adopt (9.14) as the basis of a calculational method for problems for which we cannot determine the potential directly from Coulomb's law. In particular we will consider problems where several conducting regions are fixed at some potential and we wish to find the potential everywhere in space. For simplicity we will consider only two-dimensional geometries. The approach, known as the *relaxation method*, is based on the following algorithm:

1. Divide the region of interest into a grid or lattice of cells spanning the region (see Fig. 9.6). The region must be enclosed by a surface (curve in two dimensions) with specified values of the potential along the curve.

2. The cells are either boundary or interior cells. Assign to a boundary cell, a cell whose center is within a region of fixed potential, the potential of that region.

3. Assign all interior cells an arbitrary potential (preferably a reasonable guess).

4. The first step is to compute new values for V for each interior cell. Each new value is obtained by finding the average of the initial values of potential of the four nearest neighbor cells. This is the first iteration of the relaxation process.

5. Repeat the process outlined in (4) using the values of V obtained in the previous iteration. This iterative process is continued until each interior cell potential does not change within the desired level of accuracy.

We apply **Program Laplace**, which implements the above algorithm, in Problems 9.10 and 9.11 to calculate the potential for various geometries.

```
PROGRAM Laplace
DIM V(100,100)
CALL assign(V,nx,ny,min_change)
CALL iterate(V,nx,ny,min_change,iterations)
END


SUB assign(V(,),nx,ny,min_change)
    INPUT prompt "number of cells in x-direction = ": nx
    INPUT prompt "number of cells in y-direction = ": ny
    INPUT prompt "potential of rectangle in volts = ": V0
    INPUT prompt "percentage change = ": min_change
    LET min_change = min_change/100
    FOR col = 1 to nx              ! fix potential on  rectangle
        LET V(col,1) = V0
        LET V(col,ny) = V0
    NEXT col
    FOR row = 1 to ny
        LET V(1,row) = V0
        LET V(nx,row) = V0
    NEXT row
    ! set initial potentials of interior cells
    FOR col = 2 to nx - 1
        FOR row = 2 to ny - 1
            LET V(col,row) = 0.9*V0
        NEXT row
    NEXT col
END SUB
```

```
SUB iterate(V(,),nx,ny,min_change,iterations)
   DIM Vave(100,100)
   LET iterations = 0
   DO
      LET dmax = 0
      LET iterations = iterations + 1
      FOR col = 2 to nx - 1
         FOR row = 2 to ny - 1
            ! compute average of potential of neighboring cells
            LET Vave(col,row) = V(col+1,row) + V(col-1,row)
            LET Vave(col,row) = Vave(col,row) + V(col,row+1) + V(col,row-1)
            LET Vave(col,row) = 0.25*Vave(col,row)
            ! compute percentage change in potential
            LET diff = abs((V(col,row) - Vave(col,row))/Vave(col,row))
            IF diff > dmax then LET dmax = diff
         NEXT row
      NEXT col
      FOR col = 2 to nx - 1     ! update potential at each cell
         FOR row = 2 to ny - 1
            LET V(col,row) = Vave(col,row)
         NEXT row
      NEXT col
      CALL output(V,nx,ny,iterations)
   LOOP until dmax <= min_change    ! continue until desired convergence
END SUB

SUB output(V(,),nx,ny,iterations)      ! print results
   PRINT
   PRINT "iterations = ", iterations
   FOR row = 1 to ny
      FOR col = nx to 1 step -1
         PRINT using "###.###": V(col,row);
      NEXT col
      PRINT
   NEXT row
END SUB
```

PROBLEM 9.10 Numerical solution of the potential inside a rectangular region

a. Use **Program Laplace** to determine the potential $V(x, y)$ inside a square region with linear dimension $L = 10$ cm. The boundary of the square is at a potential of 10 volts. Before you do the computation, guess the exact form of $V(x, y)$ and set the initial values of the potential of the interior cells to be within 5% of the exact answer. Choose the area of each cell to be 1 cm^2. How many iterations are necessary to achieve 1% accuracy?

b. Consider the same geometry as in part (a), but choose the initial potential of the interior cells to be zero except for $V(5, 5) = 4$. Describe the time evolution of the potential distribution of the interior cells. Does the potential distribution evolve to the correct solution? Are the final results independent of your initial guess? What is the effect of a poor initial guess? Note that the way the program is written $V(x, y)$ cannot equal zero for any interior cell. (The nature of the relaxation of the cell values towards an eventual equilibrium distribution is closely related to the process of *diffusion*, the subject of Chapter 11.)

c. Modify **SUB assign** in **Program Laplace** so that each side of the rectangle can have a different potential. Use 10 cells on each side, and fix the potentials of the sides to be 5, 10, 5, and 10 volts respectively (see Fig. 9.6). Sketch the equipotential surfaces. What happens if the potential is 10 volts on three sides and 0 on the fourth? Start with a reasonable guess for the initial values of the potential of the interior points, and iterate until 1% accuracy is obtained.

d. Repeat part (c) with 20 cells on a side. How does the greater number of cells improve your results?

e. We have discussed only a very simple implementation of the relaxation method. More general relaxation methods and the nature of their convergence are discussed in many texts (cf. Koonin). How do your results differ if the potential at each site is computed sequentially?

PROBLEM 9.11 The capacitance of concentric squares

a. Modify **Program Laplace** to treat a concentric square boundary (see Fig. 9.7). The potential of the outer square conductor is set at 10 volts and the inner square conductor, which is placed at the center of the outer square, is set at 5 volts. The linear dimensions of the exterior and interior squares are $L_1 = 5$ cm and $L_2 = 25$ cm respectively. Choose a convenient grid and compute the potential distribution between the two squares. Sketch the equipotential surfaces. Remember to change the program so that the potential of the interior square remains fixed.

b. A system of two conductors with a charge Q and $-Q$ respectively has a capacitance C which is defined as the ratio of Q to the potential difference between the two conductors. Determine the capacitance of the concentric square conductors considered in part (a). In this case the potential difference is 5 volts. The charge Q can be determined from the property that near a conducting surface the surface charge density σ is given by $\sigma = E_n/\epsilon_0$. E_n is the magnitude of the electric field normal to the surface and can be approximated by the relation $-\Delta V/\Delta r$, where ΔV is the potential difference between a boundary cell and the adjacent interior cell a distance Δr away. (We imagine that the two squares continue indefinitely in the third direction.) Use the results of part (a) to calculate ΔV for each point next to the two square surfaces. Use this information to obtain a reasonable estimate for E_n for the two surfaces and the charge per unit length on each electrode. Are the charges equal and opposite in sign? Calculate the capacitance in farads. How does the magnitude of the capacitance compare to the capacitance of a system of two concentric cylinders of radii $2\pi r_1 = 4L_1$ and $2\pi r_2 = 4L_2$?

c. Move the inner square 1 cm off center and repeat the computations of parts (a) and (b). How do the potential surfaces change? Is there any qualitative difference if we set the center conductor potential to -5 volts instead of $+5$ volts?

Laplace's equation holds only in charge-free regions. If there is a charge density $\rho(x, y, z)$ in the region, we must use *Poisson's* equation which can be written in differential form as

$$\nabla^2 V(\vec{r}) = \frac{\partial^2 V}{\partial x^2} + \frac{\partial^2 V}{\partial y^2} + \frac{\partial^2 V}{\partial z^2} = -\frac{\rho(\vec{r})}{\epsilon_0} \ . \tag{9.15}$$

The quantity $\rho(\vec{r})$ is the charge density. In Problem 9.12 we make measurements of V in the neighborhood of the cell at x, y which contains a source charge. The result of these measurements is consistent with the difference form of Poisson's equation given in two dimensions by

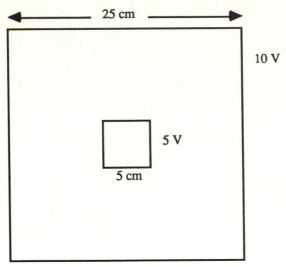

Fig. 9.7 Geometry of two concentric squares considered in Problem 9.11.

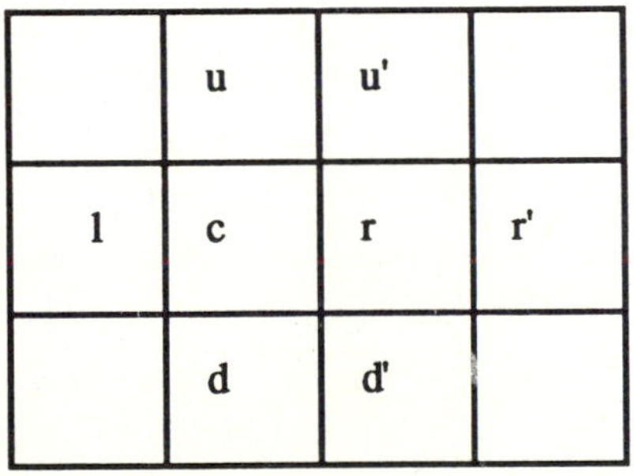

Fig. 9.8 A single point charge is at cell c.

$$V(x,y) \approx \frac{1}{4}[V(x+\Delta x, y) + V(x - \Delta x, y) + V(x, y + \Delta y) + V(x, y - \Delta y)]$$

$$+\frac{1}{4}\Delta x \Delta y \frac{\rho(x,y)}{\epsilon_0}] \quad . \tag{9.16}$$

Note that $\rho(x,y)\Delta x \Delta y$ is simply the total charge in the cell centered at x, y. The quantity ϵ_0 is related to Coulomb's constant by $K = 1/4\pi\epsilon_0$ and is given by $8.85 \times 10^{-12} \mathrm{C^2 N^{-1}\ m^{-2}}$.

PROBLEM 9.12 The difference equation form of Poisson's equation

a. Place a single $1.0\,\mu C$ charge at cell $(0,0)$ indicated by c in Fig. 9.8. In this case we cannot find the potential of cell c directly, since a point charge is located there. Use Coulomb's law and **Program fieldline** to find the approximate potential at the nearest neighbor cells (labeled u, d, l, and r) of cell c. Use these results to obtain the average potential $<V_c>$.

b. Find the average potential $<V_r>$ of cell r by averaging over its nearest neighbors u', r', d', and c. Take the potential of cell c to be $<V_c>$, the average found in part (a). Then compute the potential V_r of cell r directly and calculate the difference between $<V_r>$ and V_r.

c. Repeat the calculations of part (a) and (b) for a point charge of $2\,\mu C$ at the origin. Repeat the calculations for a point charge of $-4\,\mu C$ at the origin. Show that the difference between $<V_r>$ and V_r is proportional to the charge at $(0,0)$. The nature of this difference indicates that the potential at a cell approximately equals the average potential of its nearest neighbors plus a term proportional to the charge in the cell. In principle, we could find the constant of proportionality by averaging the potential of the point charge over the finite spatial extent of the cell.

PROBLEM 9.13 Numerical solution of Poisson's equation

a. Consider a square of linear dimension $L = 25$ cm fixed at 10 volts. Assume that each interior cell has a uniform charge density ρ such that $\frac{1}{4}A\rho/\epsilon_0 = 3$ volts/cm^2. Modify Program Laplace to compute the potential distribution for this case. Compare the equipotential surfaces obtained for this case with that found in Problem 9.11.

b. Find the potential distribution if the charge distribution of part (a) is restricted to a square of area 25 cm^2 at the center.

9.5   EXTENSIONS

Although we illustrated the relaxation method for Laplace's and Poisson's equations in the context of electrostatics, similar equations apply in magnetostatics for the components of the vector potential. In addition, such diverse areas as steady-state heat flow, static deflections of elastic membranes, and irrotational fluid flow are also described by similar equations.

Some of the more interesting extensions of the topics treated here are in plasma physics and in stellar systems. The complex nature of the phenomena in both areas is due to the long-range nature of the force which implies that the motion of an individual particle is influenced by the motion of all the other particles.

REFERENCES AND SUGGESTIONS FOR ADDITIONAL READING

Forman S. Acton, *Numerical Methods That Work,* Harper & Row (1970). Chapter 18 discusses solutions to Laplace's equation using the relaxation method and alternative approaches.

Charles K. Birdsall and A. Bruce Langdon, *Plasma Physics via Computer Simulation,* Mc-Graw-Hill (1985).

David M. Cook, *The Theory of the Electromagnetic Field,* Prentice-Hall (1975). One of the first books to introduce numerical methods in the context of electromagnetism.

J. M. Dawson, "Particle simulations of plasma," *Rev. Mod. Phys.* **55**, 403 (1983).

Robert M. Eisberg and Lawrence S. Lerner, *Physics,* Vol. 2, McGraw-Hill (1981). An introductory level text which uses numerical methods to find the electric field lines and solutions to Laplace's equation.

R. H. Good, "Dipole radiation: Simulation using a microcomputer," *Am. J. Phys.* **52**, 1150 (1984). The author reports on a graphical simulation of dipole radiation.

R. W. Hockney and J. W. Eastwood, *Computer Simulation Using Particles,* McGraw-Hill (1981).

Steven E. Koonin, *Computational Physics,* Benjamin/Cummins (1986). See Chapter 6 for a discussion of the numerical solution of elliptic partial differential equations of which Laplace's and Poisson's equations are examples.

Edward M. Purcell, *Electricity and Magnetism,* 2nd ed., Berkeley Physics Course, Vol. 2, McGraw-Hill, Inc. (1985). A well known text which discusses the relaxation method.

T. Tajima, A. Clark, G. G. Craddock, D. L. Gilden, W. K. Leung, Y. M. Li, J. A. Robertson and B. J. Saltzman, "Particle simulation of plasmas and stellar systems," *Am. J. Phys.* **53**, 365 (1985). The authors discuss a unified approach to the simulation of galaxies and electron plasmas.

P. B. Visscher, *Fields and Electrodynamics*, John Wiley & Sons, to be published. An intermediate level text which incorporates computer simulations and analysis into its development. Of special interest is the author's development of a discrete version of electrodynamics which satisfies Gauss' law, conservation of energy, etc., for arbitrary lattice spacing.

Gregg Williams, "An introduction to relaxation methods," *Byte* **12**, 111 (January, 1987). The author discusses the application of relaxation methods to the solution of the two-dimensional Poisson's equation.

APPENDICES

APPENDIX A SUMMARY OF THE CORE SYNTAX OF BASIC, FORTRAN AND PASCAL

The comparisons in the following are to be used as a guide only. BASIC refers to Microsoft BASIC on the IBM PC.

BASIC	True BASIC	FORTRAN	Pascal
Arithmetic operations			
$+ - */$	same	same	same
$2\hat{\ }3$	$2\hat{\ }3$	$2**3$	-
Declaration of variables			
			var
-	-	integer i	i : integer;
-	-	real x	x : real;
any variable ending in $		character a*5	a : packed array[1..5] of char;
dim a(5)	dim a(5)	dimension a(5)	a : array[1..5] of real;
Assigment			
$x = 5$	let $x = 5$	$x = 5$	x := 5;
Logical relations			
=	=	.eq.	=
<>	<>	.ne.	<>
>	>	.gt.	>
<	<	.lt.	<
>=	>=	.ge.	>=
<=	<=	.le.	<=
and	and	.and.	and
or	or	.or.	or

BASIC	True BASIC	FORTRAN	Pascal
Arithmetic functions			
sqr(x)	sqr(x)	sqrt(x)	sqrt(x)
fix(x)	truncate(x,0)	int(x)	trunc(x)
int(x)	int(x)	-	-
abs(x)	same	same	same
sin(x)	same	same	same
cos(x)	same	same	same
tan(x)	same	same	same
exp(x)	same	same	same
log(x)	log(x)	alog(x)	ln(x)
-	log10(x)	alog10(x)	-
-	max(x,y)	amax1(x,y)	-
-	-	max0(i,j)	-
-	min(x,y)	amin1(x,y)	-
-	-	min0(i,j)	-
rnd	rnd	depends	depends

Loops

BASIC	True BASIC
10 for $i = 1$ to n	for $i = 1$ to n
20 $x = x + 1$	let $x = x + 1$
30 next i	next i
10 while $i > 10$	do while $i < 10$
20 $i = i + 1$	let $i = i + 1$
30 wend	loop
10 while $idum = 0$	do
20 $i = i + 1$	let $i = i + 1$
30 if $i >= 10$ then goto 50	loop until $i >= 10$
40 wend	
50 ' mimics a repeat until loop	

FORTRAN

```
        do 10 i = 1, n
            x = x + 1
10      continue

        do 10 idum = 1,10000
            if (i .ge. 10) go to 100
            i = i + 1
10      continue
100     continue

        do 10 idum = 1,10000
            i = i + 1
            if (i .ge. 10 ) go to 100
10      continue
100     continue
```

Pascal

```
for i := 1 to n do begin
    x := x + 1
end;

while i < 10 do
   begin
      i := i + 1
   end;


repeat
   i := i + 1
until i >= 10;
```

Decision statements

BASIC

```
10      if i > 1 then i = 0
20      if i > 1 then i = 0 else i = -1



30      if i > 1 then i = 0 : j = 2 else i = -1
```

True BASIC

```
if i > 1 then let i = 0
if i > 1 then
   let i = 0
else
   let i = -1
end if

if i > 1 then
   let i = 0
   let j = 2
else
   let i = -1
end if
```

FORTRAN

```
if (i .gt. 1) i = 0
if (i .gt. 1) then
    i = 0
else
    i = -1
end if

if (i .gt. 1) then
    i = 0
    j = 2
else
    i = -1
end if
```

Pascal

```
if i > 1 then i := 0;
if i > 1 then
    i := 0
else
    i := -1;


if i > 1 then
    begin
        i := 0;
        j := 2
    end
else
    i := -1;
```

APPENDIX B: EXAMPLES OF INPUT AND OUTPUT STATEMENTS

Input and output statements depend on the computer hardware as well as the computer language. The following programs in Microsoft BASIC, True BASIC, FORTRAN 77, and Pascal write data to the file test.dat, read the file test.dat, print the result on the screen, and for personal computers show the result on an attached printer.

```
10   'Program IO
20   ' example of input/output in Microsoft BASIC on the IBM PC
30   x = 5.76
40   open "test.dat" for output as #1
50   print #1, x
60   close #1
70   open "test.dat" for input as #2
80   input #2, x
90   close #2
100  print using "###.##";x          ' output to screen
110  lprint using "###.##;x          ' output to printer
120  end


Program IO
! example of input/output in True BASIC
let x = 5.76
open #1: name "test.dat", access output, create new
print #1: x
close #1
open #2: name "test.dat", access input
input #2: x
close #2
print using "###.##": x
open #1: printer
print #1: x                    ! output to printer
close #1
end
```

```
Program IO(output,data);
(* example of input/output in Turbo Pascal on the IBM PC *)
var
  x : real;
  data : text;
begin
  x := 5.76;
  assign(data,'test.dat');       (* assign name of file to file variable *)
  rewrite(data);                 (* open file for output *)
  writeln(data,x:1:2);
  (* not necessary if file used again in same program *)
  close(data);
  reset(data);                   (* open file for input *)
  readln(data,x);
  close(data);
  writeln(x:6:2);                (* name:total length:decimal places *)
  writeln(lst,x:6:2);            (* output to printer *)
 end.


Program IO(output,data);
(* example of input/output in VAX Pascal *)
var
  x : real;
  data : text;
begin
  x := 5.76;
  open(data,'test.dat');
  rewrite(data);
  writeln(x);
  close(data);
  open('test.dat',history :=old);
  reset(data);
  readln(x);
  close(data);
  writeln(x:6:2);
 end.
```

```fortran
*       Program IO
*       example of input/output in VAX FORTRAN 77
        x = 5.76
        open(1,file='test.dat',status='unknown')
        write(1,*) x
        close(1)
        open(2,file='test.dat',status='unknown')
        read(2,*) x
        close(2)
        write(5,10) x
10      format(f6.2)
        stop
        end
```

Appendix C INDEX OF TRUE BASIC PROGRAMS—PART I

We list the page numbers of the True BASIC programs given in Part I of this text.

Index of True BASIC Simulation Programs

Index of Programs Illustrating True BASIC Syntax

APPENDIX D   LISTINGS OF FORTRAN PROGRAMS: PART I

In the following we list our FORTRAN 77 translations of many of the True BASIC programs given in the text. In general we have written the True BASIC programs so that they can be translated into FORTRAN and Pascal in a straightforward manner. The FORTRAN programs were run on a VAX 11/750.

Unfortunately there does not exist a one-to-one correspondence between the graphics statements used by the various languages. Among the languages available for microcomputers, True BASIC has the important advantage of allowing the user to establish a screen coordinate system which is independent of the number of pixels. In addition True BASIC allows the largest value of the vertical coordinate to be at the top of the screen.

Since the development of FORTRAN preceded the widespread availability of graphics displays, standard FORTRAN includes no graphics statements or subroutines. As an example of the use of a graphics package with FORTRAN, our programs illustrate the use of PLOT 10 (Tektronix), a common graphics package available on the VAX and other computers. On most computers PLOT 10 can also be called from Pascal. A brief description of the PLOT 10 graphics subroutines used in the programs is given in Table D1.

TABLE D1 Summary of core graphics PLOT 10 subroutines

Subroutine	Description
initt(ibaud)	initialize graphics at baud rate ibaud
dwindo(xmin,xmax,ymin,ymax)	establish window coordinates
movea(x,y)	move pen to coordinate (x,y)
pointa(x,y)	plot point at (x,y)
drawa(x2,y2)	draw line from current coordinate to (x2,y2)
a1out(nchar,iarray)	output first nchar characters of iarray; iarray is an array of characters
tsend	dump output buffer
finitt(ix,iy)	end graphics, move pen to col ix and row iy

CHAPTER 2

```
*       beginning of main program
        PROGRAM example
        CALL start(y,x,dx,n)
        CALL Euler(y,x,dx,n)
        STOP
        END
*       end of main program

        SUBROUTINE start(y,x,dx,n)
*       initial value of x
        x = 1
*       maximum value of x
        xmax = 2
*       initial value of y
        y = 1
*       magnitude of step size
        dx = 0.1
        n = (xmax - x)/dx
        RETURN
        END

        SUBROUTINE Euler(y,x,dx,n)
*       loop n times
        DO 10 i = 1,n
*           slope at beginning of interval
            slope = 2.0*x
*           estimate of total change during interval
            change = slope*dx
*           new value of y
            y = y + change
*           increment value of x
            x = x + dx
            WRITE(6,*)x,y
10      CONTINUE
        RETURN
        END
```

```
        PROGRAM cool
*       Euler approximation for coffee cooling problem
        CALL start(t,temp,rmtemp,r,dt,ncalc)
        CALL Euler(t,temp,rmtemp,r,dt,ncalc)
        STOP
        END


        SUBROUTINE start(t,temp,rmtemp,r,dt,ncalc)
*       initial time
        t = 0.0
*       initial coffee temperature (C)
        temp = 83
*       room temperature (C)
        rmtemp = 32
*       cooling constant (min-1)
        r = 0.1
*       time step (min)
        dt = 0.1
*       duration (min)
        tmax = 2
*       total number of steps
        ncalc = tmax/dt
        RETURN
        END


        SUBROUTINE Euler(t,temp,rmtemp,r,dt,ncalc)
        DO 10 icalc = 1,ncalc
*          beginning of interval
           change = -r*(temp - rmtemp)
           temp = temp + change*dt
*          time
           t = t + dt
           CALL output(t,temp)
10      CONTINUE
        RETURN
        END
```

```
      SUBROUTINE output(t,temp)
*     print results
      WRITE(6,*)t,temp
      RETURN
      END



      PROGRAM cooler
*     modified program
      CALL start(t,temp,rmtemp,r,dt,ncalc,nprt)
*     print initial values
      CALL output(t,temp)
      DO 100 iprt = 1,nprt
          CALL Euler(t,temp,rmtemp,r,dt,ncalc)
*         print results
          CALL output(t,temp)
100   CONTINUE
      STOP
      END

      SUBROUTINE start(t,temp,rmtemp,r,dt,ncalc,nprt)
*     initial time
      t = 0.0
*     initial coffee temperature (C)
      temp = 83.
*     room temperature (C)
      rmtemp = 32.
*     cooling constant (min-1)
      WRITE(6,*)'cooling constant r = '
      READ(5,*) r
*     time step (min)
      WRITE(6,*)'time interval dt = '
      READ(5,*) dt
*     duration (min)
      WRITE(6,*)'duration = '
      READ(5,*) tmax
```

```
*       time (min) between successive printing
        prtper = 0.5
*       number of times results are printed
        nprt = tmax/prtper
*       number of iterations between printing
        ncalc = prtper/dt
        WRITE(6,17)
17      FORMAT(5x,'time',7x,'temperature')
*       skip line
        WRITE(6,*)
        RETURN
        END


        SUBROUTINE Euler(t,temp,rmtemp,r,dt,ncalc)
        DO 10 icalc = 1,ncalc
            change = -r*(temp - rmtemp)
            temp = temp + change*dt
10      CONTINUE
        t = t + dt*ncalc
        RETURN
        END


        SUBROUTINE output(t,temp)
*       print results
        WRITE(6,*)t,temp
        RETURN
        END
```

CHAPTER 3

```
        PROGRAM fall
*       freely falling particle
*       initial conditions and parameters
        CALL start(y,v,t,g,dt,height)
*       output parameters
        CALL prtpar(dt,ncalc)
*       print initial values
        CALL prttab(y,v,g,t)
*       10000 is a dummy number chosen to be very large
        DO 100 i = 1,10000
*           difference equation
            CALL Euler(y,v,accel,t,g,dt,ncalc)
*           print results after ncalc steps
            CALL prttab(y,v,accel,t)
*           end calculation if y > height
            IF (y.gt.height) STOP
100     CONTINUE
        STOP
        END

        SUBROUTINE start(y,v,t,g,dt,height)
*       initial time (sec)
        t = 0.0
*       initial displacement (m)
        y = 0.0
*       initial height above ground
        height = 10.0
*       initial velocity (m/s)
        v = 0.0
        WRITE(6,*)'timestep dt = '
        READ(5,*)dt
*       magnitude of acceleration due to gravity
        g = 9.8
        RETURN
        END
```

```
        SUBROUTINE prtpar(dt,ncalc)
        prtper = 0.1
*       number of steps between printing
        ncalc = prtper/dt
*       heading
        WRITE(6,13)
13      FORMAT(5x,'time(s)',8x,'y(m)',7x,'velocity(m/s)',4x,'accel(m/s*s)'/)
        RETURN
        END


        SUBROUTINE prttab(y,v,accel,t)
        WRITE(6,15)t,y,v,accel
15      FORMAT(4F15.5)
        RETURN
        END


        SUBROUTINE Euler(y,v,accel,t,g,dt,ncalc)
        DO 10 icalc = 1,ncalc
*          velocity at beginning of interval
           y = y + v*dt
*          y positive downward
           accel = g
           v = v + accel*dt
10      CONTINUE
        t = t + dt*ncalc
        RETURN
        END
```

```
      PROGRAM styrofoam
*     initial conditions and parameters
      CALL start(y,v,t,g,vt2,dt,height)
*     output parameters
      CALL prtpar(t,dt,n0,ncalc)
*     print initial values
      CALL prttab(y,v,g,t)
      CALL Euler(y,v,accel,t,g,vt2,dt,n0)
*     print results at t = 0
      CALL prttab(y,v,accel,t)
*     10000 is a dummy large number
      DO 100 i = 1,10000
*         generalization of subroutine in Program fall
          CALL Euler(y,v,accel,t,g,vt2,dt,ncalc)
*         print results after ncalc steps
          CALL prttab(y,v,accel,t)
*         end program if y > height
          IF (y.gt.height) STOP
100   CONTINUE
      STOP
      END
```

```
       SUBROUTINE start(y,v,t,g,vt2,dt,height)
*      initial time (sec)
       t = -0.132
*      initial displacement (m)
       y = 0.0
*      initial height above ground
       height = 4.0
*      initial velocity (m/s)
       v = 0.0
       WRITE(6,*)'timestep dt = '
       READ(5,*)dt
*      magnitude of acceleration due to gravity
       g = 9.8
       WRITE(6,*)' terminal velocity (m/s) = '
       READ(5,*)vterm
       vt2 = vterm*vterm
       RETURN
       END

       SUBROUTINE prtpar(t,dt,n0,ncalc)
       prtper = 0.1
*      number of steps between printing
       ncalc = prtper/dt
       n0 = -t/dt
*      heading
       WRITE(6,13)
13     FORMAT(5x,'time(s)',8x,'y(m)',7x,'velocity(m/s)',4x,'accel(m/s*s)'/)
       RETURN
       END

       SUBROUTINE prttab(y,v,accel,t)
       WRITE(6,15)t,y,v,accel
15     FORMAT(4F15.5)
       RETURN
       END
```

```
        SUBROUTINE Euler(y,v,accel,t,g,vt2,dt,ncalc)
        DO 10 icalc = 1,ncalc
*           velocity at beginning of interval
            y = y + v*dt
*           y positive downward
            accel = g*(1.0 - sign(1.0,v)*v*v/vt2)
            v = v + accel*dt
10      CONTINUE
        t = t + dt*ncalc
        RETURN
        END
```

CHAPTER 4

```
        PROGRAM planet
*       planetary motion
*       use new velocity to update position
*       define dimension of arrays
        DIMENSION pos(2),vel(2)
        CALL start(pos,vel,GM,dt,nplot,ncalc)
*       plot position of "earth"
        CALL output(pos)
        DO 100 iplot = 1,nplot
           CALL Euler(pos,vel,GM,dt,ncalc)
           CALL output(pos)
100     CONTINUE
        STOP
        END


        SUBROUTINE start(pos,vel,GM,dt,nplot,ncalc)
        DIMENSION pos(2),vel(2)
*       astronomical units
        GM = 4.0*(3.14159)**2
        WRITE(6,*)'time step (yrs) = '
        READ(5,*)dt
        WRITE(6,*)'duration (yrs) = '
        READ(5,*)tmax
        WRITE(6,*)'plot period (yrs) = '
        READ(5,*)pltper
*       number of steps between plots
        ncalc = pltper/dt
        nplot = tmax/pltper
        WRITE(6,*)'initial x position = '
        READ(5,*)pos(1)
*       initial y position and x velocity
        pos(2) = 0
        vel(1) = 0
        WRITE(6,*)'initial y velocity = '
        READ(5,*)vel(2)
```

```
*       assumed maximum value of semi-major axis
        r = 2*pos(1)
*       screen not square, aspect ratio = horizontal dist./vertical dist.
*       VT100 value
        aspect = 1.25
*       initialize graphics for plot10
        CALL initt(1200)
        x = aspect*r
        CALL dwindo(-x,x,-r,r)
*       draw sun at origin with radius 0.1
        CALL disk(0.0,0.0,0.1)
        RETURN
        END


        SUBROUTINE disk(x0,y0,radius)
*       draw filled disk
        angle = 0.0
        da = 3.14/200
        DO 100 i = 1,200
            x = radius*cos(angle)
            y = radius*sin(angle)
*           move cursor to point on circle
            CALL movea(x0 + x,y0 + y)
*           draw line to opposite point on circle
            CALL drawa(x0 - x,y0 - y)
            angle = angle + da
100     CONTINUE
        RETURN
        END
```

```
          SUBROUTINE Euler(pos,vel,GM,dt,ncalc)
          DIMENSION pos(2),vel(2),accel(2)
          DO 10 icalc = 1,ncalc
              r = sqrt(pos(1)*pos(1) + pos(2) *pos(2))
              DO 5 i = 1,2
                  accel(i) = -GM*pos(i)/(r*r*r)
                  vel(i) = vel(i) + accel(i)*dt
                  pos(i) = pos(i) + vel(i)*dt
5             CONTINUE
10        CONTINUE
          RETURN
          END


          SUBROUTINE output(pos)
*         plot orbit
          DIMENSION pos(2)
          CALL pointa(pos(1),pos(2))
          RETURN
          END



          PROGRAM planet2
*         solar system with two planets
          DIMENSION pos(2,2),vel(2,2)
          CALL start(pos,vel,GM,dt,nplot,ncalc)
          CALL output(pos)
          DO 100 iplot = 1,nplot
              CALL Euler(pos,vel,GM,dt,ncalc)
              CALL output(pos)
100       CONTINUE
          STOP
          END
```

```fortran
      SUBROUTINE start(pos,vel,GM,dt,nplot,ncalc)
      DIMENSION pos(2,2),vel(2,2)
*     astronomical units
      GM = 4.0*(3.14159)**2
      WRITE(6,*)'time step (yrs) = '
      READ(5,*)dt
      WRITE(6,*)'duration (yrs) = '
      READ(5,*)tmax
      WRITE(6,*)'plot period (yrs) = '
      READ(5,*)pltper
*     number of steps between plots
      ncalc = pltper/dt
      nplot = tmax/pltper
*     planet one initial coordinates
      pos(1,1) = 1.0
      pos(1,2) = 0.0
      vel(1,1) = 0.0
      vel(1,2) = sqrt(GM/pos(1,1))

*     planet two initial coordinates
      pos(2,1) = 4**(1/3)
      pos(2,2) = 0.0
      vel(2,1) = 0.0
      vel(2,2) = sqrt(GM/pos(2,1))
*     assumed maximum value of semi-major axis
      r = 2*pos(2,1)
*     screen not square, aspect ratio = horizontal dist./vertical dist.
*     VT100 value
      aspect = 1.25
*     initialize graphics for plot10
      CALL initt(1200)
      x = aspect*r
      CALL dwindo(-x,x,-r,r)
*     draw sun at origin with radius 0.1
      CALL disk(0.0,0.0,0.1)
      RETURN
      END
```

```
      SUBROUTINE disk(x0,y0,radius)
      angle = 0.0
      da = 3.14/200
      DO 100 i = 1,200
          x = radius*cos(angle)
          y = radius*sin(angle)
*         move cursor to point on circle
          CALL movea(x0 + x,y0 + y)
*         draw line to opposite point on circle
          CALL drawa(x0 - x,y0 - y)
          angle = angle + da
100   CONTINUE
      RETURN
      END


      SUBROUTINE Euler(pos,vel,GM,dt,ncalc)
      DIMENSION pos(2,2),vel(2,2),a(2,2),r(2)
      DO 10 icalc = 1,ncalc
*         compute distance dr between 2 planets
          dx = pos(2,1) - pos(1,1)
          dy = pos(2,2) - pos(1,2)
          dr = sqrt(dx*dx + dy*dy)
          accel = GM/(dr*dr*dr)
*         acceleration of planet 1 due to planet 2
          a(1,1) = -0.01*accel*dx
          a(1,2) = -0.01*accel*dy
*         acceleration of planet 2 due to planet 1
          a(2,1) = -0.001*a(1,1)
          a(2,2) = -0.001*a(1,2)
```

```
          DO 5 ip = 1,2
             dist2 = pos(ip,1)**2 + pos(ip,2)**2
             r(ip) = sqrt(dist2)
             DO 2 i = 1,2
                accel = a(ip,i) - GM*pos(ip,i)/(r(ip)**3)
                vel(ip,i) = vel(ip,i) + accel*dt
                pos(ip,i) = pos(ip,i) + vel(ip,i)*dt
2            CONTINUE
5         CONTINUE
10    CONTINUE
      RETURN
      END


      SUBROUTINE output(pos)
*     plot orbit
      DIMENSION pos(2,2)
*     planet 1
      CALL pointa(pos(1,1),pos(1,2))
*     planet 2
      CALL pointa(pos(2,1),pos(2,2))
      RETURN
      END
```

CHAPTER 5

```
      PROGRAM sho
*     simple harmonic oscillator
      CALL start(pos,vel,w2,dt,ncalc)
      t = 0.
*     10000 is a large dummy number
      DO 10 i = 1,10000
         CALL output(pos,vel,t)
         CALL Euler(pos,vel,w2,dt,ncalc)
         t = t + ncalc*dt
10    CONTINUE
      STOP
      END
```

```
        SUBROUTINE start(pos,vel,w2,dt,ncalc)
        WRITE(6,*)'enter initial position (meters)'
        READ(5,*)pos
*       initial velocity  (m/s)
        vel = 0.0
*       natural (angular) frequency
        WRITE(6,*)'enter ratio of k/m'
        READ(5,*)w2
        WRITE(6,*)'enter time step (sec) ( < 0.05)'
        READ(5,*)dt
        prtper = 0.05
        ncalc = prtper/dt
        WRITE(6,15)
15      FORMAT(15x,'time',14x,'position',12x,'velocity')
        WRITE(6,*)
        RETURN
        END


        SUBROUTINE Euler(pos,vel,w2,dt,ncalc)
*       Euler-Cromer algorithm
        DO 10 icalc = 1,ncalc
            accel = -w2*pos
            vel = vel + accel*dt
            pos = pos + vel*dt
10      CONTINUE
        RETURN
        END


        SUBROUTINE output(pos,vel,t)
        WRITE(6,25)t,pos,vel
*       each number has 20 spaces including 4 decimal places
25      FORMAT(3F20.4)
        RETURN
        END
```

```
      PROGRAM rc
      CALL start(R,tau,V0,w,tmax,dt)
      CALL screen(shift,V0,tmax)
      CALL scope(shift,R,tau,V0,w,tmax,dt)
      STOP
      END

      SUBROUTINE start(R,tau,V0,w,tmax,dt)
*     amplitude of external voltage
      V0 = 1.0
      WRITE(6,*)'external voltage frequency (hertz) = '
      READ(5,*)f
*     angular frequency
      w = 2.0*3.14159*f
      WRITE(6,*)'resistance (ohms) = '
      READ(5,*) R
      WRITE(6,*)'capacitance (farads) = '
      READ(5,*) C
      WRITE(6,*)'time step dt = '
      READ(5,*) dt
*     relaxation time
      tau = R*C
*     period of external voltage source
      T = 1/f
      IF (T.gt.tau) then
         tmax = 2*T
      ELSE
         tmax = 2*tau
      ENDIF
      RETURN
      END
```

```
        SUBROUTINE screen(shift,V0,tmax)
        CHARACTER*25 title
        tmin = 0.0
        Vmin = -V0
*       shift of y screen coordinates for top plot
        shift = 2.5*V0
*       maximum y screen coordinate
        ymax = shift + 1.1*(V0 - Vmin)
        CALL initt(1200)
        CALL dwindo(1.1*tmin,1.1*tmax,1.1*Vmin,ymax)
        title = 'source voltage'
        CALL axis(tmin,tmax,Vmin,V0,title)
        title = 'resistor voltage drop'
        CALL axis(tmin,tmax,Vmin+shift,V0+shift,title)
        RETURN
        END


        SUBROUTINE scope(shift,R,tau,V0,w,tmax,dt)
        ntime = tmax/dt
        t = 0.0
*       values at t = 0
        Vs0 = V(V0,w,t)
        Vr0 = Vs0
        Q = 0.0
        DO 100 itime = 1,ntime
            t = t + dt
            cur = V(V0,w,t)/R  - Q/tau
            Q = Q + cur*dt
            Vs = V(V0,w,t)
            Vr = cur*R
            CALL movea(t-dt,Vs0)
            CALL drawa(t,Vs)
            CALL movea(t-dt,Vr0+shift)
            CALL drawa(t,Vr+shift)
            Vs0 = Vs
            Vr0 = Vr
100     CONTINUE
        RETURN
        END
```

```
      FUNCTION V(V0,w,t)
      V = V0*cos(w*t)
      RETURN
      END


      SUBROUTINE axis(xmin,xmax,ymin,ymax,title)
      CHARACTER*25 title
      ntick = 10
      dx = (xmax - xmin)/ntick
      dy = (ymax - ymin)/ntick
*     determine location of axes
      IF (xmin*xmax.lt.0.0) then
         x0 = 0.0
      ELSE
         x0 = xmin
      ENDIF
      IF (ymin*ymax.lt.0.0) then
         y0 = 0.0
      ELSE
         y0 = ymin
      ENDIF
*     draw vertical axis then horizontal axis
      CALL movea(x0,ymin)
      CALL drawa(x0,ymax)
      CALL movea(xmin,y0)
      CALL drawa(xmax,y0)
*     length of vertical tick mark on x axis
      xlen = 0.1*dy
*     length of horizontal tick mark on y axis
      ylen = 0.1*dx
*     draw tick marks
      DO 50 i = 0,ntick-1
         col = xmin + i*dx
         row = ymin + i*dy
         CALL movea(col,y0-xlen)
         CALL drawa(col,y0+xlen)
         CALL movea(x0-ylen,row)
         CALL drawa(x0+ylen,row)
50    CONTINUE
```

```
*       print title
        CALL movea(xmin + 7.0*dx,ymax)
        WRITE(6,11)title
11      FORMAT(a25)
*       print maximum x and y values
        CALL movea(xmax-0.5*xlen,y0)
        WRITE(6,13)xmax
        CALL movea(x-4.0*ylen,ymax+ylen)
        WRITE(6,13)ymax
13      FORMAT(f5.1)
        RETURN
        END
```

CHAPTER 6

```
        PROGRAM md
        DIMENSION x(1024),y(1024),vx(1024),vy(1024)
        DIMENSION ax(1024),ay(1024)
        CALL start(x,y,vx,vy,N,Sx,Sy,dt,dt2,nsnap,ntime)
        CALL accel(x,y,ax,ay,N,Sx,Sy,virial,zpe)
        virial = 0.0
        zpe = 0.0
        DO 100 isnap = 1,nsnap
           DO 10 itime = 1,ntime
              CALL move(x,y,vx,vy,ax,ay,N,Sx,Sy,dt,dt2,flx,fly,virial,zke,zpe)
10         CONTINUE
           CALL output(flx,fly,virial,zke,zpe,Sx,Sy,dt,N,ntime)
100     CONTINUE
        STOP
        END
```

```
SUBROUTINE start(x,y,vx,vy,N,Sx,Sy,dt,dt2,nsnap,ntime)
DIMENSION x(1024),y(1024),vx(1024),vy(1024)
WRITE(6,*)'enter number of particles'
READ(5,*)N
WRITE(6,*)'enter box sizes'
READ(5,*)Sx,Sy
WRITE(6,*)'enter time step'
READ(5,*)dt
dt2 = dt*dt
WRITE(6,*)'enter maximum velocity component'
READ(5,*)vmax
WRITE(6,*)'enter # of snapshots and timesteps between them'
READ(5,*)nsnap,ntime
WRITE(6,*)'enter random number seed'
READ(5,*)iseed
WRITE(6,*)'enter starting conf. 1=old,2=hot,3=cold'
READ(5,*)icf
IF (icf.eq.1) then
*        read old configuration
         DO 10 i = 1,N
            READ(8,12)x(i),y(i),vx(i),vy(i)
12          FORMAT(4(2x,f10.5))
10       CONTINUE
ELSEIF (icf.eq.3) then
*        ordered (cold) starting configuration
         area1 = Sx*Sy/N
         ys = 0.5*sqrt(3.0)
         a = sqrt(area1/ys)
         Ly = 2*int(.5*(1.0 + Sy/(a*ys)))
         Lx = N/Ly
```

```
            DO 30 ix = 1,Lx
               DO 20 iy = 1,Ly
                  i = (iy - 1)*Ly + ix
                  y(i) = (iy - 0.5)*a*ys
                  IF (mod(iy,2).eq.0) then
                     x(i) = (ix - 0.25)*a
                  ELSE
                     x(i) = (ix - 0.75)*a
                  ENDIF
                  vx(i) = vmax*(2*ran(iseed) - 1)
                  vy(i) = vmax*(2*ran(iseed) - 1)
20             CONTINUE
30          CONTINUE
         ELSE
*           random (hot) starting configuration
            DO 40 i = 1,N
               x(i) = Sx*ran(iseed)
               y(i) = Sy*ran(iseed)
               vx(i) = vmax*(2*ran(iseed) - 1)
               vy(i) = vmax*(2*ran(iseed) - 1)
40          CONTINUE
         ENDIF
         DO 50 i = 1,N
            vxcum = vxcum + vx(i)
            vycum = vycum + vy(i)
50       CONTINUE
         vxcum = vxcum/N
         vycum = vycum/N
         DO 60 i = 1,N
            vx(i) = vx(i) - vxcum
            vy(i) = vy(i) - vycum
60       CONTINUE
         RETURN
         END
```

```
SUBROUTINE move(x,y,vx,vy,ax,ay,N,Sx,Sy,dt,dt2,flx,fly,virial,zke,zpe)
DIMENSION x(1024),y(1024),vx(1024),vy(1024)
DIMENSION ax(1024),ay(1024)
DO 10 i = 1,N
   xnew = x(i) + vx(i)*dt + 0.5*ax(i)*dt2
   ynew = y(i) + vy(i)*dt + 0.5*ay(i)*dt2
   CALL cellp(xnew,ynew,vx(i),vy(i),Sx,Sy,flx,fly)
   x(i) = xnew
   y(i) = ynew
   vx(i) = vx(i) + 0.5*ax(i)*dt
   vy(i) = vy(i) + 0.5*ay(i)*dt
10    CONTINUE
CALL accel(x,y,ax,ay,N,Sx,Sy,virial,zpe)
DO 20 i = 1,n
   vx(i) = vx(i) + 0.5*dt*ax(i)
   vy(i) = vy(i) + 0.5*dt*ay(i)
   zke = zke + vx(i)*vx(i) + vy(i)*vy(i)
   virial = virial + ax(i)*x(i) + ay(i)*y(i)
20    CONTINUE
RETURN
END

SUBROUTINE accel(x,y,ax,ay,N,Sx,Sy,virial,zpe)
DIMENSION x(1024),y(1024),ax(1024),ay(1024)
DO 1 i = 1,n
   ax(i) = 0.0
   ay(i) = 0.0
1     CONTINUE
DO 20 i = 1,(n-1)
   DO 10 j = (i+1),n
      dx = x(i) - x(j)
      dy = y(i) - y(j)
      CALL sep(dx,dy,Sx,Sy)
      r = sqrt(dx*dx + dy*dy)
      CALL FU(r,force,pot)
      ax(i) = ax(i) + force*dx
      ay(i) = ay(i) + force*dy
      zpe = zpe + pot
```

```
*              Newton's third law used to determine force on particle j
               ax(j) = ax(j) - force*dx
               ay(j) = ay(j) - force*dy
10       CONTINUE
20       CONTINUE
         RETURN
         END

         SUBROUTINE FU(r,force,pot)
         ri = 1/r
         ri3 = ri*ri*ri
         ri6 = ri3*ri3
         ri12 = ri6*ri6
         g = 24*ri*ri6*(2*ri6 - 1)
         force = g*ri
         pot = 4*(ri12 - ri6)
         RETURN
         END

         SUBROUTINE sep(dx,dy,Sx,Sy)
         IF (abs(dx).gt.0.5*Sx) dx = dx - sign(Sx,dx)
         IF (abs(dy).gt.0.5*Sy) dy = dy - sign(Sy,dy)
         RETURN
         END

         SUBROUTINE cell(xnew,ynew,Sx,Sy)
         IF (xnew.lt.0) xnew = xnew + Sx
         IF (xnew.gt.Sx) xnew = xnew - Sx
         IF (ynew.lt.0) ynew = ynew + Sy
         IF (ynew.gt.Sy) ynew = ynew - Sy
         RETURN
         END
```

```
SUBROUTINE cellp(xnew,ynew,vx,vy,Sx,Sy,flx,fly)
IF (xnew.lt.0) then
    xnew = xnew + Sx
    flx = flx - vx
ENDIF
IF (xnew.gt.Sx) then
    xnew = xnew - Sx
    flx = flx + vx
ENDIF
IF (ynew.lt.0) then
    ynew = ynew + Sy
    fly = fly - vy
ENDIF
IF (ynew.gt.Sy) then
    ynew = ynew - Sy
    fly = fly + vy
ENDIF
RETURN
END

SUBROUTINE output(flx,fly,virial,zke,zpe,Sx,Sy,dt,N,ntime)
data iff /0/
IF (iff.eq.0) then
    iff = 1
    write(6,*)'ke  pe  tot   pflux  pvirial   pideal'
ENDIF
pflux = ((flx/Sx) + (fly/Sy))/(2*dt*ntime)
zke = 0.5*zke/ntime
zpe = zpe/ntime
tot = zke + zpe
```

```
         pideal = zke/(Sx*Sy)
         pvirial = pideal + (.5/(Sx*Sy))*virial/ntime
         write(6,13)zke,zpe,tot,pflux,pvirial,pideal
13       format(6(1x,e13.6))
         zke = 0
         zpe = 0
         fly = 0
         flx = 0
         virial = 0
         RETURN
         END
```

CHAPTER 7

```
         PROGRAM maptable
         character*1 choice
*        iterate one-dimensional map f(x)
*        idum is a large dummy number
         DO 100 idum = 1,10000
             CALL start(x,r)
             CALL map(x,r)
             WRITE(6,*)'continue y/n? '
             READ(5,13)choice
13           FORMAT(a1)
             IF (choice.eq.'n') STOP
100      CONTINUE
         STOP
         END

         SUBROUTINE start(x,r)
         WRITE(6,*)'growth parameter (0 < r < 1) = '
         READ(5,*) r
         WRITE(6,*)'initial value of x (0 < x < 1) = '
         READ(5,*) x
         RETURN
         END
```

```
        SUBROUTINE map(x,r)
        DIMENSION xs(8)
        CHARACTER*1 choice
        iter = 0
        DO 100 idum = 1,1000
*           print 20 rows of 8 iterations each
            DO 50 irow = 1,20
                DO 10 i = 1,8
                    xs(i) = 4*r*x*(1 - x)
                    x = xs(i)
                    iter = iter + 1
10              CONTINUE
            WRITE(6,15)(xs(k),k=1,8)
15          FORMAT(8f9.6)
50          CONTINUE
            WRITE(6,*) 'number of iterations = ', iter
            WRITE(6,*) 'more iterations y/n?'
            READ(5,17)choice
17          FORMAT(a1)
            IF (choice.ne.'y')RETURN
100     CONTINUE
        RETURN
        END
```

CHAPTER 8

```
        PROGRAM oscillators
*       calculate displacement of N coupled oscillators
        DIMENSION u(0:21),vel(20)
        CALL start(N,u,vel,kc,k,dt,tmax)
        CALL screen(N,nplot,tmax,dy)
        CALL move(N,u,vel,kc,k,dt,nplot,tmax,dy)
        STOP
        END
```

```
       SUBROUTINE start(N,u,vel,kc,k,dt,tmax)
       DIMENSION u(0:21),vel(20)
       WRITE(6,*) 'number of particles = '
       READ(5,*) N
       WRITE(6,*) 'time step = '
       READ(5,*) dt
       WRITE(6,*) 'duration = '
       READ(5,*) tmax
       WRITE(6,*) 'spring constant kc = '
       READ(5,*) kc
*      coupling to walls
       k = 1
*      initial displacement of first two oscillators
       u(1) = 0.5
       u(2) = 0.0
*      set initial velocities equal to zero
        DO 10 i = 1,N
           vel(i) = 0
10     CONTINUE
       RETURN
       END


       SUBROUTINE screen(N,nplot,tmax,dy)
*      distance between plots on screen
       dy = 2
       CALL initt(1200)
       CALL dwindo(-1.0,tmax + 1.0,-dy,3.0*dy)
       ntick = 100
*      distance between ticks
       dx = tmax/ntick
*      "height" of tick marks
       hy = 0.1*dx
*      number of oscillators to be graphed
       nplot = min(4,N)
*      draw tick marks
       sy = -1.0
```

```
      DO 30 j = 1,nplot
          CALL movea(0.0,sy)
          CALL drawa(tmax,sy)
          DO 20 i = 1,ntick
             sx= i*dx
                CALL movea(sx,sy)
             CALL drawa(sx,sy+hy)
20        CONTINUE
          sy = sy + dy
30    CONTINUE
      RETURN
      END
```

```
        SUBROUTINE move(N,u,vel,kc,k,dt,nplot,tmax,dy)
        DIMENSION u(0:21),vel(20)
        DIMENSION a(20)
        DO 1000 idum = 1,1000
            t = t + dt
*           accel of particles not connected to wall
            DO 40 i = 2,(N - 1)
                a(i) = kc*(u(i + 1) + u(i - 1) - 2*u(i))
40          CONTINUE
*           accel of end masses
            a(1) = kc*(u(2) - u(1)) - k*u(1)
            a(N) = kc*(u(N - 1) - u(N)) - k*u(N)
*           Euler-Cromer algorithm
            DO 50 i = 1,N
                vel(i) = vel(i) + a(i)*dt
                u(i) = u(i) + vel(i)*dt
50          CONTINUE
            row = -1
            DO 60 i = 1,nplot
                CALL pointa(t,u(i)+row)
                row = row + dy
60          CONTINUE
            IF (t.ge.tmax) RETURN
1000    CONTINUE
        RETURN
        END
```

CHAPTER 9

```
        PROGRAM Laplace
        DIMENSION V(100,100)
        CALL assign(V,nx,ny,change)
        CALL relax(V,nx,ny,change,iter)
        STOP
        END
```

```
      SUBROUTINE assign(V,nx,ny,change)
      DIMENSION V(100,100)
      WRITE(6,*)'number of cells in x-direction = '
      READ(5,*) nx
      WRITE(6,*)'number of cells in y-direction = '
      READ(5,*) ny
      WRITE(6,*)'potential of rectangle in volts = '
      READ(5,*) V0
      WRITE(6,*)'minimum % change to stop = '
      READ(5,*) change
      change = change/100
      DO 100 i  = 1,nx
*         fix potential on rectangle
          V(i,1) = V0
          V(i,ny) = V0
100   CONTINUE
      DO 200 j = 1,ny
          V(1,j) = V0
          V(nx,j) = V0
200   CONTINUE
*     initialize potentials of interior cells
      DO 400 i  = 2,nx - 1
         DO 300 j  = 2,ny - 1
            V(i,j) = 0.9*V0
300      CONTINUE
400   CONTINUE
      RETURN
      END
```

```
          SUBROUTINE relax(V,nx,ny,change,iter)
          DIMENSION Vave(100,100),V(100,100)
          iter = 0
          DO 1000 idum = 1,1000
             dmax = 0
             iter = iter + 1
             DO 200 i = 2,nx - 1
                DO 100 j = 2,ny - 1
*                   compute average of potential of neighboring cells
                    Vave(i,j) = V(i+1,j) + V(i-1,j)
                    Vave(i,j) = Vave(i,j) + V(i,j+1) + V(i,j-1)
                    Vave(i,j) = 0.25*Vave(i,j)
*                   compute percentage change in potential
                    diff = abs((V(i,j) - Vave(i,j))/Vave(i,j))
                    IF (diff.gt.dmax) dmax = diff
100          CONTINUE
200       CONTINUE
*         update potential at each cell
          DO 400 i = 2,nx - 1
             DO 300 j = 2,ny - 1
                V(i,j) = Vave(i,j)
300          CONTINUE
400       CONTINUE
          CALL output(V,nx,ny,iter)
*         continue until change is less than minimum desired change
          IF (dmax.lt.change) RETURN
1000 CONTINUE
     RETURN
     END


     SUBROUTINE output(V,nx,ny,iter)
     DIMENSION V(100,100)
     WRITE(6,*)'number of iterations = ',iter
     DO 100 j = ny,1,-1
        WRITE(6,13)(V(i,j), i = 1,nx)
13      FORMAT(10F8.4)
100  CONTINUE
     RETURN
     END
```

APPENDIX E LISTING OF PASCAL PROGRAMS: PART I

In the following we list our Pascal versions of many of the True BASIC
programs given in Part I of the text. The programs were run using Macintosh
Pascal. Relatively minor changes are needed for other versions of Pascal.

Since the development of Pascal preceded the widespread availability of
graphics displays, Pascal does not include graphics procedures. True BASIC
allows the programmer to establish a screen coordinate system in accordance
with the usual mathematical convention for which the largest value of the vertical coordinate is at the top of the screen. In contrast the graphics procedures
available in most microcomputer versions of Pascal differ from this convention
and require the smallest value of the vertical coordinate to be at the top of the
screen. Although it is possible to write procedures to convert the graphics procedures given in microcomputer versions of Pascal to procedures similar to those
used by True BASIC, we have related the x and y coordinates to the appropriate
number of screen pixels on the Macintosh screen.

The graphics procedures used in the Pascal programs are from the Macintosh
toolbox and can be called from other programming languages on the Macintosh.
A brief description of the graphics procedures used in the programs is given in
Table E1.

TABLE E1 Summary of common Macintosh Pascal graphics procedures

Procedure	Description
moveto(x,y)	move pen to position (x,y)
lineto(x2,y2)	draw line from current position to (x2,y2)
paintoval(top,left,bottom,right)	draw filled ellipse inscribed in rectangle with integer coordinates top, left, bottom, right
framerect(top,left,bottom,right)	draw rectangle
eraserect(top,left,bottom,right)	erase area inside rectangle
paintrect(top,left,bottom,right)	fill in rectangle
drawstring(strg)	print string beginning at current location

In Table E2 we list some of the important graphics procedures used in Turbo
Pascal (Borland International) as implemented on the IBM PC and compatibles.

TABLE E2 Summary of "core" graphics procedures in Turbo Pascal on the IBM PC

Procedure	Description
HiRes	high resolution mode (640 x 200 dots)
GraphMode	(320 x 200) monochrome graphics
GraphColorMode	(320 x 200) color graphics
TextMode	25 lines of 80 characters
Plot(x,y,color);	plot point at coordinate (x,y)
Draw(x1,y1,x2,y2,color);	draw line from (x1,y1) to (x2,y2)
Circle(x,y,radius,color);	draw circle with specified radius centered at (x,y)
FillShape(x,y,fc,bc);	fill in area with color specied by fc; enclose (x,y) by a closed boundary of color specified by bc

CHAPTER 2

```
program example(output);
var                              (* variable declarations *)
    y, x, dx : real;
    n : integer;


procedure initial (var y, x, dx : real;
                    var n : integer);
var
    xmax : real;
begin
    x := 1.0;                    (* initial value of x *)
    xmax := 2.0;                 (* maximum value of x *)
    y := 1;                      (* initial value of y *)
    dx := 0.1;                   (* magnitude of step size *)
    n := trunc((xmax - x) / dx)
end;
```

```
      procedure Euler (var y, x, dx : real;
                       var n : integer);
      var
         slope, change : real;
         i : integer;
      begin
         for i := 1 to n do              (* loop n times *)
            begin
               slope := 2.0 * x;         (* slope at beginning of interval *)
               change := slope * dx;     (* estimate of total change during interval *)
               y := y + change;          (* new value of y *)
               x := x + dx;              (* increment value of x *)
               writeln(x, y)
            end
      end;


begin                                    (* main *)
      initial(y, x, dx, n);
      Euler(y, x, dx, n)
end.



program cool(output);          (* Euler approximation for coffee cooling problem *)
var                            (* variable declarations *)
      t, temperature, room_temp, r, dt : real;
      ncalc : integer;

      procedure initial (var t, temperature, room_temp, r, dt : real;
                         var ncalc : integer);
      var
         tmax : real;
      begin
         t := 0.0;                        (* initial time *)
         temperature := 83;               (* initial coffee temperature (C) *)
         room_temp := 22;                 (* room temperature (C) *)
         r := 0.1;                        (* cooling constant (1/min) *)
         dt := 0.1;                       (* time step (min) *)
         tmax := 2.0;                     (* duration (min) *)
         ncalc := trunc(tmax / dt)        (* total number of steps *)
      end;
```

```
procedure output (t, temperature : real);
begin
    writeln(t, temperature)          (* print results *)
end;


procedure Euler (var t, temperature, room_temp, r, dt : real;
                 var ncalc : integer);
var
    change : real;
    icalc : integer;
begin
    for icalc := 1 to ncalc do           (* loop ncalc times *)
        begin
            change := -r * (temperature - room_temp);
            temperature := temperature + change * dt;
            t := t + dt;                 (* time *)
            output(t,temperature)
        end
end;

begin                            (* main *)
    initial(t, temperature, room_temp, r, dt, ncalc);
    Euler(t, temperature, room_temp, r, dt, ncalc)
end.
```

CHAPTER 3

```
program fall (input, output);     (* freely falling body *)
const
    g = 9.8;                      (* magnitude of acceleration due to gravity *)
var
    y, v, accel, t, dt, height : real;
    ncalc : integer;
```

```pascal
procedure initial (var y, v, t, dt, height : real);
begin
    t := 0.0;                      (* initial time (sec) *)
    y := 0.0;                      (* initial displacement (m) *)
    height := 10.0;                (* initial height of object above ground *)
    v := 0.0;                      (* initial velocity *)
    write('timestep dt = ');
    readln(dt)
end;


procedure print_parameters (var dt : real;
                            var ncalc : integer);
var
    print_period : real;
begin
    print_period := 0.1;               (* sec *)
    ncalc := round(print_period / dt); (* number of steps between printing *)
    write(' time(s)     ');            (* heading *)
    write('y (m)    ');
    write('vel (m/s)    ');
    writeln('accel (m/s*s)');
    writeln
end;


procedure print_table (y, v, accel, t : real);
(* print results in tabular form *)
begin
    writeln(t : 6 : 2, y : 12 : 2, v : 12 : 2, accel : 12 : 2)
end;
```

```
        procedure Euler (var y, v, accel, t, dt : real;
                         ncalc : integer);
    var
        icalc : integer;
    begin
        for icalc := 1 to ncalc do
            begin
                y := y + v * dt;
                accel := g;
                v := v + accel * dt
            end;
        t := t + dt * ncalc
    end;


begin                     (* main *)
    initial(y, v, t, dt, height);        (* initial conditions and parameters *)
    print_parameters(dt, ncalc);
    print_table(y, v, g, t);             (* print initial values *)
    repeat
        Euler(y, v, accel, t, dt, ncalc);
        print_table(y, v, accel, t)
    until y > height
end.
```

CHAPTER 4

```
program planet (input, output);
(* planetary motion *)
(* use updated velocity to update position *)
type vector = array[1..2] of real;      (* define array dimensions *)
var
    pos, vel : vector;
    GM, dt, rmax : real;
    ncalc, nplot, iplot : integer;
```

```
procedure initial (var pos, vel : vector;
                   var GM, dt, rmax : real;
                   var nplot, ncalc : integer);
const
   pi = 3.14159;
var
   plot_period, tmax : real;
begin
   GM := 4.0 * pi * pi;              (* astronomical units *)
   writeln('time step = ');
   readln(dt);
   writeln('duration (yrs) = ');
   readln(tmax);
   writeln('plot period (yrs) = ');
   readln(plot_period);
   ncalc := round(plot_period / dt);    (* # of iterations between plots *)
   nplot := round(tmax / plot_period);
   writeln('initial x position  = ');
   readln(pos[1]);
   rmax := 2.0 * pos[1];        (* assumed maximum value of semi-major axis *)
   pos[2] := 0.0;     (* initial y position *)
   vel[1] := 0.0;      (* initial x velocity *)
   writeln('initial y velocity = ');
   readln(vel[2]);
   paintoval(130, 230, 170, 270)              (* paint sun at origin *)
end;
```

```
procedure Euler (var pos, vel : vector;
                 GM, dt : real;
                 ncalc : integer);
var
    accel : vector;
    icalc, i : integer;
    r : real;
begin
    for icalc := 1 to ncalc do
        begin
            r := sqrt(pos[1] * pos[1] + pos[2] * pos[2]);
            writeln(r);
            for i := 1 to 2 do
                begin
                    accel[i] := -GM * pos[i] / (r * r * r);
                    vel[i] := vel[i] + accel[i] * dt;
                    pos[i] := pos[i] + vel[i] * dt
                end
        end
end;

procedure orbit (pos : vector;
                 rmax : real);
(* plot orbit *)
const
    x0 = 250;
    y0 = 150;
    aspect = 0.6667;
var
    i, j : integer;
begin
    i := round(x0 + (250 / rmax) * pos[1] * aspect);
    j := round(y0 - (150 / rmax) * pos[2]);
    paintoval(j - 1, i - 1, j + 1, i + 1)
end;
```

```
    begin                              (* main *)
        initial(pos, vel, GM, dt, rmax, nplot, ncalc);
        orbit(pos, rmax);
        for iplot := 1 to nplot do
            begin
                Euler(pos, vel, GM, dt, ncalc);
                orbit(pos, rmax)
            end
    end.
```

CHAPTER 5

```
    program sho (input, output);              (* simple harmonic oscillator *)
    var
        dataout : text;
        pos, vel, w2, dt, t : real;
        ncalc, iprt, nprt : integer;


        procedure initial (var pos, vel, w2, dt : real;
                            var ncalc, nprt : integer);
        var
            prt_period, total_time : real;
            fname : string;
        begin
            write('initial position (meters) = ');
            readln(pos);
            vel := 0.0;                    (* initial velocity (m/s) *)
            write('ratio of k/m = ');
            readln(w2);
            write('time step (sec) = ');
            readln(dt);
            write('time between printing data = ');
            readln(prt_period);
            write('total time of simulation = ');
            readln(total_time);
            ncalc := round(prt_period / dt);
            nprt := round(total_time / prt_period);
            write('name of data file = ');
            readln(fname);
```

```
        open(dataout, fname);
        rewrite(dataout);
        writeln(dataout, 'time' : 11, 'position' : 11, 'velocity' : 11);
        writeln(dataout);
        writeln('time' : 11, 'position' : 11, 'velocity' : 11);
        writeln
    end;


    procedure Euler (var pos, vel, w2, dt : real;
                        ncalc : integer);        (* Euler-Cromer algorithm *)
    var
        accel : real;
        icalc : integer;
    begin
        for icalc := 1 to ncalc do
            begin
                accel := -w2 * pos;
                vel := vel + accel * dt;
                pos := pos + vel * dt
            end
    end;


    procedure outdat (pos, vel, t : real);
    begin
        writeln(t : 11 : 4, pos : 11 : 4, vel : 11 : 4);
        writeln(dataout, t : 11 : 4, pos : 11 : 4, vel : 11 : 4)
    end;

begin                             (* main *)
    initial(pos, vel, w2, dt, ncalc, nprt);
    t := 0.0;
    for iprt := 1 to nprt do
        begin
            outdat(pos, vel, t);
            Euler(pos, vel, w2, dt, ncalc);
            t := t + ncalc * dt
        end;
    close(dataout)
end.
```

CHAPTER 6

```
program md (input, output);
const
    c = 32768;                    (* needed to obtain random numbers *)
    Nmax = 30;                    (* maximum number of particles *)
type
    component = array[1..Nmax] of real;
var
    x, y, vx, vy, ax, ay : component;
    N, nave, nset, iset, iave : integer;
    Lx, Ly, dt, dt2 : real;
    virial, xflux, yflux, pe, ke, time : real;

    procedure initial (var x, y, vx, vy : component;
                       var N, nave, nset : integer;
                       var Lx, Ly, dt, dt2 : real);
    var
        irow, icol, nrow, ncol, i : integer;
        ax, ay, xscale, yscale, Mx, My : real;
        vscale, vmax, vxcum, vycum : real;
        fname : string;
        datain : text;
        newconf : char;
    begin
        write('number of particles = ');
        readln(N);
        write('box size Lx and Ly = ');
        readln(Lx, Ly);
        write('time step = ');
        readln(dt);
        dt2 := dt * dt;
        write('number of time steps between averages = ');
        readln(nave);
        write('number of sets of averages = ');
        readln(nset);
        write('new configuration  y/n? ');
        readln(newconf);
```

```
if (newconf = 'y') then
   begin                              (* begin on triangular lattice *)
      write('number of particles per row = ');
      readln(nrow);
      write('maximum speed = ');
      readln(vmax);
      ncol := N div nrow;
      (* near neighbor distances in each direction *)
      ay := Ly / nrow;
      ax := Lx / ncol;
      i := 0;
      for icol := 1 to ncol do
         for irow := 1 to nrow do
            begin
               i := i + 1;
               y[i] := ay * (irow - 0.5);
               if ((irow mod 2) = 0) then
                  x[i] := ax * (icol - 0.25)
               else
                  x[i] := ax * (icol - 0.75);
                  vx[i] := random * vmax / c;   (* random velocities *)
                  vy[i] := random * vmax / c;
                  (* sum vx and vy so that net velocity is 0 *)
                  vxcum := vxcum + vx[i];
                  vycum := vycum + vy[i]
            end;
      vxcum := vxcum / N;
      vycum := vycum / N;
      for i := 1 to N do
         begin   (* net velocity set equal to 0 *)
            vx[i] := vx[i] - vxcum;
            vy[i] := vy[i] - vycum
         end
   end
```

```pascal
    else                          (* old configuration *)
        begin
            write('name of file containing configuration is ');
            readln(fname);
            write('fractional change in speed = ');
            readln(vscale);
            open(datain, fname);
            reset(datain);
            readln(datain, N, Mx, My);
            xscale := Lx / Mx;
            yscale := Ly / My;
            for i := 1 to N do
                begin
                    readln(datain, x[i], y[i], vx[i], vy[i]);
                    x[i] := x[i] * xscale;
                    y[i] := y[i] * yscale;
                    vx[i] := vx[i] * vscale;
                    vy[i] := vy[i] * vscale
                end;
            close(datain)
        end
end;
```

```pascal
            procedure periodic (var xtemp, ytemp, xflux, yflux : real;
                             px, py, Lx, Ly : real);
        begin
           if xtemp < 0.0 then
              begin
                 xtemp := xtemp + Lx;
                 xflux := xflux - px
              end;
           if xtemp > Lx then
              begin
                 xtemp := xtemp - Lx;
                 xflux := xflux + px
              end;
           if ytemp < 0.0 then
              begin
                 ytemp := ytemp + Ly;
                 yflux := yflux - py
              end;
            if ytemp > Ly then
              begin
                 ytemp := ytemp - Ly;
                 yflux := yflux + py
              end
        end;


            procedure separation (var dx, dy : real;
                              Lx, Ly : real);
        begin
           if abs(dx) > 0.5 * Lx then
              dx := dx * (1.0 - Lx / abs(dx));
           if abs(dy) > 0.5 * Ly then
              dy := dy * (1.0 - Ly / abs(dy))
        end;
```

```
procedure f (r : real;
                var force, potential : real);
var
    ri, ri3, ri6, g : real;
begin
    ri := 1.0 / r;
    ri3 := ri * ri * ri;
    ri6 := ri3 * ri3;
    g := 24.0 * ri * ri6 * (2.0 * ri6 - 1.0);
    force := g * ri;
    potential := 4.0 * ri6 * (ri6 - 1.0)
end;


procedure accel (var x, y, ax, ay : component;
                    N : integer;
                    Lx, Ly : real;
                    var pe : real);
var
    i, j : integer;
    dx, dy, r, force, potential : real;
begin
    for i := 1 to N do
        begin
            ax[i] := 0.0;
            ay[i] := 0.0
        end;
    for i := 1 to (N - 1) do
        for j := (i + 1) to N do
            begin
                dx := x[i] - x[j];
                dy := y[i] - y[j];
                separation(dx, dy, Lx, Ly);
                r := sqrt(dx * dx + dy * dy);
                f(r,force,potential);
```

```
                    ax[i] := ax[i] + force * dx;
                    ay[i] := ay[i] + force * dy;
                    ax[j] := ax[j] - force * dx;
                    ay[j] := ay[j] - force * dy;
                    pe := pe + potential
              end
    end;


procedure Verlet (var x, y, vx, vy, ax, ay : component;
                      N : integer;
                      Lx, Ly, dt, dt2 : real;
                      var virial, xflux, yflux, pe, ke : real);
var
    i : integer;
    xnew, ynew : real;
begin
    for i := 1 to N do
        begin
            xnew := x[i] + vx[i] * dt + 0.5 * ax[i] * dt2;
            ynew := y[i] + vy[i] * dt + 0.5 * ay[i] * dt2;
            (* partially update velocity using old acceleration *)
            vx[i] := vx[i] + 0.5 * ax[i] * dt;
            vy[i] := vy[i] + 0.5 * ay[i] * dt;
            (* periodic boundary condition and flux calculation  *)
            periodic(xnew, ynew, xflux, yflux, vx[i], vy[i], Lx, Ly);
            x[i] := xnew;
            y[i] := ynew
        end;
    accel(x, y, ax, ay, N, Lx, Ly, pe);      (* compute new acceleration *)
    for i := 1 to N do
    (* complete update of velocity using new acceleration *)
        begin
            vx[i] := vx[i] + 0.5 * ax[i] * dt;
            vy[i] := vy[i] + 0.5 * ay[i] * dt;
            ke := ke + 0.5 * (vx[i] * vx[i] + vy[i] * vy[i]);
            virial := virial + x[i] * ax[i] + y[i] * ay[i]
        end
    end;
```

```pascal
procedure results (N, nave : integer;
                    Lx, Ly, dt : real;
                    var virial, ke, pe, xflux, yflux, time : real);
var
    pflux, pvirial, E, T : real;
begin
    if time = 0.0 then
        writeln('time,T,E,pflux,pvirial');
        time := time + dt * nave;
        ke := ke / nave;
        pe := pe / nave;
        E := (pe + ke) / N;                  (* energy per particle *)
        T := ke / N;                         (* temperature *)
        ke := 0.0;
        pe := 0.0;
        (* reduced pressure from flux calculation *)
        pflux := ((xflux / (2.0 * Lx)) + (yflux / (2.0 * Ly))) / (dt * nave);
        xflux := 0.0;
        yflux := 0.0;
        (* reduced pressure from virial calculation *)
        pvirial := (N * T) / (Lx * Ly) + 0.5 * virial / (Nave * Lx * Ly);
        virial := 0.0;
        writeln(time : 9 : 3, T : 9 : 4, E : 9 : 4, pflux : 9 : 4, pvirial : 9 : 4)
end;
```

```pascal
    procedure save_conf (var x, y, vx, vy : component;
                              N : integer;
                              Lx, Ly : real);
    var
        fname : string;
        dataout : text;
        i : integer;
    begin
        write('name of file containing configuration is ');
        readln(fname);
        open(dataout, fname);
        rewrite(dataout);
        writeln(dataout, N, Lx, Ly);
        for i := 1 to N do
            writeln(dataout, x[i], y[i], vx[i], vy[i]);
        close(dataout)
    end;


begin                              (* main *)
    initial(x, y, vx, vy, N, nave, nset, Lx, Ly, dt, dt2);
    pe := 0.0;
    accel(x, y, ax, ay, N, Lx, Ly, pe);
    time := 0.0;
    pe := 0.0;
    ke := 0.0;
    xflux := 0.0;
    yflux := 0.0;
    virial := 0.0;
    for iset := 1 to nset do
      begin
        for iave := 1 to nave do
        Verlet(x, y, vx, vy, ax, ay, N, Lx, Ly, dt, dt2, virial, xflux, yflux, pe, ke);
        results(N, nave, Lx, Ly, dt, virial, ke, pe, xflux, yflux, time)
      end;
    save_conf(x, y, vx, vy, N, Lx, Ly)
end.
```

CHAPTER 7

```
program map_graph (input, output);
var
    x, r : real;
    iterate : integer;

    procedure parameter (var x, r : real;
                              var interate : integer);
    begin
        write('r = ');
        readln(r);
        write('initial x = ');
        readln(x);
        write('iterate of f(x) = ');
        readln(iterate)
    end;

    function f (x, r : real;
                  iterate : integer) : real;
    (* f defined by recursive procedure *)
    var
        y : real;
    begin
        if iterate > 1 then
            begin
                y := f(x, r, iterate - 1);
                f := 4 * r * y * (1.0 - y)
            end
        else
            f := 4 * r * x * (1 - x)
    end;
```

```
        procedure map (r : real;
                         iterate : integer);
const
    min = 50;
    max = 250;
    scale = 200;
var
    delta, margin, x, y : real;
    m, n, i, j : integer;
begin
    n := 200;                    (* number of points at which f(x) is computed *)
    delta := 1.0 / n;
    (* draw axes *)
    moveto(min, min);
    lineto(min, max);
    lineto(max, max);
    (* draw line y = x *)
    moveto(min, max);
    lineto(max, min);
    x := 0;
    y := f(x, r, iterate);
    i := min;
    j := round(max - y * scale);
    moveto(i, j);
    for m := 1 to n do
        begin
            x := x + delta;
            y := f(x, r, iterate);
            i := round(min + x * scale);
            j := round(max - y * scale);
            lineto(i, j)
        end
end;
```

```
procedure draw (x, r : real;
                iterate : integer);
const
   n = 100;      (* number of iterations of map *)
   min = 50;     (* used for screen coordinates *)
   max = 250;
   scale = 200;
var
   y, y0, x0 : real;
   i, j, m : integer;
begin
   x0 := x;
   y0 := 0.0;
   for m := 1 to n do
      begin
         y := f(x, r, iterate);
         i := round(min + scale * x);
         j := round(max - scale * y0);
         moveto(i, j);
         j := round(max - scale * y);
         lineto(i, j);
         i := round(min + scale * y);
         lineto(i, j);
         x0 := y;
         y0 := y;
         x := y
      end
   end;

begin                          (* main *)
   parameter(x, r, iterate);
   map(r, iterate);
   draw(x, r, iterate)
end.
```

CHAPTER 8

```pascal
program waves (input, output);
    var
        A, v, lambda, dt, xmax, space, xscale, yscale : real;
        ntime : integer;

    procedure initial (var A, v, lambda, dt : real);
    begin
        write('v (cm/sec) = ');
        readln(v);
        A := 1.0;  (* amplitude of wave *)
        lambda := 2.0 * 3.14159;     (* cm *)
        write('time (sec) between plots = ');
        readln(dt)
    end;

    procedure screen (A, lambda, dt : real;
                        var xmax, space, xscale, yscale : real;
                        var ntime : integer);
    const
        x0 = 250;
        y0 = 300;
    var
        iaxes, ntick, itick, i, j : integer;
        ymax, dx, dy, row, t : real;
    begin
        xmax := 6.0 * lambda;
        xscale := 250 / xmax;
        ntime := 5;                    (* number of times wave is plotted *)
        space := 0.5 * A;              (* spacing between plots *)
        ymax := ntime * (space + 2 * A);
        yscale := 300.0 / ymax;
        dx := lambda / 4.0;
        write('distance between tick marks = ', dx);
        dy := A / 10.0;  (* height of tick mark *)
        row := A;
        ntick := round(xmax / dx);
```

```
for iaxes := 1 to ntime do
    begin
        i := round(x0 + xscale * (-xmax));
        j := round(y0 - yscale * row);
        moveto(i, j);
        i := round(x0 + xscale * xmax);
        lineto(i, j);
        for itick := -ntick to ntick do
            begin
                i := round(x0 + itick * dx * xscale);
                j := round(y0 - yscale * row);
                moveto(i, j);
                j := round(y0 - yscale * (row + dy));
                lineto(i, j)
            end;
        row := row + space + 2.0 * A
    end
end;

function u (A, v, x, t : real) : real;
begin
    u := A * cos(x - v * t)
end;
```

```
        procedure wavemotion (A, v, xmax, dt, space, xscale, yscale : real;
                              ntime : integer);
    const
        x0 = 250;
        y0 = 300;
    var
        row, dx, t, x : real;
        i, j, itime, ipoint, npoint : integer;
    begin
        npoint := 200;
        dx := xmax / npoint;
        t := 0.0;
        row := A;                   (* y coordinate on screen for u = 0 *)
        for itime := 1 to ntime do
            begin
                t := t + dt;
                x := -dx * npoint;
                i := round(x0 + xscale * x);
                j := round(y0 - yscale * (u(A, v, x, t) + row));
                moveto(i, j);
                for ipoint := -npoint + 1 to npoint do
                    begin
                        x := dx * ipoint;
                        i := round(x0 + xscale * x);
                        j := round(y0 - yscale * (u(A, v, x, t) + row));
                        lineto(i, j)
                    end;
                row := row + space + 2.0 * A
            end
    end;

begin                           (* main *)
    initial(A, v, lambda, dt);
    screen(A, lambda, dt, xmax, space, xscale, yscale, ntime);
    wavemotion(A, v, xmax, dt, space, xscale, yscale, ntime)
end.
```

CHAPTER 9

```
program Laplace (input, output);
type
    matrix = array[1..100, 1..100] of real;
var
    V : matrix;
    nx, ny, iterations : integer;
    change : real;

    procedure assign (var V : matrix;
                        var nx, ny : integer;
                        var change : real);
    var
        col, row : integer;
        V0 : real;
    begin
        write('number of cells in the x direction = ');
        readln(nx);
        write('number of cells in the y direction  = ');
        readln(ny);
        write('potential of rectangle in volts = ');
        readln(V0);
        write('repeat until % change  = ');
        readln(change);
        change := change / 100.0;
        for col := 1 to nx do                (* fix potential on rectangle *)
            begin
                V[col, 1] := V0;
                V[col, ny] := V0
            end;
```

```
      for row := 1 to ny do
         begin
            V[1, row] := V0;
            V[nx, row] := V0
         end;
      (* set initial potential of interior cells *)
      for col := 2 to nx - 1 do
         for row := 2 to ny - 1 do
            V[col, row] := 0.9 * V0
end;

procedure outdat (var V : matrix;
                        nx, ny, iterations : integer);
var
   col, row : integer;
begin
   writeln;
   writeln('iterations = ', iterations);
   for row := 1 to ny do
      begin
         for col := 1 to nx do
            write(V[col, row] : 7 : 3);
         writeln
      end
end;
```

```pascal
procedure iterate (var V : matrix;
                   var nx, ny, iterations : integer;
                   change : real);
var
   Vave : matrix;
   diff, dmax : real;
   row, col : integer;
begin
   iterations := 0;
   repeat
      dmax := 0.0;
      iterations := iterations + 1;
      for col := 2 to nx - 1 do
         for row := 2 to ny - 1 do
            begin
               Vave[col, row] := V[col + 1, row] + V[col - 1, row];
               Vave[col, row] := Vave[col, row] + V[col, row + 1] + V[col, row - 1];
               Vave[col, row] := 0.25 * Vave[col, row];
               (* compute percentage change in potential *)
               diff := abs((V[col, row] - Vave[col, row]) / Vave[col, row]);
               if diff > dmax then
                  dmax := diff
            end;
      for row := 2 to ny - 1 do
         for col := 2 to nx - 1 do
            V[col, row] := Vave[col, row];
      outdat(V, nx, ny, iterations)
   until dmax <= change          (* continue iterations until desired accuracy *)
end;


begin                           (* main *)
   assign(V, nx, ny, change);
   iterate(V, nx, ny, iterations, change)
end.
```

SUBJECT INDEX: PART I

PLOT POINTS 27, 28
PLOT TEXT 28, 30
PRINT 16, 88, 135
PRINT USING 30, 88
PROGRAM 17
READ 136
RND 124
SELECT CASE 207, 209
SET BACK 28, 29
SET COLOR 28, -29
SET CURSOR 28, 29
SET WINDOW 27, 28, 59
sgn 45
SUB 16
subroutine 16–20
TRUNCATE 158
UNTIL 39
WHILE 39

transport properties 153–157
triangular lattice 140, 141
truncation error 25

U
universality 168–170

V
van der Waals equation 139
velocity autocorrelation function 143, 144, 146, 157
Verlet algorithm *See* numerical integration
velocity space *See* particle orbits
virial 134, 135, 150

W
wave properties
dispersion 195, 196
group velocity 195
motion 191–196
period 194
phase velocity 195
wave equation 192
wavelength 194
wave number 194